Sherlock's World

Fandom & Culture

PAUL BOOTH AND KATHERINE LARSEN, SERIES EDITORS

Sherlock's World

Fan Fiction and the Reimagining
of BBC's *Sherlock*

Ann K. McClellan

UNIVERSITY OF IOWA PRESS Iowa City

University of Iowa Press, Iowa City 52242

Copyright © 2018 by the University of Iowa Press

www.uipress.uiowa.edu

Printed in the United States of America

The University of Iowa Press is a member of Green Press Initiative
and is committed to preserving natural resources.

Printed on acid-free paper

Library of Congress Cataloging-in-Publication Data
Names: McClellan, Ann K. author.
Title: Sherlock's world : fan fiction and the reimagining of BBC's Sherlock /
by Ann K. McClellan.
Description: Iowa City : University of Iowa Press, 2018. | Series: Fandom &
culture | Includes bibliographical references and index. |
Identifiers: LCCN 2018013981 (print) | LCCN 2018016600 (ebook) |
ISBN 978-1-60938-617-7 | ISBN 978-1-60938-616-0 (pbk. : alk. paper)
Subjects: LCSH: Sherlock (Television program : 2010–) |
Television viewers—Attitudes.
Classification: LCC PN1992.77.S475 (ebook) | LCC PN1992.77.S475 M33 2018
(print) | DDC 791.45/72—dc23
LC record available at https://lccn.loc.gov/2018013981

For my mother,

who first introduced me

to the great detective

CONTENTS

ACKNOWLEDGMENTS

Several friends, family members, and colleagues have played significant roles in the life and development of this book.

Much of the research for this book would not have been possible without the financial support of Plymouth State University. A sabbatical release, numerous professional development awards, a 2014 Plymouth State University Research Advisory Council grant for archive research at the Richard Lancelyn Green Bequest in Portsmouth, UK, and a 2016 Summer Visiting Fellowship at Richmond, the American International University in London, all further supported my Sherlock Holmes research.

Several colleagues, in person and virtually, have helped refine and shape the book. Thanks to Kristina Busse at *Transformative Works and Cultures* for her encouragement and for always keeping me up to date on new developments in fan culture, both in the journal and on the immortal AO3. Similar thanks to Kathy Larsen for her wonderful leadership of the fan studies area at PCA and for her support for my fan studies research over the years. She, along with Louisa Stein and Paul Booth, gave wonderful feedback on the manuscript; you all helped make this a better book, and any remaining errors of judgment or thinking are all mine. Thanks, too, to all of the reviewers and editors I've worked with over the past few years while publishing excerpts of the book in progress. I miss the kind of collaborative writing and research community I had in graduate school (Scott Hermanson, Jeff Miller, Cathrine Frank), so I highly value the thoughtful feedback I've been given that makes my work smarter.

Significant thanks and appreciation also go to the wonderful team at the University of Iowa Press. First, to editor Catherine Cocks who initially approached me about writing a book on *Sherlock* fanfiction; years of my life and reams of pages are due to you. More recently, Ranjit Arab, Meredith Stabel, and all of the wonderful people at the University of Iowa Press gave me the support and guidance necessary to finalize the book for publication.

To my wonderful students, colleagues, and friends who have listened to me fangirl about *Sherlock* for over six years and who have supported my research and obsessions: thank you. In particular, student extraordinaire Ryan French cut short his Christmas vacation to help me prepare the images and format the manuscript. Your dedication, patience, and support are much to be lauded. For Liz, my former department chair and dear '80s friend, who told me about this NPR story she'd heard about a new modern-day Sherlock Holmes TV show coming to PBS—without you, this obsession would never have developed. Pat and Al Cantor, thank you for the movie and dinner breaks from research and writing and for the endless questions about my work. To Matt Cheney, for keeping me up-to-date on current methodological approaches and for live tweeting *Sherlock* episodes with me. No spoilers! To Jeannette, for being my fanfic buddy and for relentlessly analyzing *Sherlock* episodes with me each season. To Lynne Bates, for Friday nights and reminders to keep calm and carry on. To my best friend and colleague, Cathie LeBlanc: thank you so much for your support, intellectually and emotionally, over the past several years. You've been my biggest fan and best supporter of my work. Everyone should have such a supportive and celebratory friend in their lives. Thank you for the hours and hours of car rides discussing episodes, fanfic storylines, organization, frustrations, and triumphs. Thank God for intellectually curious friends!

Lastly, I want to offer appreciation for my family who, even after my twenty-plus years in academia, still don't really understand what I do but are proud and support me anyway.

IT'S *SHERLOCK'S* WORLD AND WE'RE JUST LIVING IN IT
World Building, Canon, and Fanfiction

With more than twelve million viewers in the United Kingdom, *Sherlock* is one of the most-watched television series in BBC history.[1] Set in contemporary London, thirtysomething Sherlock and John (no longer fussy old Holmes and Watson) solve crimes with the help of smartphones, texting, online forums, and the internet. The show has become an international hit, its stars and creators greedily sought-out worldwide by obsessive fans and faithful Sherlockians alike. In their modernization of Sir Arthur Conan Doyle's nineteenth-century world, *Sherlock* creators Steven Moffat and Mark Gatiss make London as much a character of their show as the actors themselves. Episodes highlight iconic modern images of London—the London Eye, Big Ben, the Gherkin, the Tower of London—as well as solidify the domestic interior of 221b Baker Street so that all of these factors combine to create a uniquely identifiable—and transferable—fictional world that is simultaneously grounded in the reality of twenty-first-century London.[2] In addition, Benedict Cumberbatch and Martin Freeman as Sherlock and John are stylized and presented in the show as such contrasting opposites (tall to short, dark to light, flamboyant to restrained) that each actor's characterization becomes a type in and of itself. *Sherlock's World* investigates the constructs underlying the show's fictional world and analyzes how contemporary fans engage with—and challenge—that world through their fanfiction writing. As fans delve deeper into alternative storylines, characterizations, genres, and themes, they move further away from the confines of the show. Using (and confronting) the frameworks of fanfiction genres (role playing, slash, genderswap, alternate universe, and, ultimately, real person fic), *Sherlock* fan writers both contest and concretize the canonical structures defining the particular fictional universe.

Sherlock's World starts from the assumption that fanfictions are art objects and treats them with the respect, depth, appreciation—and love— that is their due; as such, to write (and read) fanfiction literature, fans need to understand the components, mannerisms, nuances, and style of the original fictional world. Similar to adaptation theory, the appeal of fanfic comes from the pleasure of "repetition with variation. . . . Recognition and remembrance are part of the pleasure (and risk) of experiencing an adaptation," both of which are motivated by "the desire to repeat particular acts of consumption" (Hutcheon 4–5). Fan authors must also study the specific tropes, iconic settings, and characterizations that govern the primary text, known as its canon, and then recreate a recognizable version of that world for other audiences. Fanfiction is not simply a derivative copy of the original text, however;[3] through the process of adapting the original text's characters, settings, and storylines into a new medium, fans transform fictional worlds into something that is recognizable but new. Such a transformation allows authors to delve into the conventions of the original world: to explore and/or explode canonical settings and environments, to reinforce and/or challenge characterization, and to reinforce and/or break down boundaries between fiction and reality. Ultimately, I argue that fictional worlds and characterization are intrinsically linked; specifically, I maintain that fanfiction worlds are primarily defined by character, and as long as the characters remain canonically consistent—or compliant—within fanfiction, the fictional world remains intact, no matter how radical the changes.

World Building

So what do we mean by *worlds* and *world building*? Well, generically, a fictional world is a vast, detailed, coherent narrative space with related objects and characters and a common set of values, ethics, and beliefs (Hills, *Fan Culture* 137; Ryan, *Narrative* 91). Observers and users can interact with the fictional world in some way, although its full extent and boundaries may never be realized or experienced by any single individual because of its extensive size and depth. Fictional worlds contain complex systems of categorization and creation, including everything from basic physical laws to weather, species stability, social values, and ethics, all of which are internally consistent and presented as if they are real, no matter how far they stray from our actual physical world. Such details must be inventive, complete, and consistent through all their various iterations. Beyond being a system of categorization, fictional worlds are also experiential and contain everything that affects the characters, including the basic elements impacting a life (culture, society, worldviews, and customs) (Wolf 25). Like the physical elements, these defining cultural components give the impression of a much larger universe beyond the boundaries of a specific scene, event, or text. Thus, worlds are not the same as settings or even geographic environments but rather larger conceptual constructs that imply history, action, and storylines that happen outside or beyond the constructed boundaries of the established universe.

Analysis of world building can take two basic approaches: from the creator's standpoint or from the reader's. Fantasy author J. R. R. Tolkien is often cited as one of the first literary authors to articulate the concept of world building, particularly from the author's point of view. In his 1947 essay, "On Fairy Stories," Tolkien defined the necessary components of fantasy literature, including giving the text an "inner consistency of reality" in what he called "sub-creation" (138). (Tolkien's use of "sub" implies the fictional world is secondary to, under, or related to the actual world.)[4] Writers create a "Secondary World into which both designer and spectator can enter, to the satisfaction of their senses while they are inside; but in its purity it is artistic in desire and purpose" (Tolkien 142). This focus on sensory experience becomes essential in contemporary online worlds, such as video games, where participants must see, hear, navigate, and experience multiple layers of the digital world to fully immerse themselves in the environment. Such realism, even in a fantasy environment, is core to Tolkien's vision:

> Probably every writer making a secondary world, a fantasy, every sub-creator, wishes in some measure to be a real maker, or hopes that he is drawing on reality; hopes that the peculiar quality of this secondary world (if not all the details) are derived from Reality, or are flowing into it. If he indeed did achieve a quality that can fairly be described by the dictionary definition: "inner consistency of reality," it is difficult to conceive how this can be, if the world does not in some way partake

of reality. The peculiar quality of the joy in successful Fantasy can thus be explained as a sudden glimpse of the underlying reality, or truth. (Tolkien 155)

Tolkien's emphases on the real, Reality (capitalized or uncapitalized), and truth are striking in their implied incongruity with fantasy. Being a real maker, he implies, means being taken seriously as an artist, and this includes making fictional and fantasy worlds as complete, consistent, truthful, and realistic as possible—even if they include fantastical animals, magic, or other mystical events. All must be portrayed with the utmost seriousness and realism as if they existed in an alternate world. Such "Realism of Presentation," C. S. Lewis explains, requires immediacy, vividness, and sharply observed or imagined detail (57). Stories do not have to contain real content—that is, plots, characters, species, and/or elements true to life—but they must be presented *as if* they were real. "Realism of Presentation" allows authors to invent totally unreal, yet believable, possible worlds because they remain internally consistent within their established systems (Lewis 59).

This emphasis on realism is likewise important for Lin Carter's foundational text, *Imaginary Worlds* (1973). Carter is perhaps the first fantasy writer and critic to explicitly label fictional content as a world, defining imaginary worlds as stories situated in "settings completely made up by the author, whether such settings consist of a single country or an entire world, or even an imaginary period of the remote past or the distant future" (Carter 7). Carter insisted on the term "world" rather than geography or environment because setting involves more than one specific scene (Carter 176, 180, 188); worlds are expansionist, implying that they broaden beyond the limits of the story and the extension of the narrative and other elements into new media outlets (Mittell, "Strategies" 263).[5] The author's role is to convince the reader that the invented fictional world is real and that it exists beyond the specific characters, scenes, and instances of the narrative itself. Carter's interest in setting, place, and geography adds a new emphasis on *systems* (such as geography and physics), which provide the focus for Nelson Goodman's *Ways of Worldmaking* (1976). For Goodman,

Worldmaking consists of taking apart and putting together, often conjointly: on the on [sic] hand, of dividing wholes into parts and partitioning kinds into sub-species, analyzing complexes into component features, drawing distinctions; on the other hand, of composing wholes and kinds out of parts and members and subclasses, combining features into complexes, and making connections. Such composition or decomposition is normally effected or assisted or consolidated by the application of labels: names, predicates, gestures, pictures, etc. (Goodman 7–8)

We can see new emphases here on identification, organization, and categorization (all of which will be essential for our analysis of fanfiction genres), with world building becoming more a specific practice for writers and creators rather than a theory. A quick search today for "world building" on Amazon, for example, will quickly produce various how-to books for burgeoning fantasy writers and Dungeons & Dragons enthusiasts. For Goodman, world building requires authors to break down the elements of a world into their component parts, to understand the underlying structures within a world and to apply them, in new formulations, to a newly imagined construction. The process means that much world building activity happens in the background while constructing the story (Wolf 30). Thus, worlds are not random but are rather systems, a form of "enworldedness" that "constitute(s) a self-organizing, self-enclosed, and self-referential totality" that both encloses and also excludes (Hayot 32, 40).

Fantasy clearly isn't the only genre with storyworlds; at some level, all fiction is about creating believable alternatives to our daily lives. Possible Worlds theory in the 1980s and 1990s postulated an infinite number of possible versions of the actual world (that is, the real world) within our universe. To be considered viable, these alternative satellite worlds must be specifically linked to the one central system understood to be the real world (Ryan, *Narrative* 99–100). Literary theorists like Pavel, Dolezel, Eco, and Ryan, then, applied this approach to fiction, asking whether a fictional statement can ever be true, since it is, at heart, made up (that is, fiction) and exists in a constructed text. These theorists were particularly interested in the semantic elements of fictional worlds and in how language constructs and delimits reality. Texts in this formulation become one of many possible (fictional) worlds in which writers and creators imagine alternative experiences, characters, rules, laws, and social values (Ryan, "Story/Worlds/Media" 31–32). Such "What if?" stories (Mittell, "Strategies" 274) are foundational to fanfiction, since so many explore potential storylines introduced (but not developed) within the source text, including imagining characters, worlds, and plotlines that seem completely divergent from the original world.

Not all writers decide to invent original worlds, however; many (both professional and amateur) choose to adapt or create within already established worlds with set characters, settings, and elements. Creating within an established world can put important limits and restrictions on what a writer can do, depending on whether the world is closed or still open.[6] A closed world is one that its author (the designated authority on the world's canon) has declared finished; that is, no new narratives, characters, or extensions are to be developed. The closed world, as it exists, is complete and whole. An open world, by contrast, is one in which new texts and stories are still being created (Wolf 270). Since Sir Arthur Conan Doyle died in 1930, his world of 221b Baker Street is technically closed; no new official additions to Doyle's Sherlock Holmes adventures can be made (of course, there have been Holmesian pastiches and parodies since the character was first created, although many of these have been the subject of copyright and licensing lawsuits from the Sir Arthur Conan Doyle Estate). In comparison, the BBC's *Sherlock* television show has the potential to produce new episodes; theoretically, the full trajectory of the characters and storylines are still ripe for speculation, which makes it an open text. Both closed and open texts provide excellent fodder for fanfiction, in particular;[7] they provide an already established world with developed characters, a known setting, and genre-specific plotlines. The open-endedess of the television show, however, provides fans with ample opportunities to speculate on character and relationship arcs, conflict and cliffhanger resolutions, and broader plot development while still remaining within the constructs of the original world, perhaps one explanation as to why the serial nature of the show increases its popularity with fans.

Sherlock's openness depends upon the seemingly contradictory coexistence of narrative coherence and plot gaps. On the one hand, while the characters within a series carry over from one episode to the next, each episode must be complete in itself. On the other hand, sufficient gaps within the plot, character development, and timeline are necessary to warrant the show's continuation. *Sherlock*'s use of season cliffhangers has been a particularly effective technique for garnering immediate fan reaction and investment in the future of the show. By leaving audiences hanging on an undetermined conclusion, show writers Steven Moffat and Mark Gatiss not only guarantee viewers will return, they also open up the seasons' resolutions to fan culture. With a two-plus-year gap between seasons, fans have plenty of time to speculate on possible solutions and to play within the show's narrative world with fanfiction, fan vids, art, and cosplay. Gaps in the storyline raise feelings of anticipation and retrospection in the viewer, leading her to either anticipate how the show will answer her questions in future installments or to fill the gaps herself with her own imagination, or both. Consequently, gaps filled by episodes in the subsequent season will change viewers' perceptions of what was previously seen.

As we'll see in the first chapter, on transmedia storytelling, *Sherlock*'s creators have made significant use of various social media platforms to foster the impression that the show remains open for interpretation, appropriation, and expansion, particularly through authorized transmedial extensions—branches of storytelling and world building developed in media formats tangential to and outside of the original TV series—like BBC character blogs, Twitter accounts, and partnerships with merchandisers such as Big Chief Studios and the Project Factory. Unauthorized extensions emerge in fanfiction, fan art, vidding, cosplay, and other fandom activities. Audiences can thus imagine a larger *Sherlock* world based on the individual extensions they encounter. Often, these transmedial worlds are so extensive that any one participant will not or cannot experience every additive component; therefore, every individual's conceptualization of the world will be incomplete at some level. In fact, incompleteness is a major characteristic of a world (Wolf 38; Ryan "Story/World/Text," 34; Hayot 60–61). This seems at odds, however, with several other claims that worlds are complete entities; both Eric Hayot and Mark Wolf simultaneously claim that worlds are both complete and incomplete (Hayot 54; Wolf 33). But how can this be true? What seems at first contradictory in fact provides helpful insight into how transmedial worlds work. One foundational characteristic of worlds is their internal uniformity. Characters, actions, and environments must all be logically consistent within the stories from which the world is built (Van Levenworth 332); any haphazardness creates divisiveness and leads readers to experience them as separate texts rather than as parts of a larger construct. To maintain world consistency, each additional story added must take into account all of the stories already included (Wolf 205). Such consistency adds to the overall complexity of the world (another major characteristic) and contributes to the audience's perception of the world as detailed, real, and expansive. The scope of the world thus implies that it is always already complete and that it exists beyond the boundaries of the audience's individual experience.

Because the world is so expansive, however, and because it has so many extensions and iterations, no one can ever experience its totality. The *desire* for completeness, for an encyclopedic knowledge of the world, prompts readers and users to seek out other extensions to increase their understanding and experience of the world, to become informational "hunter-gatherers," to borrow Henry Jenkins's term (*Textual Poachers*, 26). But since the world is always increasing in size and scope, they will never gain a finalized vision of its complete form. In a sense, then, no world can ever be closed or complete. It remains, by definition, incomplete—not because the world isn't finished from the creator's point of view, necessarily, but rather because the audience's *experience* of the world can never be complete.

This desire to address unanswered questions and to fill in the gaps left within texts and worlds is a foundational issue in reader response theory, reception studies, and adaptation studies and in transmedia storytelling as well. Reader response theorist Wolfgang Iser argues that the act of reading itself is comprised of filling in gaps between the known and the hidden, between scenes and storylines. Much like how film editing implies action and connections between shots, readers are given glimpses into characters' minds and actions but are never provided with the entire story. Rather, the reader's active participation completes the narrative; by filling in the gaps in the narrative, the reader brings the text to life and gives it meaning. Iser's ideas about gaps are particularly insightful in regard to fan production and creativity. He explains:

> With a literary text we can only picture things which are not there; the written part of the text gives us the knowledge, but it is the unwritten part that gives us the opportunity to picture things; indeed, without the elements of indeterminacy, the gaps in the text, we should not be able to use our imagination. (283)

This indeterminacy makes the fictional world even more believable because this is how most people experience the actual world (Wolf 62). Not only is it the reader's role to fill in the narrative gaps with her imaginings, but the number of possible realizations is infinite. As Iser explains, "one text is potentially capable of several different realizations, and no reading can ever exhaust the full potential, for each individual reader will fill the gaps in his own way, thereby excluding the various other possibilities; as he reads, he will make his own decisions as to how the gap is to be filled" (280). The text/world is inexhaustible, and yet it "is this very inexhaustibility that forces [the reader] to make this decision" (Iser 280). That is, the openness of the textual gaps mandates that the audience complete it; otherwise, there is no meaning.

Transmedia audiences, however, are not motivated necessarily by their desire for fulfillment or resolution—that is, by their desire to know the answer to the puzzle or to gain a complete understanding of the world. Rather, the pleasure in experiencing and participating in the world comes from the constant deferment of completion. Pleasure comes from delayed gratification, from the suspense of wondering what will be the next development, mystery, or conclusion. Fanfiction operates from a similar position in that stories about the world proliferate across fandom, even when fans are faced with episode or series gaps or even with the potential discontinuation of a franchise. In a sense, the reader and the world work in opposition to one another: the reader seeks out multiple extensions to refill and satisfy her desire for knowledge, resolution, and completeness, while each extension keeps adding new mysteries and developments that both answer old questions and introduce new ones. The world only exists when the audience pieces the different texts together and actively makes connections between perhaps seemingly unrelated characters and plotlines; without the reader, the world risks remaining a group of isolated but connected individual texts.[8]

As a result, worlds are not just fictional places but *experiential* sites of immersion.[9] In comparison to Coleridge's "willing suspension of disbelief," entering a fictional world requires instead an *active creation* of belief (Murray 110). World creation happens both unconsciously and consciously as the reader is presented with complex and detailed characters, events, and environments that, while not necessarily advancing the storyline of the text, require the reader to construct a rich background and a larger system within which the storyworld takes place (Hayot 2; Wolf 2).[10] These storyworlds create a mental model in the reader's mind, where she builds and experiences the narrative (Koten 50). The textual world thus becomes part of the reader's worldview through a blending of semiotic and personal experiences. Active participation within a world—building an online avatar, acting as dungeon master for a Dungeons & Dragons role-playing game (RPG), or, for our purposes, creating transformative fan works like fanfiction, videos, and art—all contribute to the audience's sense of *worldness*, that is, the world's overall sense of "coherence, completeness, and consistency within the world's environment," all of which combine into a "collective creation of belief" in the audience (Pearce 20). Producers and audiences share an understanding of the world's distinguishing features, including the origin of the world, its social structures, and character backstories and conflicts; the construction and description of physical spaces within the world, including both the geography and historical events, help establish the topos or general material layout (think George R. R. Martin's prefatory maps for Westeros in the *Game of Thrones* novels). For many theorists, the reader's active engagement in world building leads to greater investment and immersion—that is, "the experience through which a fictional world acquires the presence of an autonomous, language-dependent reality populated with live human beings" (Ryan, *Narrative* 14). On the surface, immersion could easily replace the definition for *world* itself; however, the composite elements of the world by themselves do not create the sense of immersion and belief within readers. Rather, active participation in the world builds a stronger connection to the broader fiction and to its sense of coherence, completeness, and consistency. Focusing on audience engagement not only aligns with contemporary participatory culture, it also recognizes the importance of readers imagining, creating, and taking ownership of worlds within their own minds, all important elements for writing and reading fanfic.

Fans' shared mental image of the world's distinguishing features mostly originates from "the first version of the world presented" (Klastrup and Tosca 1). The question of the "first version of the world" is an interesting one for Sherlock Holmes fans, however, since so many post-Doyle Sherlockian texts and images have overtaken the authenticity of the original text. For instance, Holmes's deerstalker hat is never mentioned in any of Doyle's sixty original stories; it first appears in an early Sidney Paget illustration for *The Strand Magazine* in 1891.[11] Similarly, Holmes's famous meerschaum pipe is not a product of Doyle's imagination but rather a stage prop introduced in 1899 by American actor William Gillette. And yet, both of these iconic symbols now have the power to evoke Holmes's character in just a single iteration.

Much of *Sherlock*'s world comes directly from Sir Arthur Conan Doyle's original Victorian stories, and yet the BBC's modern reimagining and transmediation adds more layers of storytelling and episodic extensions that continually move the storylines and characters further and further from the original source text. While this risks destabilizing the world, it also renders each transmedial extension more independent of the power of its central object; that is, the world becomes less dependent on one character, text, or storyline for its existence (Wolf 247). The more diverse and wide-ranging the transmedial world, the more important the role of the audience. The world becomes a blueprint fans use to imaginatively create a mental image of the world (Herman vii), and a cult figure such as Sherlock Holmes becomes a perfect candidate for deep media storytelling or world building—that is, linked, immersive stories that engage audiences beyond the typical one-to-two-hour movie or television episode (Rose 3)—since he occupies a cohesive narrative world, encounters other characters and experiences detachable events easily fragmented into segments that can be used in other stories, and possesses a living textuality that encourages audience appropriation and transformation.[12]

Holmes's Nineteenth-Century World

Sherlock Holmes first appeared in the novella *A Study in Scarlet* in *Beeton's Christmas Annual* (1887), but it wasn't until publication of "A Scandal in Bohemia" in *The Strand Magazine* in 1891 that he really caught the public's attention.[13] Sir Arthur Conan Doyle, Holmes's creator, theorized that the development of a single, defined character within disparate episodic stories would grab—and keep—readers' interest in ways that longer serialized narratives could not. The problem with serialized novels, Doyle argued, was that

> sooner or later, one missed one number and afterwards it had lost all interest. Clearly the ideal compromise was a character which carried through, and yet installments which were each complete in

themselves, so that the purchaser was always sure that he could relish the whole contents of the magazine. I believe that I was the first to realize this and "The Strand Magazine" the first to put it into practice. (Doyle, *Memories* 95–96)

Doyle couldn't have known that this new genre, the short story series, had come about at a perfectly timed moment in cultural history. The 1870 and 1880 Education Acts had recently allowed for state-funded, nondenominational compulsory public education for children aged five to ten, which led to the rise of an increasingly literate middle class—a middle class likewise benefitting from new labor laws and increased leisure time often spent reading new, affordably priced periodicals such as *The Strand*, one of the most popular magazines in the late nineteenth and early twentieth centuries. No other magazine, British or American, reached circulation levels anywhere near *The Strand*'s, especially while Arthur Conan Doyle was publishing his Sherlock Holmes stories there (Pound 32).[14] Including one of Doyle's stories was enough to double sales (to approximately 500,000) and quadruple audience figures to two million, with many waiting in long queues outside lending libraries to obtain the most recent edition (Wiltse 108; Pound 92). In no time, Sherlock Holmes and his indomitable Doctor Watson became cult figures with the public.

In 1893—a mere six years from Holmes's original appearance in *A Study in Scarlet* and a meager eighteen months from his rise to fame in "A Scandal in Bohemia" in *The Strand*—Doyle decided to kill off his erstwhile hero, citing dissatisfaction and embarrassment over his literary creation.[15] The notorious publication, "The Final Problem," appeared in the December 1893 edition of *The Strand*, and its consequences were immediately felt all over the world. Over twenty thousand subscribers immediately cancelled their subscriptions to the magazine. Fanlore reports sympathetic mourners bearing black armbands over their sleeves; readers wept in the streets. Doyle received hate mail labeling him "a brute." He was amazed at the public's response: "They say that a man is never appreciated until he is dead and the general protest against my summary execution of Holmes taught me how many and numerous were his friends" (Doyle, *Memories* 99–100).

Perhaps the biggest indicator of fan investment in Doyle's Sherlock Holmes, and the most analogous to contemporary fan production, is the number of literary pastiches and adaptations that have been produced over the past century.[16] Hundreds of Sherlockian parodies appeared between 1893 and 1900 during Doyle's hiatus from the Holmes stories, including: Cunnin' Toil's "The Adventures of Picklock Holes" published in *Punch* (1893); Charles Brookfield and Seymor Hicks's play, *Under the Clock, or Sheerluck* (1893); Charles Hamilton's ninety-seven literary parodies including characters "Herlock Sholmes" and "Dr. Jotson"; and the first silent Sherlock Holmes film, *Sherlock Holmes Baffled* (1900), followed by the first talking Holmes film, *The Return of Sherlock Holmes* (1929) (Campbell 107, 108; Duncan 190). Arguably, one of the most famous nineteenth-century pastiches, William Gillette's drama, *Sherlock Holmes* (1899), was an adaptation of a play Doyle himself had written for the stage but had been unsuccessful in producing. In addition to professionally produced pastiches, 1890s magazine promotions and letter columns in *The Strand*'s companion periodical, *Tit-Bits*, encouraged fans to recreate Sherlock Holmes's London, imagining new adventures for the detective and his partner, Dr. Watson. Readers were encouraged to write and submit their own Sherlock Holmes pastiches, to participate in fandom quizzes on Holmes's methods, or to vote on their favorite Sherlock Holmes stories, thus creating fan communities and norms similar to contemporary online fan boards such as LiveJournal and Archive of Our Own.[17] Throughout the twentieth century, thousands of writers, amateur and professional, were drawn to Doyle's characters and his mysterious world of London landmarks, darkened alleyways, and cozy sitting rooms.[18]

Although Doyle was frustrated at the revenue unauthorized pastiches and parodies took from his bank account, he was sometimes famously lenient with proposed changes to his characters and stories, while at other times he was incredibly strict regarding what he found acceptable for Holmes's world. In response to Gillette's question, "May I marry Holmes?" for his 1899 play adaptation, Doyle famously responded, "You may marry or murder or do what you like with him" (Doyle, *Memories* 102). He complained, however, that neither Sidney Paget's nor any other subsequent illustrations or impersonations of Holmes accurately matched his description of the character in the original stories (Doyle, *Memories* 106). In light of the BBC's updated version, interestingly, Doyle had vehemently rejected any kind of modernization, including telephones, motor cars, and other modern conveniences (Doyle, *Memories* 106; Carr 207).[19] Ironically, some of the most popular mid-twentieth-century film versions of Sherlock Holmes, including both Arthur Wontner's take as the great detective (1931–37) and the legendary Basil Rathbone's portrayals (1939–46), were set in modern times, most notably with Rathbone in fedora and trench coat battling Nazis in *Sherlock Holmes and the Voice of Terror* (1942).

After almost a decade of increasing public demand and its associated growing financial incentive, in 1901 Doyle finally decided to publish a new serialized Holmes novella, *The Hound of the Baskervilles*; however, he asserted, this was not a return of the famous detective but rather a cleverly backdated adventure that had taken place within the timeline of the original stories. Readers lined up outside *The Strand*'s offices the morning the first installment was published, employees were offered bribes for advance copies, and *The Strand*'s circulation jumped immediately to more than thirty thousand copies (Stashower 237). The novella continued to be a massive best seller when published subsequently in book form, a success that was enough to encourage Doyle's return to writing Holmes stories. The day in October 1903 that Holmes officially returned from the dead in "The Adventure of the Empty House" is a matter of literary history: "The scenes at the railway-bookstalls," wrote one witness, "were worse than anything I ever saw at a bargain-sale" (quoted in Carr 202).

Doyle continued to publish Sherlock Holmes tales right up until his death from a heart attack in 1930. Faced with a future without the great detective, dedicated fans established "keep Holmes alive" societies as sites to share their love of the detective and his adventures and to analyze his method. Today over seven hundred Sherlock Holmes organizations exist worldwide, but the first were formed in San Francisco, Chicago, Boston, and of course London. Perhaps the most famous was the New York society, the Baker Street Irregulars, begun in 1934 by Christopher Morley, a literary journalist working at the *Saturday Review of Literature*. Its initial charge was to honor Holmes's life and achievements and, above all, to revere and practice his science of deduction. The equally famous Sherlock Holmes Society of London, also begun in the early 1930s, played a major role in bringing Holmes back into the public eye for the 1951 Festival of Britain. Initially, the Public Libraries Commission had suggested an exhibit on Sherlock Holmes, but many festival committee members thought the detective too out-of-date and unappealing to a larger audience. In response, Sherlockians began a letter-writing campaign to the *Times* demanding that Holmes be featured as site of Britishness in the exhibition. Letters allegedly from Dr. Watson, Inspector Lestrade, even Mycroft Holmes himself flowed in, some of which claimed to have mementoes of Holmes that they offered to share for the exhibition (Sherlock Holmes Society). The result was the first reconstruction of the sitting room at 221b Baker Street, which later became the foundation of today's Sherlock Holmes Museum.

These early Sherlockian fan societies also introduced one of the singular elements of Sherlockian fandom: "The Great Game." Generally attributed to Ronald Knox's 1911 paper "Studies in the Literature of Sherlock Holmes," originally delivered at Oxford University, the "Great Game" refers to the unusual assertion that Sherlock Holmes and John Watson were real people and that Conan Doyle's stories were actually Watson's personal memoirs; Arthur Conan Doyle, in these circumstances, is relegated to the role of Watson's editor and/or literary agent.[20] In his founding satirical essay, Knox argued that even the most popular of texts, like that of Doyle's Holmes, could be treated as objects of serious research if one used the elements of the Higher Criticism, recently established in the nineteenth century as a method for interpreting the Bible as a historical document. Mystery novelist and Sherlock Holmes Society member Dorothy L. Sayers was instrumental in establishing the rules of the Great Game early on in the preface to her book, *Unpopular Opinions*, one of the most important being that the game must be played with all the "solemnity of a country cricket match at Lord's, the slightest touch of extravagance or burlesque ruining the atmosphere" (quoted in Hall 4), leading many serious academics to question the validity of the Holmes stories as worthy fodder for serious literary analysis and of Sherlock Holmes scholars as one of their number. Referring to the Holmes stories as "the sacred writings"—the *canon*—players of the game meet in their various societies to honor the characters' real lives and produce mock-scholarly essays tracing the origins of Holmes's family tree and the layout of 221b or speculating on Holmes's relationship with Irene Adler and whether the two ever had an illegitimate child. Lacking the internet as venue, the Baker Street Irregulars established a literary journal (essentially equivalent to a modern-day fanzine) to share their creations. *The Baker Street Journal*, dedicated solely to publishing Great Game scholarship on the sacred writings, was founded in 1946 and, other than a brief hiatus between 1949 and 1951, it remains the most popular publication for Sherlockian scholarship today.

Historically, many academics have disparaged Great Game scholarship, but our new vantage point within cultural studies makes it possible to look back and recognize such work for what it was: early-twentieth-century fan production. Just as in contemporary fan practices, Great Game scholars and Sherlockians created a community with shared norms, expectations, and behaviors, including a gift economy of shared work and fan creations (stories, specialized pamphlets, Christmas cards, artwork) within communal spaces (*The Baker Street Journal*, society meetings). While the original letters to Sherlock Holmes at 221b Baker Street perhaps lack the tongue-in-cheek positioning that characterizes postmodernism, from the beginning Great Game scholars assumed an ironic stance toward academic scholarship and the boundaries between fiction and reality, both of which imply the kind of play in which contemporary writers and fan producers engage.[21] Perhaps one of the reasons researchers have not explicitly identified early Sherlock Holmes history and research as fandom is because most Sherlockians—whether as part of the seriousness of the Great Game or due to other identity issues—would deny they were fans in the first place. Rather, most Sherlockians prefer the labels "admirer, enthusiast, devotee, aficionado," even when "they are fully aware of the cultural hierarchies at play" between these terms and the term *fan* (Pearson, "Barbies" 106–7). With the pioneering work in fan studies from the likes of Camille Bacon-Smith, Henry Jenkins, Matt Hills, however, such cultural attitudes toward fans have changed. With new models of deep media and transmedia storytelling, fans have become an integral part of media's global marketplace. As Jenkins himself articulates, "We should no longer be talking about fans as if they were somehow marginal to the ways the culture industries operate" ("Afterword" 362). Instead, as this analysis of *Sherlock* illustrates, fans are now fundamental to the ways in which producers develop, create, and maintain new media projects.[22]

In an amazingly short period of time, Sherlock Holmes became one of the most famous media icons of our time. In his analysis of the cult film favorite, *Casablanca*, Umberto Eco theorized three defining characteristics of the cult text. First, the text must come "completely furnished" with an identifiable and complete narrative world that the reader can return to again and again (198). The narrative world of 221b Baker Street was fully functioning even in Doyle's lifetime and a site of fan tourism. "I do not think that I ever realized what a living personality Holmes had become to the more guileless readers," Doyle wrote in his *Memories and Adventures*, "until I heard of the very pleasing story of the *char-a-banc* of French schoolboys who, when asked what they wanted to see first in London, replied unanimously that they wanted to see Mr. Holmes's lodgings in Baker Street" (108). The continuing popularity for Sherlockian pilgrimages to 221b Baker Street, now the Sherlock Holmes Museum, testifies to Holmes's modern cult status.

Second, the cult text must be encyclopedic; that is, it must contain innumerable details, quotations, and objects that can be extracted from the source and proliferated on their own. "In order to transform a work into a cult object," Eco argues, "one must be able to break, dislocate, unhinge it so that one can remember only parts of it, irrespective of their original relationship to the whole" (200). The Great Game of Sherlockian pseudo-scholarship is dedicated to mining these hidden elements from the original stories, with entire journals dedicated to publication of the results. Holmes has become so detached from his origins that his most famous line, "Elementary, my dear Watson," is a complete fabrication that does not exist in any of the original stories.[23] One doesn't need to mention the name of Sherlock Holmes at all to invoke the myth behind the cult; his famous silhouette (deerstalker hat, meerschaum pipe, Inverness cape, magnifying glass) is sufficient, but the image itself can be broken down, disasssembled into its individual components, and each alone is enough to summon the entirety of the narrative world.

Ultimately, the cult text escapes from the author's control and becomes a text of texts with no origin other than its own proliferation (Eco 199). Sherlock Holmes is not now and has never been a purely literary figure. Much like the genre in which he initially appeared, Holmes has himself become a "subject of sheer seriality," "a proliferating cultural icon, a literary simulacrum without origin or end" (Kestner 116, quoting from a 1993 essay by literary critic Laurie Langbauer). From this point of view, then, limiting investigation of Holmes's popularity to the literary stories alone is insufficient, since it ignores the intersection of text with modern media developments such as advertising, radio, film, television, and the internet. The connection between Holmes's popularity and the rise of media culture is nowhere more evident than in the ubiquitous uses of his image and name over the last century to sell everything from tobacco to gin to citrus. Rather than seeing Holmes as a "meeting place for different discourses," we need to recognize that Holmes himself *is* a discourse (Plakotaris 41). By analyzing how this discourse is disseminated across media platforms, ranging from literary series to television to fanfiction, we gain a better understanding of the relationship between audience reception and the production of texts.

Fanfiction and Fan Studies: A Primer and History

Although many academics and general audiences may be un-aware of fan studies as a field, the discipline actually has a forty-plus-year critical history within academia and an even longer trajectory within communities generated by print traditions such as science fiction and fantasy. For science fiction writers before the 1960s, fanfiction (technically called fan_fiction) meant any original writing published by amateur writers (predominantly men in those days) in what were known as zines, fan magazines created, printed, and distributed by fans of the field. Sometimes handwritten, sometimes typed, zines were mimeographed or photocopied collections of original stories mailed to interested parties who subscribed to fandom lists through popular science fiction magazines or at regional conventions (Jamison, *Fic* 75). In contrast to our current understanding of the term, pre-1960s fan fiction focused primarily on producing original science fiction stories, rather than building on existing TV shows, films, or books written by other authors or creating narratives about the lives of fans themselves (for example, the TV series *The Big Bang Theory* or Rainbow Rowell's popular 2013 book, *Fan Girl*). However, with the rise of new technological forms—that is, the shift from print to media culture, particularly the predominance of film and television media and, later, the internet—the conditions of fan production and fan activity changed as well.

The 1960s saw two dramatic shifts in fan activities. First, spurred by the popularity and influence of the 1960s sci-fi TV show *Star Trek*, fan culture shifted genres from original fiction produced by amateur writers to fiction situated within, and responding to, already published fictional worlds. Rather than write their own original fiction, fans wrote about characters from *Star Trek* or *The Man from U.N.C.L.E.*, to name just two examples. Second, Western media fandom came to be dominated by female, rather than male, fans (Jamison, *Fic* 75). The first shift gave rise to our contemporary understanding of fanfiction (no space) as a cultural practice and literary genre. As Lev Grossman explains, fanfiction is comprised of "stories and novels that make use of the characters and settings from other people's professional creative work." Such fans believe they have the right to "take possession of characters and settings of other people's narratives and tell their own tales about them—to expand and build upon the original, and, when they deem it necessary, to tweak it and optimize it for their own purposes" (Grossman). In the case of *Star Trek*, in particular, female fans began writing and circulating stories about the USS *Enterprise* crew in romantic relationships with one another, denoted by the slash mark. Joining the names or initials of primary characters in this way (Kirk/Spock, for example) indicated an erotic or explicitly sexual relationship between those characters. This type of writing produced some of the most popular stories circulated among female fans—enough to support an entire fanzine industry (Coppa, *Fanfiction Reader* 19; Sawyer, quoted in Jamison, *Fic* 84).[24]

While *Star Trek* is often cited as ground zero for contemporary fan practices, more recently critics have started to broaden our conceptualization of the genre by looking at earlier forms of authorized and unauthorized writings, ranging from Homer's collections of the *Odyssey* and *Iliad* stories to Shakespeare's reimaginings of Thomas Kyd's *Spanish Tragedy* in *Hamlet* or, more recently, to late nineteenth- and early twentieth-century Sherlock Holmes pastiches, parodies, and comics. In the aforementioned examples, authors adopt the main characters, geography, and major plot elements of an already established fictional world and create new narratives that then exist outside the original text. Fanfic can provide backstory on individual characters, fill in gaps left within original storylines, create new plotlines, extend the world and its characters beyond the boundaries of the original source, place the characters into new situations or worlds, and more.[25] Fanfiction authors bring a "What if?" mentality to the world and imagine various hypothetical possibilities for character development and story that are clearly outside the established boundaries of the canon (Mittell, "Strategies" 274–75). "What if?" narratives are not intended to replace or merely reproduce "what is" stories, that is, the narrative as it already exists; rather, they are valued for the ways they *expand* the fictional world to offer readers new versions of characters, place, and themes (Parrish 5.11). When written by amateurs, such stories are seen as unauthorized versions of the authorized or canonical world; that is, they are not condoned by the original producers or creators or acknowledged as authentic extensions of the original world, they are not copyrighted, and they are not due any financial remuneration—fanfiction creators do not get paid for their work.

Technological developments in the 1980s and 1990s had dramatic impact on the volume and pervasiveness of fanfiction in the following decades. The laborious work of editing, collating, and distributing fanzines in the 1960s and 1970s was replaced by instantaneous internet publishing, with virtually no roadblocks to publication and access. Digital listserves followed by message boards, fan sites, online journal and blog platforms, and contemporary social media sites all provided fans with ready access to multiple fandoms, new genres of writing and fan activity, and vast communities with common interests. The rise of digital platforms, particularly contemporary social media sites, also helped solidify fandom practices and community mores so that it became easier for fans and audiences alike to understand and articulate what fandom *is* and what it *does*. In the words of fan scholar Anne Jamison: "The Internet changed fanfiction. Period" (*Fic* 113).

Francesca Coppa, in *The Fanfiction Reader* (2017), has provided a helpful breakdown of the major characteristics of contemporary fanfiction. Using the fandom motif of the *5+1* format—five times something happened or didn't happen, plus one extra item—Coppa articulates six main elements:

1. Fanfiction is created outside of the literary marketplace. (2)
2. Fanfiction is fiction that rewrites and transforms other stories. (4)
3. Fanfiction is fiction that rewrites and transforms stories currently owned by others. (6)
4. Fanfiction is written within and to the standards of a particular fannish community. (7)
5. Fanfiction is speculative fiction about character rather than about the world. (12)

(+1) Fanfiction is made for free, but not "for nothing." (14)

Coppa begins by making important distinctions between contemporary fanfiction and pastiche—that is, professionally published literature written in the style of another writer or about previously created and published characters. For many fans and scholars, the fact that fanfiction is done outside the literary marketplace is a key defining characteristic and what differentiates it from something like Gregory Maguire's *Wicked* (a retelling of the *Wizard of Oz* from the Wicked Witch of the West's point of view), Peter Carey's *Jack Maggs* (a retelling of Charles Dickens's *Great Expectations*), or even Nicholas Meyer's *Seven-Per-Cent Solution* (a fictional portrayal of Arthur Conan Doyle's Sherlock Holmes meeting real-life psychoanalyst Sigmund Freud for therapy). Often, fan works are gifted to other fans—that is, they are offered freely as gestures of good will, friendship, and camaraderie, with no other expectation than general appreciation.[26] While Coppa claims fan works are done for love rather than profit (*Fanfiction* 3), another way to frame the difference would be to think about motivation. Fans write for other fans, without plan for or thought of economic gain, which further supports Coppa's fourth requirement: the importance and influence of the fan community.

One of the most important elements determining what constitutes fanfiction is that it is written, published, and accessed within a community environment created by fans, for fans. Internet platforms like LiveJournal.com, Fanfiction.net, and Archive of Our Own (AO3.org) provide fans with safe spaces where they can share their ideas, writing, theories, insecurities, and even sexual kinks, ideally without fear of reprisal, copyright threats, or shame. While this isn't always the case, fandom moderators work collaboratively to create rules and standards of behavior intended to provide community-based guidelines for publication and critique. These shared understandings of fandom also help create fan-based genres, tropes, warnings, and shortcuts that help fan writers and readers find each other by interest, whether fandom (*Sherlock* versus *Elementary* or Robert Downey Jr. as Sherlock Holmes), story type (alternate universe, slash, RPF), or trope (male pregnancy or mpreg, first time). Some common tags or tropes, such as rape, noncon (nonconsensual sex), or incest, also serve to help warn readers away from kinds of fic that might trigger damaging emotional or psychological reactions (Busse, *Framing* 117). Fan communities likewise assist fans to expand their understanding of the source world by providing sites for knowledge sharing and archiving (Jenkins, *Textual Poachers*). Thus, the context in which a fanfiction is created and disseminated is integral to its meaning and reception. The recent spate of fanfiction debacles in the news (like Caitlin Moran reading *Sherlock* fanfiction excerpts to the cast at a media event or UK TV talk show host Graham Norton sharing fan comments, art, and fanfiction with celebrities on his show) raise considerable anger and concern among fans, who understand the unique situations within which fandom tropes, expectations, and storylines are created and welcomed. To remove these from their context can be as damaging as viewing Andy Warhol's *Campbell's Soup Cans* in a magazine ad in *People Magazine*. Context matters. As Francesca Coppa concludes: "No work of art can or should be divorced from its cultural surroundings (both ethos and pathos, writer and reader)" (*Fanfiction* 215).

The fact that fanfiction "rewrites and transforms" previously published stories (Coppa's second and third points) has been an important factor in copyright disputes involving derivative versus transformative works. Several contemporary fan scholars, such as Henry Jenkins, Paul Booth, Janet Murray, Louisa Stein, and Kristina Busse, have described fanfiction as seeking to rework, repair, dismiss, enact, and play with the text (Jenkins, *Textual Poachers* 165; Booth, *Digital Fandom* 75; Murray 170; Stein and Busse 195).[27] Fan writers do not reproduce the original plotlines, characters, and world of the source text; *they rewrite them*, adding their own views, politics, and affective needs. Revision is thus a key element of fanfiction and what, according to US copyright law, protects it from legal suit; but revision also makes fanfiction *transformative*. That is, rewriting the original text transforms the original cult text into a new work of art. For some theorists, this transformation is also *performative*: fanfictions make someone else's characters and world perform according to different rules and storylines (Coppa, "Writing Bodies" 230); such enacted events transform the original events by making them part of the readers' personal experiences (Murray 170). Similarly, the act of writing allows fans to perform their emotional attachment to and identity within a specific fan community (Bury 37, 75).

Fan studies, and fanfiction studies in particular, has roots in 1970s and 1980s British cultural studies, particularly in Stuart Hall's popular culture paradigm of incorporation and resistance, and in early reception studies. Reception studies looked at audience composition, behaviors, and specific viewing practices and ultimately argued that, rather than being passive consumers, media subcultures (interest-based audiences) had the power to subvert dominant ideologies through their own countercultural readings of popular texts. The first wave of fan studies scholarship adopted this subculture view toward fans and emphasized their active, rather than passive, participation in contemporary media production and reception. Early 1990s fan studies scholarship (Jenkins *Textual Poachers*; Penley "Feminism"; Bacon-Smith) concentrated on the ways fan writers have been seen as outsiders to traditional society, as members of culturally subordinate groups, particularly women, and on how, as a result, fan practice has often been viewed as an artistic resistance to dominant social mores.[28] The resistance model has not necessarily always been viewed as a positive one, however.

In this first wave of fan studies scholarship in the early 1990s, Henry Jenkins argued that our modern day understanding of the fan as over-invested and excessively emotional comes from early twentieth-century portrayals of female film audiences (*Textual Poachers* 12), and his portrayal of fan authors as "textual poachers," while foundational for fanfiction studies, has more recently been challenged as negatively labeling fan practices. Building off the work of French theorist Michel de Certeau, Jenkins argues that fans "appropriate popular texts and reread them in a fashion that serves different interests, as spectators who transform the experience of watching television into a rich and complex participatory culture" (Jenkins, *Textual Poachers* 23). While the passage positively praises fans for enriching other media by transforming it into a participatory experience, the word *appropriation*—like *poaching*—implies that readers are taking something that doesn't belong to them. *Poaching* historically has meant hunting on someone else's land, taking livestock or sustenance that legally belongs to another, without permission. Jenkins does clarify that while de Certeau sees poaching as an "impertinent raid on the literary preserve that takes away only those things that are useful or pleasurable to the reader" (24), he sees it as a countercultural move whereby fans can influence and even change contemporary cultural images and dominant messages, thus challenging artistic, cultural, and legal attitudes regarding textual ownership. Other critics, however, remain concerned that the theoretical term *poaching* reinforces negative stereotypes of fan activity (Parrish 1.5). Both Parrish and Constance Penley argue that "Brownian motion" is perhaps a more apt description of fan practices like fanfiction. Defined as "the tactical maneuvers of the relatively powerless when attempting to resist, negotiate, or transform the system and products of the relatively powerful" (Penley, "Brownian Motion" 139), Brownian motion better signals the in-between relationship among unauthorized, subcultural fan audiences and authorized cultural producers and creators.

Much of *Sherlock's World* engages with this exact power dynamic between corporate producers and fan creators, and the book looks at the ways in which *Sherlock*'s producers set up the show's world and how fans embrace, challenge, and expand that world through their fanfiction. Fanfiction, then, is tactical, intentional, with clear motivations and strategies for responding to and transforming cult texts. It provides means for the relatively powerless to respond to and challenge dominant cultural messages about gender, sexuality, power, and more. Rather than poaching from the authorized text, under the Brownian motion concept fans are characterized as seeking to negotiate and transform the original source as a mode of resistance, until fanfiction becomes "nearly indivisible from world building" (Parrish 1.5). While *Sherlock's World* doesn't get into the motivations underlying why fans write *Sherlock* fanfic, it does look at the ways fanfic uses genre and tropes to interrogate the boundaries of the *Sherlock* world through the themes of identity, sexuality, gender, and place.

By the late 1990s and early 2000s, other fan scholars had begun to raise concerns about viewing fans as subversive, homogenous groups and had shifted their emphasis to fans as individuals with personal emotional relationships to specific texts (Busse, *Framing* 8). These "fandom as a way of life" texts (Abercrombie and Longhurst; Hills, *Fan Culture*; and Sandvoss) all looked at how fans engage with particular fandoms, objects, and communities to perform a particular identity. The engagement of second-wave fan studies with performance and the materiality of fandom (fan objects, memorabilia, cinematic tourism, and so on) remains an important element in current fan scholarship and raises important questions about class, economics (who can afford to perform fandom, where, and for whom?), race and gender (cosplay debates, the Gamergate controversy that followed the eruption of vicious online harassment of women in the videogame and media worlds), and identity. While much of first- and second-wave fan studies scholarship focused on ethnographic approaches, interviews, and surveys of specific fan audiences and subgroups, the next wave of fan studies seemed to move away from such human-focused research to a more abstract, conceptual approach to audience and reception studies.

Third-wave fan studies takes a much broader, industrial approach to fan practices, looking at the combined practices of audiences and media industries to analyze the various ways they work conjointly and in opposition. Foundational books such as Henry Jenkins's *Convergence Culture* (2006) look at the ways contemporary media production is changing how fans access and consume new media. Rather than critique either media corporations or fans themselves, Jenkins instead posits new models for how the two demographics work *together*. He looked at how open source technologies like YouTube, Tumblr, and Twitter allowed audiences to adapt, remix, and renew already existing media, and he encourages media producers to open up similar spaces for audience engagement and creation and to partner with amateur producers to reach new audiences. In 2014, for example, *Doctor Who* fan Billy Hanshaw created and uploaded on YouTube his own original title sequence for the TV series. After receiving more than 60,000 views in its first weekend, *Who* showrunner (and *Sherlock* co-creator) Steven Moffat contacted Hanshaw and negotiated the rights to use the new intro for the show (Youngs). While such partnerships between media moguls and individual fans bring opportunities for greater audience collaboration and influence, they also run the risk of alienating fans from their labor and co-opting fan work into larger corporate structures and profits.

Jenkins's work continues to focus on potential collaborations between media industrialists and fan producers (Jenkins, Ford, and Green 2013), but more importantly, he has also brought in educators and civic leaders from across the country to imagine ways teachers, students, and media professionals can bring about change in approaches to, and appropriations of, new media and various texts (Jenkins, *Reading in a Participatory Culture*; Jenkins, et al., *By Any Media Necessary*; The Civic Imagination Project). This democratization of fandom comes at a pivotal time, with calls for more attention to, and inclusion of, underrepresented groups within fandom. Most readers will readily acknowledge that fandom is a *human* activity, not just a white, Western one, so it's surprising that most fans and fan scholars only focus on predominantly white, middle-class, Western characters and/or fandoms. While fandom has done a good job of addressing gender and sexuality in popular culture, it has done much less well with transnational fandoms, with race and ethnicity in the United States and worldwide, with ability/disability, and with other underrepresented groups. The move toward greater representation and inclusion is an important way in which fan studies continues to change how we view ourselves and our culture and how we represent the human experience.

Current work in fan studies often focuses on changing interdisciplinary understandings of fandom, whether behavior-based, identity-based, or object-based. Fans can be defined (and studied) by the things they do, by who they are, or by what they produce. *Sherlock's World* falls into the third category. Along with its attempts to contextualize contemporary fan practices within a broader historical understanding of Sherlock Holmes fandom, *Sherlock's World* brings literary analysis together with the broader interdisciplinary frameworks of media studies, literary studies, and world building. By focusing solely on *Sherlock* fanfiction, this book provides a much-needed in-depth analysis of a particular fan practice (fanfiction) within a specific fandom (*Sherlock*) within a particular world (Sherlock Holmes).

World Building in Fanfiction:
Canon, Characterization, and Compliance

So how does fanfiction build a fictional world? In three primary ways: by reinforcing the canonical storyline; by incorporating the iconic geographic place/space, which includes location, geography, and objects; and by building on the given characters.

Fictional worlds with the most recognizable characters, settings, objects, and syntax are often the most commercially successful—and the most frequently appropriated for fanfiction (Wolf 278). Iconic fictional worlds like those in *The Lord of the Rings*, *Star Wars*, *Game of Thrones*, and, of course, Sherlock Holmes are constantly invoked across popular culture in licensed merchandise, spin-offs, comics, video games, and webisodes, as well as in unlicensed pastiches, parodies, and other fan products. Fans' fascination with the fictional world drives them to seek out additional extensions through which to (re)immerse themselves in the universe by consuming additional related paratexts.[29] Fanfiction's reliance on, and simultaneous impulse to challenge, canon can result in interesting conflicts, however. On the one hand, the most unforgiveable sin in any fanfic universe is departing from canon and getting basic facts wrong, a fault known as *noncompliance* (Pugh 40); at the same time, however, fans also seek to creatively modify, remix, alter, and extend the original story and characters (Jenkins, "Afterword" 362). Often, these explorations focus on

"What if?" stories that examine alternative storylines, conclusions, and different universes. Sometimes fans are motivated to create their own stories by their frustrations with the source text, whether with a particular storyline or character or with the show's implicit views on issues such as race, sexuality, or class. According to Camille Bacon-Smith, as specific canonical content becomes unstuck from the source text and its authors, fan writers are able to fragment, recombine, and transform that content into new and even unreal combinations (Bacon-Smith 293). Fanfiction's position between canon and original fiction provides room for exactly the kind of limited play that allows fans to challenge dominant societal narratives.[30] Canon is necessary both for world building and as something to write *against* (Pugh 40).

Originally referring to the accepted set of texts and religious law within biblical scripture, the term *canon* was applied to literary studies in the early twentieth century to describe the most important and influential literary works, particularly within the Western tradition.[31] At a more focused level, the term is applied to a particular body of work by a group of writers in a particular literary period or genre (Romantic poets, for example) or to the body of work by one author. In the arena of fanfiction and world building, specifically, canon refers to the major storylines, significant characters, settings, objects, and themes that dominate a particular media text or world. For many critics (and fans), canon is central to all fanfiction. "Charting the canonical events, characters, and settings featured in a storyworld is a central mode of engagement" for fans, according to Jason Mittell ("Strategies" 256).[32] Fanfiction authors "know their work fits into a structure that includes both the source products and all the diction that has grown around them" (Bacon-Smith 56), so fans' knowledge of canon becomes another form of cultural capital whereby they both showcase and share their knowledge by participating in larger fan communities (Bury 100). The source text becomes a fetishized object, but rather than viewing it as "a solitary, pristinely autonomous object," as happens in literary study (Sandvoss 21), within fandom the ur-text becomes a site for proliferation and expansion.

Canon has special significance for Sherlock Holmes scholarship, in particular, referring to Doyle's original so-called sacred writings, the sixty stories and novels comprising the Sherlock Holmes collection. If one includes the various pastiches, comics, parodies, radio dramas, and film and

TV versions over the past century, however, the Sherlockian canon is immense. This wealth constituted an important creative element for Moffat and Gatiss when they created their own modern-day *Sherlock* television show: "There's an enormous amount of stuff and everything is canonical, the Billy Wilder film [*The Private Life of Sherlock Holmes*], the Basil Rathbone films—they can all be drawn upon as a *Sherlock* source" (Morgan). *Sherlock*'s official canon comprises the 13 extant episodes (although one might argue that *The Abominable Bride* special, originally aired in 2015, technically counts as an alternate universe episode and thus should not be considered part of the *Sherlock* canon). General plotlines include John and Sherlock's original meeting in the lab at St. Bart's Hospital, their encounters with Moriarty, John's marriage to Mary Morstan, and the main cases covered in each episode. In the contemporary digital age, however, no TV show, film, or text stands alone without various paratexts framing, commenting on, and extending its world. Paratexts, according to theorist Gerard Genette, include all the ancillary materials framing a text's reception. In print books, this can be title pages, prefaces, epigraphs, footnotes, or even book jackets, cover images, and illustrations. These all act as messages to the reader and ultimately become indistinguishable from the text itself. In the case of film or television, paratexts include trailers, movie posters, DVD covers, summary descriptions, the title sequence, marketing materials, and so on. For *Sherlock*, framing extends to all of the DVD packaging and DVD extras; the original unaired pilot included on the season one DVD; audio commentaries; "Making of" episodes aired on PBS *Masterpiece*, along with the BBC's marketing materials and press packs, images, co-merchandizing (the reissued Arthur Conan Doyle Sherlock Holmes books with Cumberbatch and Freeman on the cover and the *Sherlock*-themed Cluedo game); and tie-in websites: all combine to create a substantial transmedial canon from which fans can pull. Indeed, Moffat and Gatiss were right: Everything is canon for *Sherlock* and its fans.

Because of the depth of paratexts surrounding a show like *Sherlock* (which has had only four seasons; imagine *Supernatural*, with its thirteen seasons of twenty-plus episodes—so far!), what counts as canon can be a contested topic within fandom. Do you use the 221b furniture and props from the unaired pilot for your setting or do you use the aired version from "A Study in Pink"? Do you base Sherlock's sexuality on his initial conversation at Angelo's restaurant from the pilot or from the first episode, since

Cumberbatch and Freeman portrayed the two iterations very differently? Each fanfiction acts as a particular interpretation of the various canonical elements, a form of *epitext*, to use another of Genette's terms—that is, a form of commentary or metadiscourse on the canonical world. Fans take the content of the show and the materials surrounding the source text and craft their own interpretation of the world—or an original conception of how the world might be altered, changed, or adapted to other situations and frameworks. As a result, sometimes fans interpret the show in ways that do not necessarily align with the original creators' vision. One hotly debated topic within *Sherlock* fandom, for example, is the nature of John and Sherlock's relationship on the show. Moffat and Gatiss have written numerous scenes, starting from the very first episode, in which various characters indicate a belief that Sherlock and John are gay. Moffat and Gatiss, however, as well as the lead actors, Cumberbatch and Freeman, have maintained numerous times in press conferences and media events that the characters are just close friends.[33] Contrary to this position, a substantial majority of *Sherlock* fanfiction is nonetheless about a romantic and/or sexual relationship between John and Sherlock. For *Sherlock* fans, a Johnlock pairing is canon, and, they argue, textual evidence within the TV episodes supports this interpretation, even though the show's creators and actors flatly deny such an interpretation. Fanfiction and canon, then, provide a public/private space for fans and showrunners to debate who has the authority to interpret a text and to determine canon.[34]

Not only do fans and corporations sometimes disagree on what counts as canon in particular franchises, sometimes fans remember or have different interpretations of the same text, episode, or scene. As Anne Jamison explains,

> Fans often regard their recollections as canon, when in fact every reading already includes a variety of interpretations beyond the base facts and usually places the fan into a group of like-minded readers. The fanfiction writer is constantly engaged in creating her own individualized version of canon: she foregrounds certain facts and scenes and overlooks others; she makes some aspects of the story much more central to her reading than they may be in the source text; and she reads the text within her own cultural context, thus affecting her very individual responses. (*Fic* 108)

Mostly, these individualized interpretations align with the events portrayed in the source; however, sometimes fan canon—or *fanon*—is completely disconnected from the source text and created wholly and completely within the fandom world. Fanon can range from an event or characteristic never portrayed in the original text to repeated motifs, minor facts, or simply fun elements added to the world. In Sir Arthur Conan Doyle's Sherlock Holmes world, Sherlock's deerstalker, meerschaum pipe, and Inverness cape can all be read as forms of cultural fanon: none of these characteristics existed in Doyle's original texts; rather, they come from various influential media outlets (Sidney Paget's original illustrations, William Gillette's stage performances and promotional images, Basil Rathbone's 1940s movie costumes, and so on). The Sherlockian Great Game scholars, similarly, contributed to the detective's fanon by portraying Doyle as Watson's literary agent (much to the Doyle estate's dismay) and by speculating on Watson's gender (as in Rex Stout's essay, "Watson Was a Woman"). Similarly, *Sherlock* fandom adopts its own tropes: John Watson loves jam, John has a secret stash of red underwear, forensics specialist Anderson has a dinosaur fetish—the list goes on. Some of these fanon tropes can be identified with particular fanfictions, but most cannot be traced back to a single fan-created source. Fanon just *is*, and fans love it. Ultimately, only a fine line separates canon and fanon in the world of fanfiction; all traceable elements come down to individual interpretations of the source text combined with the influence of the networked fan community. Those elements on which fandom agrees become articles of faith and are put to use in fanfiction to (re)construct the source world (Busse, *Framing* 110).

One way *Sherlock* fan writers establish canon is through detailed descriptions of the setting, at both macro and micro levels. At the macro level, viewers know *Sherlock* takes place in contemporary London in a world closely aligned with the politics, physics, and social rules of the actual world. At the micro level, audiences recognize that the majority of the episodes take place in John and Sherlock's flat, the famous 221b Baker Street apartment in London (even though the majority of exterior and interior shots are filmed on location or in the studio in Cardiff, Wales). The *Sherlock* world's verisimilitude depends on the consistency and detailed descriptions of the physical spaces and objects included in the canon (even if they're not realistic). Not only must the show's creators give the impression that the objects, furniture, location, and so on, of a specific place in the canon is real and believable within the constraints of that world, they must also imply that a larger world exists beyond the borders of the specific iteration and that it can be mapped and traveled through at length (Ryan, *Narrative* 124; Klastrup, *Towards a Poetics* 26). These objects, places, and spaces become diegetic objects with important symbolic value and usefulness for the fan, and they act as "especially intense site[s] of interpretive force" (Hayot 68), so much so that any overlap between the fictional world and the actual world, whether through cinematic tourism or purchase of commercial objects, becomes an additional site for immersion and realism.[35] (More details about the specific settings and objects within *Sherlock*'s physical world are discussed in chapter 1.)

Another major element in establishing *Sherlock*'s canonical world in fanfiction is characterization, which includes everything from physical descriptions and mannerisms to clothing/costuming, speech patterns, and behavior. For *Sherlock*, the main body of characters includes some from the original Arthur Conan Doyle canon—Sherlock Holmes, John Watson, Mycroft Holmes, and Moriarty—as well as new recurring characters such as Molly Hooper. Others, although introduced in the original stories (Mrs. Hudson, Mary Morstan, Inspector Lestrade, Bill Wiggins, and so on), are more fully developed in the television show. For many critics and fans, canonical characterization is the most important element of fanfiction and world building alike; while fans may go along with substantial changes to the world's setting, plotlines, and themes, they will rebel if a writer's characterization veers too far from their vision of the original character (Ryan, "Story/Worlds/Media" 32; Pugh 65–66; Mittell, "Strategies" 260; Gregoriou 54). Fan authors must therefore be somewhat mimetic in their reproduction of distinct characters if their world is to be consistent and compliant with the canon (Pugh 70); otherwise, they may be accused of writing the protagonists OOC—out of character—and will risk losing readers.[36]

In fanfiction, both authors and audiences come to new texts already familiar with the setting and characters. Characters have established voices, whether they come from print texts or other media extensions, and readers' impressions of characters' physicality may likewise be influenced by prior knowledge of the actors who played the roles on-screen as well as other roles the actors may have played in other productions (both items will be covered in more detail in chapter 6 on real person fiction) (Coppa,

"Writing Bodies" 6). Fan authors study the source text in depth, analyzing its stylistic and linguistic codes to reproduce and invoke the source's composition (Bacon-Smith 159; Pearce 20). This syntax can range from a particular character's speech pattern and catchphrases (in *Sherlock*'s case, for example, "The game is on!" or "When you have eliminated the impossible, whatever remains, however improbable, must be the truth.") to a character's costuming to the generic structure of an episode (the mystery or police procedural). Our impression of the fanfiction character thus results from a combination of background schemata and explicit and implicit textual cues (Gregoriou 54). Ultimately, character becomes the tool whereby fans explore scenarios and challenge the boundaries of canon, and fans push the boundaries of characterization through their explorations of genre.

In general literary terms, genres are "patterns/forms/styles/structures which transcend individual art products, and which supervise both their construction by artists and their reading by audiences" (Ryall, quoted in Klastrup and Tosca 102). They are discursive practices that use layered "generic codes to associate media texts, characters, and narratives, to draw on already established meanings, and to make texts personally meaningful" (Stein, "Emotions-Only" 2.2). Writers and readers use generic conventions to create structural and thematic shortcuts to render the text's basic narrative assumptions visible. Interestingly, genre identification dominates most critical discussion and archiving of contemporary fanfiction. Codes or tags range from identifying (fanfic) genres such as slash (same-sex romantic or sexual pairings), genderswap (characters switch sex or gender identity), or alternate universe (protagonists appear in a different world or setting) to specific story tropes or trajectories, such as a "coffee shop AU" (a specific type of alternate universe story in which the primary action takes place in a coffee shop), "Aliens Made Them Do It" (a form unique to sci-fi fandom in which a character's actions are controlled by aliens), or first time fic (characters have their first sexual encounter).[37]

Just as a TV show's canon includes the multiple paratextual elements that surround the source text, fanfiction is similarly framed by paratextual elements that simultaneously signal to—and steer fans away from—particular stories, tropes, and fandoms (Busse, *Framing* 202). In early online fandom, in particular, the headers preceding works were significantly influential in establishing fandom vocabulary, norms, and expectations by providing readers with the fandom, rating (for example, *G* for general audience or *M* for mature audience), characters, genre, tropes, pairings, and a general summary (Busse, *Framing* 202; see also Derecho's "Archontic Literature").[38] Fanfiction writers foregrounded commonly used terms, genres, and tropes in header tags as a kind of shorthand that helped both them and their readers to understand the subtleties, meanings, and intentions of specific fandom stories (Busse, *Framing* 209). Tags also serve as an archival system for fanfic on online sites such as Archive of Our Own, helping fans search for the specific kind of story they seek. Tagging thus works to organize, sort, and archive fanfiction at the same time that it helps writers and readers understand and work within—and against— fandom conventions and expectations.

Sherlock's World tracks fans' use of unique categories such as role playing, slash, genderswap, alternate universe, and RPF to explore what makes particular fanfictions canonical. Transforming *Sherlock*'s characters and storylines into different genre conventions allows fans to shift the emphasis from plot to character and thus to challenge the boundaries between canon and fanon, fiction and reality. To set a clear history and context for Sherlockian world building—both in the nineteenth century and today—the first chapter introduces the key elements of *Sherlock*'s world: the Arthur Conan Doyle canon, modern London, the 221b Baker Street set; it then analyzes how *Sherlock*'s transmedia texts use both exclusive and inclusive models to build the show's fictional world. Looking at the BBC companion websites and Project Factory's Sherlock: The Network, the chapter examines the ways each platform uses different immersion strategies, including participation and interactivity, to create closed and open fictional worlds, both of which give users the impression of a complete, consistent, and coherent narrative space. Chapter 2 shifts away from corporate models to look at how fans imagine, create, and perform *Sherlock*'s world through online social media role playing. Contemporary audiences use social media to challenge traditional understandings of character, world building, and fandom and to achieve greater realism; role playing Sherlock and John on Facebook, Tumblr, and Twitter allows fans to break down the barriers between the fictional world and the actual world by enacting the characters in real-time exchanges that deepen for them the verisimilitude of the world.

Chapter 3, on slash fanfiction, expands on these questions by exploring the role of characterization and identity specifically. For many critics and fans, characterization is the most important element in fanfiction and the main device rendering the world identifiable, but both slash and genderswap fanfiction alter the main characters' sexual and gender identities to explore alternative storylines, erotic fantasies, and character development. The chapter therefore explores characterization in depth, focusing particularly on the ways two key texts—Kate_Lear's "Love Song of John H. Watson" and emmagranto1's "A Cure for Boredom"—comply with or alter canonical renderings of fictional identity. Ultimately, even though most slash fanfiction significantly alters the principal characters' sexuality and sexual identities, the stories themselves remain canon compliant by grounding their physical descriptions, syntax, and mannerisms in the original world of the show. Chapter 4 builds on the previous chapter's discussions of characterization, identity, sexuality, and gender to look at genderswap and transgender fanfiction. Genderswap fanfictions explore the personal, political, and cultural effects of changing a canonical character's biological sex. In such stories, the canonically male Sherlock or John (and/or other canonical characters) is sexed (and sometimes renamed) female, with resulting changes in the ways other characters respond to and perceive that character. The chapter examines several shorter fics, including "Astronomy" and "Categories" by Parachute_Silks; Mad_Maudlin's "In Arduis Fidelis"; SomeoneElsesDream's fem!Sherlock story, "And Then You Wake"; and transgender fics such as Ishmael's "Body of Evidence," Red's "A Room Untended," and Etothepii's "Seems so Easy for Everybody Else," to explore how (primarily female) fans respond to gendered characters and portrayals on the show and how they have used *Sherlock*'s world to make broader comments about the roles of sex, gender, and trans* identities in contemporary Western culture.

As *Sherlock's World* progresses, the imaginary worlds in the genres discussed get farther and farther away from the canonical world. If world building is the most important element in fanfiction and what draws audiences to a particular text or fandom to begin with, then why would fans want to imagine their favorite characters in different forms, settings, and time periods? The book's final two chapters analyze genres that seemingly violate several important tenets of world building: alternate universe (AU) fanfiction and real person fiction (RPF or real person slash). Chapter 5 looks at these seeming violations of the fictional world by examining key alternate universe fanfictions such as Mad_Lori's *Performance in a Leading Role*, Jupiter_Ash's "A Study in Winning," and earlgreytea68's *The Bang and the Clatter*. While on the surface an actor AU, a tennis AU, and a baseball AU may seem leagues away from *Sherlock*'s twenty-first-century London, what we find is that, even though these stories appear to be completely different fictional constructs than the original text, they in fact constantly refer back to and reinforce the original canonical settings, characterization, and syntax of the show. Alternate universe stories may seem the most canon divergent; however, they are often the most canon compliant of all fanfiction genres.

Real person fiction brings the issue of characterization to its logical breaking point. Since so many of the genre-shifting stories explored in the first several chapters depend on Cumberbatch and Freeman's depictions of Sherlock and John, the assumed boundaries between generic *Sherlock* fanfiction and real person fiction about Cumberbatch and Freeman potentially blur and disappear. RPFs are fantasy-based fictions that create fictional stories about real celebrities' lives. In fanfic, these are often either slash pairings of the real actors playing specific characters in a show or they place the reader in a personal encounter or relationship with the real-life actor playing the fictional role (self-insert fic). Looking at two self-insert fic Tumblr blogs focused on Benedict Cumberbatch and Martin Freeman, as well as a novel-length RPF, *Method Act* by Splix71, chapter 6 analyzes how contemporary fans appropriate celebrities' bodies and conflate the celebrities' personal identities with their fictional characterizations, ultimately challenging the distinction between real and fictionalized personas. Using the frameworks of celebrity studies and philosophical concepts of the self and authenticity, the chapter looks back at how the previously discussed genres of fanfic base much of their approaches to canonical world building on descriptions of the real-life physical appearance and mannerisms of the actors playing Sherlock and John. If so much of *Sherlock*'s world building is grounded in the real-life bodies of Benedict Cumberbatch and Martin Freeman, the chapter asks, what happens when fans cross the boundaries between fictional world and real world? The chapter looks at RPFs that attribute *Sherlock* plot and character elements to the real-world Cumberbatch and Freeman; it then analyzes Splix71's *Method Act*, which conflates the real and fictional worlds in a body-swapping (the mind of one character is magically or scientifically transferred into another character's body), multiverse exploration of character, fiction, reality, and canon.

The book concludes with a brief epilogue speculating on post-object fandom, fan responses to season four, and speculations on *Sherlock*'s future. Creators Steven Moffat and Mark Gatiss, along with stars Cumberbatch and Freeman, have widely reported that the show's future is uncertain and that they would be satisfied if the series ended with season four's last episode, "The Final Problem." For many fans and critics, however, *Sherlock*'s fourth season veered radically from previously established canonical norms, raising the question of what happens to the fictional world when the creators themselves seem to violate the basic characterization, genre, and world conventions they have spent more than seven years establishing. Similarly, the epilogue looks at fan responses to season four, particularly with a brief foray into the genre of fix-it fics in which fans strive to fix or realign the canonical world.

World building provides the essential structure connecting a text or media franchise to the various fan extensions created around it—and responding to it. The created worlds are both familiar and outward looking, implying a sense of possibility, creativity, and adventure. Fanfiction provides one way for audiences to immerse themselves in a familiar universe and to defamiliarize that universe through a variety of genre perspectives and conventions. To understand the vast creativity and expanse of *Sherlock* fanfiction, it is best to start with the first iteration of the Sherlock Holmes world: Sir Arthur Conan Doyle's nineteenth-century London.

CHAPTER ONE
TRANSMEDIA *SHERLOCK*
Exclusive and Inclusive World Building

We begin by exploring the main characteristics of *Sherlock*'s world and how the producers extrapolate the television show's primary elements into corporate transmedial world building practices and merchandising. Described as creating a coherent, unified narrative across multiple media platforms, transmedia storytelling has become a dominant mode of programming for media producers over the past several years. Such texts do not merely adapt a primary source into new formats; rather, they offer new perspectives into the characters and the complex world of the show—what scholar Matt Hills has labeled its *hyper-diegesis* (Evans 30; Hills, *Fan Culture* 137). Many critics emphasize transmedia's interactivity (that is, its inclusivity) as the primary way in which these stories engage audiences; however, the creators must first establish the world's primary canonical elements before audiences can engage with and potentially change or add to the fictional world. Building off the show's canon, *Sherlock*'s producers, Steven Moffat and Mark Gatiss, incorporate both exclusive and inclusive models of corporate transmedia storytelling to extend the show's hyper-diegesis. In addition to merchandising and tie-in novels, the BBC's character websites provide the showrunners with a space in which to adapt additional Arthur Conan Doyle stories, but the websites also create a static window through which viewers can read about John and Sherlock's further adventures beyond the show's original programming. Viewers can go to John's blog, but they cannot interact with it; its online verisimilitude creates the *illusion* of interactivity, but users are excluded from actively engaging with the closed world portrayed on the website. In Sherlock: The Network, however, users are directly addressed by Sherlock, John, and Mycroft through video, audio files, and text messaging that directly impact the user's navigation and strategization within the game. By making the user a member of Sherlock's famed "homeless network," the audience is virtually taken inside *Sherlock*'s world as a participant and co-creator, thus establishing an additional sense of connection with the show, its characters, and its storylines. By combining these seemingly dichotomous forms of transmedia storytelling, the show is able to create the simultaneous impression that *Sherlock*'s world is both a closed, cohesive unit and one open to, and part of, the viewer's real world.

Sir Arthur Conan Doyle's Nineteenth-Century Sherlockian World

Before we can begin analyzing fans' reactions to and participation within a transmedial world, we first need to study the ur-actualization of the world's core elements, which define its worldness (Klastrup and Tosca 4).[1] Determining *Sherlock*'s ur-text is tricky, however, since there have been hundreds of textual, televisual, film, and other media portrayals of the character ever since Sir Arthur Conan Doyle's introduction of Sherlock Holmes in 1887. Showrunners Moffat and Gatiss have spoken extensively about the many different adaptations they've appropriated for their own version (Digital Spy); however, most versions can be traced back to Doyle's original incarnation of Holmes in *A Study in Scarlet* (1887). Doyle established many of the most commonly recognized Sherlockian world elements in his original fifty-six short stories and four novellas, including foggy London city streets, the 221b Baker Street flat, and many of the original characters from the stories (Holmes, Watson, Mycroft, Lestrade, Mrs. Hudson, and so on). Doyle's nineteenth-century London is instantly recognizable and has been reproduced by scores of fiction writers, dramatists, scriptwriters, and fans over the succeeding years, beginning as early as 1892, and the realism of Doyle's representation of Victorian London is perhaps the reason why so many adaptations have focused so heavily on the tales' setting and milieu.[2] Because Doyle's 221b Baker Street was so full of minute and convincing details (Holmes's Persian slipper filled with tobacco, the jackknife-speared correspondence on the mantel, the unframed portrait of Henry Ward Beecher), early fans believed the fictional place to be real, and many planned trips to visit the home of the famous detective. Even though the 221b Baker Street address did not become a reality until 1930, fans still sent hundreds of letters, both to Doyle at his home, and later to the Abbey National Bank housed in Holmes's canonical address.[3] The Abbey National Bank received so many letters addressed to Holmes over the years that they had to hire a full-time secretary to respond to each one. Thousands of fans to this day make the pilgrimage to Holmes's offices on Baker Street, even though the house did not actually exist when Doyle created the character.

This blurring between the fictional place described in Doyle's stories and the real location of 221b Baker Street in the actual world highlight the symbolic ways place and space work within transmedia storytelling. Michel de Certeau defines places as "locations of stability" while spaces are "mobile" (117). In this formulation, the concrete physical location of 221b Baker Street and its interior objects becomes a place; the flat is a destination and home for specific elements within the Sherlockian world. In contrast, spaces imply geographic topographies that must be traversed, like the vast network of London city streets. We (imaginatively) travel through England's vast spaces in the Sherlock Holmes stories, from the Ascot races in "The Adventures of the Silver Blaze" to the desolate fields of Dartmoor in *The Hound of the Baskervilles*. Detailed descriptions of places and spaces in fiction help create what Roland Barthes has termed "the reality effect": concrete details fix an atmosphere and remind the reader of the larger world of the plot (Ryan, *Narrative* 130). The fictional world, then, acts as a simulation of the actual world until the fiction risks rewriting the actual world out of existence (Polasek 195–96).[4]

Doyle's characterization of Sherlock Holmes, in particular, has also played a dominant role in establishing the ur-text for contemporary Sherlock Holmes adaptations such as the BBC version. Holmes is described as tall, thin, with dark hair, recessed gray eyes, and a hawk-like nose (Doyle, in *A Study in Scarlet*). Readers are given copious details of his physical mannerisms (his thinking pose in Doyle's "Red-Headed League") and of his particular speech patterns and common phrases ("The game is afoot," in Doyle's "Abbey Grange," or "When you have eliminated the impossible, whatever remains, however improbable, must be the truth," in *The Sign of the Four*). Interestingly, three of Holmes's most famous characteristics— his deerstalker hat, Inverness cape, and meerschaum pipe—were not included in the original world created by Doyle but rather were added to the canon by outside artists and actors (Sidney Paget, Basil Rathbone, and William Gillette, respectively). At the same time that audiences believe Holmes is an instantly recognizable character, Doyle also left significant gaps in his character's history. We don't know where Sherlock Holmes was born and raised, other than that he is descended from "a long line of Sussex squires" (Doyle, "The Musgrave Ritual"; "The Greek Interpreter") and that he is distantly related to the French painter Vernet (Doyle, "The Greek Interpreter"). We know of his brother, Mycroft, but we know nothing else of his family or personal history. We don't know which university he attended (if at all) or how he came up with his deductive reasoning technique. We know how he came to be a consulting detective (Doyle, "The Gloria Scott") but nothing about his life history after 1904, which is when Watson tells us Holmes retired to Sussex to keep bees. Yet even with all of these gaps—or, perhaps, because of them—Sherlock Holmes's London remains one of the most famous and well-known fictional worlds in literary history. From its very inception, Sherlock Holmes's world was open to audience interpretation and appropriation.

Sherlock's World

In their modernization of Doyle's nineteenth-century world, *Sherlock* creators Steven Moffat and Mark Gatiss similarly invoke London as the central place in their contemporary adaptation. As previously explained, fictional worlds must be massive yet detailed, implying both expansiveness and specificity. Audiences must be able to see, in minute detail, all of the specific elements in Sherlock Holmes's flat as clearly as they can imagine the larger London world that lies outside his doors. London and Sherlock's 221b Baker Street flat are "'invested with agency'" to the extent that they can be seen as characters in the same vein as Sherlock and John (Gregoriou 49–50).[5] The city becomes part of a larger framework that shapes the cultural values and overall milieu of the show and its characters, and it seeps into every aspect of the world and its extensions. For instance, even though the show was filmed in Cardiff and on set, *Sherlock*'s opening credits include scenes and stills from the season's episodes, but they also include views of key London landmarks from the original Doyle canon, such as Piccadilly Circus, home of the Criterion Bar, where John Watson met his former colleague, Mike Stamford, after his return from the second Afghan War in *A Study in Scarlet*; *Sherlock* adapts this meeting into a Criterion coffee shop meeting with Stamford in "A Study in Pink." The show repeatedly features exterior and interior shots from St. Bartholomew's hospital, where Sherlock Holmes and John Watson are first introduced in *A Study in Scarlet* in 1887; *Sherlock* adds multiple layers to the symbolic role of this spot by repeating the original *Study in Scarlet* meeting in "A Study in Pink" (season one, episode one, or S1E1) and also by making it the site of Sherlock's alleged suicide at the end of "The Reichenbach Fall" (S2E3). In their appropriation of several important Doyle sites, *Sherlock* reinscribes these spaces with new layers of meaning and significance, particularly for those fans familiar with the original stories.

In addition to using setting to establish canonical antecedents with the Arthur Conan Doyle stories, *Sherlock* also highlights several iconic London landmarks. The first season's credits display elements of London's famous skyline, including the London Eye Ferris wheel, Piccadilly Circus, Big Ben, the river Thames, and the Gherkin financial building; the second season strays farther afield and includes shots from Dartmoor and even Sherlock's 221b door, thus ensuring that audiences know which London world they are about to experience. Other important landmarks play significant roles in different episodes. For instance, a vibrant aerial shot of London's Buckingham Palace appears in the first half of "A Scandal in Belgravia" (S2E1) when John is being helicoptered in to meet Sherlock and Mycroft over the royal photo scandal with Irene Adler. The Tower of London is featured in "The Reichenbach Fall" (S2E3) as the site of Jim Moriarty's burglary of the Crown Jewels and his subsequent arrest by New Scotland Yard. Each of these locations helps associate the plotlines of the specific episode with actual geographical locations in the city of London. They work to remind viewers that they are vicariously taking part in a fictional world grounded in actual world locales. These iconic sites serve to reassure audiences of the authenticity of *Sherlock*'s world—especially important since the show was primarily filmed in Cardiff and on set. *Sherlock*'s London thus is both manufactured, through stock media images like the aerial shot of Buckingham Palace, and visitable, since fans can physically travel to the material sites showcased in the opening credits and key episodes.

In addition to featuring significant London landmarks and important canonical sites for the original stories, *Sherlock* also creates its own canonical settings. For example, a few key scenes in "The Blind Banker" were filmed in London's Chinatown and in a graffiti-covered skate park on the south bank of the Thames, both of which have become popular sites for fan tourism. Cinematic tourism brings fans of cult television shows, movies, and books to now sacred filming sites. Much like Doyle's anecdote of the French schoolboys who wanted to visit Sherlock Holmes's home in the early twentieth century, contemporary fans scope out filming sites for cult TV shows such as *Sherlock* and *Doctor Who* and films such as *Harry Potter* and *The Lord of the Rings* series, visits that serve to legitimate fans' investment in the cult text and to "unmediate and authenticate" the realities created by the shows (Hills, *Fan Culture* 150–51).[6] These cult geographies become sacred sites of pilgrimage and performance for fans because they support their fantasies of "entering into the cult text, as well as [allow] the 'text' to leak out into spatial and cultural practices via fans' creative transpositions and 'genres of self'" (Hills, *Fan Culture* 150–51). Such activities are evidenced by the sheer number of international fans who visit 221b Baker Street each year, the home of the Sherlock Holmes Museum, as well as the number of popular walking tours now operating in London that trace *Sherlock* filming locations. *Sherlock* fans see a visit to Speedy's Café on North Gower Street, a *Sherlock* filming location, as a rite of passage, and many seek to restage Sherlock's death at St. Bart's hospital in "The Reichenbach Fall." Iconic London locations such as Buckingham Palace, Piccadilly Circus, Big Ben, and others combine to build the "vast and detailed narrative space" necessary for *Sherlock*'s world, and they have become fetishized in the *Sherlock* fan world by fans seeking to experience that world more fully (Hills, *Fan Culture* 137).

Populating *Sherlock*'s world are the show's main characters, Sherlock Holmes and John Watson, played by Benedict Cumberbatch and Martin Freeman, respectively. Their characterizations, mannerisms, catchphrases, and physical characteristics have all become essential elements of the *Sherlock* brand on the BBC and PBS. The actors are essential to the look and sound of the show, and their centrality carries over to *Sherlock* fanfiction, helping to differentiate it from fanfiction on Sherlock Holmes/ Dr. Watson iterations featuring Robert Downey Jr./Jude Law, Johnny Lee Miller/Lucy Liu, or any number of others. Classic Hollywood films frequently assign specific tics, tags, and characteristics to individual characters so that they become immediately identifiable to audiences:

Their traits must be affirmed in speech and physical behavior, the observable projections of personality. . . . Even a simple physical reaction—a gesture, an expression, a widening of the eyes, constructs character psychology in accordance with other information. . . . Hollywood cinema reinforces the individuality and consistency of each character by means of recurrent motifs. A character will be tagged with a detail of speech or behavior that defines a major trait. (Bordwell 15)

In *Sherlock*, Benedict Cumberbatch, with his tall figure, striking eyes, dark curls, and prominent cheekbones, contrasts sharply with Martin Freeman, with his ashy blonde hair, muscular short stature, and pug nose: descriptions and depictions of these physical characteristics appear again and again in fanfiction and fan art. Each actor also brings a distinctive physicality to his character. Cumberbatch's Sherlock is frequently seen perched on the back of a chair, hands pressed together under his chin in the classic "thinking pose" of Arthur Conan Doyle's Sherlock. Cumberbatch also frequently ruffles his own curly locks and pops the collar of his signature Belstaff coat. Freeman as Watson often licks his lips, and he has a left-hand tremor, indicated by the character's frequent clenching of his left fist in times of anger or frustration.

Bordwell further notes that characters are also identified by a specific "detail of speech" that "defines a major trait" (Bordwell 15). In addition to the character's costumes, mannerisms, and physical appearance, *Sherlock*'s characters use specific catchphrases or ways of speaking that differentiate them from other members of the cast. Sherlock often tells his colleagues, for example, that certain clues or deductions are "obvious" for those who pay attention to the details. Sherlock's line "The game is on" from "A Study in Pink" is a modernized homage to the Doyle Sherlock's exclamation "The game is afoot" ("The Abbey Grange"), and it becomes a drunken joke in "The Sign of Three" (S3E2), when Sherlock can't remember the ending of his own catchphrase and John has to supply the missing word ("The game is . . . you know"). Other lines, used once in the episodes, get repeated over and over again in fanfiction, like Sherlock's comment to Anderson in "A Study in Pink" (S1E1), "You lower the IQ of the whole street." Perhaps even more popular than Sherlock's dialogue are Jim Moriarty's catchphrases from seasons one and two. In the swimming pool scene of "The Great Game" (S1E1), for instance, Moriarty's tonal "Hi" to Sherlock and John as well as his line "That's what people DO" both illustrate Andrew Scott's particular phraseology for the character. Scott's Moriarty is memorable for the way he adds surprising emphasis to words in particular lines or phrases that startle viewers out of any sense of complacency. Other Moriarty lines, such as "Daddy's had enough now" ("The Great Game"), "Honey, you should see me in a crown" ("A Scandal in Belgravia"), and "Did you miss me?" ("His Last Vow" and *The Abominable Bride*) have become memorable additions to the *Sherlock* fanon. These speech patterns, in addition to the visual, topographic, and stylistic elements, combine to create the show's syntax. In grammar, syntax includes the structural rules underlying a particular speech act. When applied to world building, syntax refers to the structural elements that give the fictional universe its particular worldness and that distinguish it from other fictional realms. In *Sherlock*'s case, this even includes other Sherlock adaptations.

In addition to the show's "vast and detailed narrative space" and stylistic syntax, *Sherlock*'s world also includes "a connected set of objects" (Wolf 19–20). Fans frequently comment on Sherlock's Belstaff coat, his Dolce and Gabbana shirts, and his bespoke Spencer Hart suits, for example, while John is more comfortably dressed in his black Haversack shooting jacket and assorted cable-knit and cardigan jumpers. Many of the characters' costumes are lovingly detailed on fan sites such as *Sherlockology*, where dedicated audiences can go to find out the specific brands, terminology, and details of their favorite characters' wardrobes—and possibly purchase versions for their own collections. In terms of objects, specifically, 221b Baker Street is replete with easily identifiable and iconic items that become important components in fans' visions of the *Sherlock* world. In the realm of theatre or film, props are meant to help establish the realism and overall atmosphere of an individual production or show. These objects can then become endowed with a metonymic meaning whereby they independently represent the world of the show. For instance, several canonical props in Sherlock's flat accrue symbolic meaning for fans, including the skull on the mantle, the blue skull painting on the living room wall, John's Union Jack pillow, the bull skull with earphones hanging over the desk, and even Sherlock and John's tea kettle and china set (as seen in "The Reichenbach Fall," S2E3). Not only are these items reimagined in various fanfictions as canonical indicators of the specific *Sherlock* world, they are also made available in the actual world through corporate merchandizing. Fans can not only reimagine Sherlock's tea kettle and china in their own fic, they can also purchase them for their own homes.[7] Such "diegetic extensions" often do not bear much symbolic weight in the actual show (Mittell, "Strategies" 259); however, they work to break down the boundaries between the fictional world and the actual world.[8] When engaging with props from the show in the real world, fans imagine they are in a real world with real objects and that they can have a real impact on the fictional world (Klastrup, "Towards a Poetics" 264).

Matthew Freeman's recent work on transmedia storytelling in the *Wizard of Oz*, *Tarzan*, and *Batman* both historicizes and frames the kinds of brand extensions—"the idea that successful brands are built by exploiting multiple contacts between the brand and the consumer" (Jenkins, *Convergence* 69)—*Sherlock*'s creators are exploiting. Freeman's body of work focuses on the "commercial exploitation of content as promotion," especially through transmedia storytelling practices throughout the twentieth century (Freeman, "Advertising" 2369). According to Freeman, transmedia stories can act as forms of advertising—both for their own media extensions and for other products that connect to the original world. By purchasing products embedded in or related to a show like *Sherlock*, for example, fans can both recreate and reenact the world of the show in their own lives. They can hang replicas of John Pinkerton's blue skull painting or Sherlock's 1635 map of the British Isles (available from Amazon) in their living rooms, and they can sit on John's Union Jack pillow (available at Amazon.co.uk). Perhaps at its most meta, fans can purchase a *Sherlock* edition of the classic board game Cluedo (Clue in North America), which was both referenced in "The Hounds of Baskerville" episode (S2E2) and seen jackknifed to the wall in the prior episode, "A Scandal in Belgravia." In these situations, fans need not purchase all available media texts to understand all the various threads of the world; buying tie-in materials like props, costumes, games, and novels, however, further links the audience to the fictional world and extends the boundaries of the transmedia world into everyday life.[9] The objects and visual content of the world, then, become a cross-promotional web whereby the consumer is constantly connected to, and immersed within, *Sherlock*'s world through a variety of branded products (Freeman, "Branding Consumerism" 19).

In addition to the set itself, the BBC has invested substantial resources into creating, producing, and reproducing *Sherlock*'s world through merchandizing and other venues. After the show's successful first season, BBC Media immediately reprinted a few core Arthur Conan Doyle Sherlock Holmes texts with pictures of their Sherlock Holmes (Benedict Cumberbatch) and John Watson (Martin Freeman) on the covers and with introductions written by the three writers and lead actors. BBC Media franchised an edition of Cluedo in the UK that featured *Sherlock* characters, settings, and imagery. They also partnered with Big Chief Studios to create and market high-end Sherlock and John dolls for collectors, with new Victorian versions to support the network's Victorian alternate universe special, *The Abominable Bride*. The BBC itself created and maintains a set of character websites, and Hartswood Studios partnered with the video game company the Project Factory to create an interactive app called Sherlock: The Network. All of these ventures are part of a contemporary phenomenon known as transmedia storytelling.

What Is Transmedia Storytelling?

While transmedia practices existed long before the twenty-first century, Henry Jenkins's *Convergence Culture* (2006) popularized the concept and helped transform it into a highly profitable and popular storytelling model in the US and beyond, with international successes ranging from Marvel's *Avengers* saga to the BBC's *Doctor Who* franchise.[10] Defined most recently by Jenkins as "a process where integral elements of a fiction get dispersed systematically across multiple delivery channels for the purpose of creating a unified and coordinated entertainment experience" ("Transmedia 202"), transmedia's success has gone hand in hand with the rising ubiquity of wireless internet and small portable devices such as tablets and smartphones, all of which provide greater access to multiple media outlets. The roots of transmedia storytelling go much deeper than contemporary digital culture, however; Matthew Freeman traces transmedia storytelling back to the rise of consumer culture and early twentieth-century advertising (Freeman, "Advertising" 2363).[11] No longer is there a single, unitary text; rather, transmedia storytelling models a collection or universe of intertextual paratexts, to borrow Gerard Genette's term. With the advent of tie-in novels, webisodes, graphic novels, video games, merchandise, and so on, transmedia worlds are built as much by the texts surrounding the narrative as they are by the films, television series, or books themselves, to the point where the narrative is so large that no one single text can contain it (Jenkins, *Convergence* 95; Evans 1-2).

Transmedia stories contain common characteristics and serve various functions across universes. Some threads offer backstory for specific characters or for the world itself, while others serve to map or lay out the key chronologies, myths/lore, or physical geography of the narrative world. They can provide alternative perspectives on key or even tangential events that may directly impact or parallel the world's main characters and events. Perhaps the two key elements to transmedia storytelling, according to Jenkins, are its radical intertextuality and its resulting additive comprehension. For Jenkins, transmedia stories must be intertextual; that is, they must speak to one another in either direct or oblique ways.[12] Without such radical intertextuality, films, novels, and television series may be crossmedial but not transmedial. Crossmedia franchises like those of Warner Brothers' *Harry Potter* involve unidirectional interaction and development. In the *Harry Potter* example, individuals can see the movies, visit Pottermore online, and play virtual Hogwarts games; they may visit Diagon Alley at the Wizarding World of Harry Potter at Universal Studios, Florida, purchase *Harry Potter* merchandise, and so on. Each of these threads, however, flows in a single direction from Rowling's novels to the new media platform/adaptation; they do not intersect with Rowling's creation or add to her story. Transmedia, by contrast, involves multiple layers of intertextuality; each form of new media directly intersects with, and affects, other forms of media within the transmedia universe. Tony Stark's panic attacks and paranoia in *Iron Man 3*, for example, only make sense if fans have seen the crossworld interaction involving Thor, Loki, and the Avengers in the first *Avengers* movie. Such intricate design and intertextuality requires an immense layer of simultaneous collaboration during creation.

Sherlock's transmedial platforms do talk to each other, but not always in consistent or unified ways. The TV episodes allude to specific cases and experiences John and Sherlock have had that haven't been fully developed on the show; however, the John and Sherlock character websites do fill in details missing from the episodes. Similarly, by repackaging the BBC Books' editions of Arthur Conan Doyle's original Sherlock Holmes novels with covers showing Cumberbatch and Freeman in their *Sherlock* costumes, the network implies that Doyle's original texts, even though they were written more than one hundred years before the TV show, are actually transmedial extensions of *Sherlock* rather than the other way around. Unfortunately, the BBC has apparently dropped their investment in *Sherlock*'s transmedial worlds, announcing after season four that John's blog will no longer be updated or maintained by the network, perhaps a clear indicator that the show has been discontinued; Sherlock's thescienceofdeduction.co.uk had been unofficially abandoned sometime around season two. Even though the network may have abandoned their transmedial extensions, however, fans continue to respond to, revise, and fill in gaps created in the show and its transmedial extensions. Fans speak to and add to Sherlock's fictional world through their own fan extensions. And while Moffat and Gatiss and the BBC cannot, perhaps, directly respond to or acknowledge fan extensions of the world due to legal concerns, together the corporate extensions and the fandom creations combine to create a great transmedial world. Each paratext must be complete on its own (that is, in an Aristotelian sense, with a beginning, middle, and end); however, the only way to experience and understand the entire transmedia world is to seek out all of the various incarnations and iterations to see how they overlap, comment on, and create a larger media world. In each new paratextual encounter, the reader's understanding of the world, and of previously read extensions, is compounded and changed. Each new paratext adds to the readers' understanding of the world as a whole as well as to their understanding of the individual texts they have already encountered. Bringing together all of the various media outlets and narrative threads constitutes "additive comprehension" (Jenkins, "Transmedia 202"), perhaps the most important factor in Jenkins's articulation. Since transmedia storytelling is, at heart, "the art of world making" (Jenkins, *Convergence* 21), the question of who controls the world is integral to fan studies and fanfiction.

John Watson's Blog: Key Features, World Building, and Verisimilitude

The BBC began actively designing transmedia projects as early as 2006 when CEO and former BBC director Mark Thompson laid out the company's new policies for 360 Degree Commissioning. The idea was to envision and develop new content simultaneously across multiple media platforms, including televisual material, interactive games, social media, webisodes, and others, right from the start of the process (Evans 34–35). The proposal from Sue Vertue, Steven Moffat, and Mark Gatiss for a modernized update of Sir Arthur Conan Doyle's Sherlock Holmes stories seemed the perfect place to start. Doyle's tales were ripe for transmedia appropriation: they contained already established and easily recognizable characters, an established world (even if it was originally Victorian), and an established Sherlock Holmes fan base. In addition, the fact that Sherlock Holmes was on the cutting edge of technology in his day, combined with the BBC's plan to modernize him into the twenty-first century, meant they could easily tap into younger audiences who would already be experienced in various social media and online formats. The combination of the tried-and-true Sherlock Holmes character and world in combination with a new, youthful audience meant that the BBC virtually could not go wrong with their formula.

The foundation of the BBC *Sherlock* transmedia platform was the development of four character websites for Sherlock Holmes, John Watson, forensic pathologist Molly Hooper, and beauty queen and fashion expert Connie Prince, all written by Joe Lidster.[13] All four websites are currently inactive: Connie's because of her character's death in S1E3, "The Great Game," and Molly's after the revelation that she was duped by "Jim from IT," aka Moriarty, in the same episode. Oddly, Sherlock's website has been similarly inactive ever since S2E1, "A Scandal in Belgravia," perhaps because John insults his blog and tells him no one is reading it. As a result, by the beginning of season two all of the BBC's transmedia efforts were dedicated to developing and maintaining John Watson's blog (Lidster), although that too has gone offline, as of the start of season four.[14]

John Watson's blog works to build the larger world through various narrative and visual elements. For instance, each of John's blog entries is organized by date, thus giving the viewer a timeline of the show's events; however, the site doesn't use any indication of year or television season, which can potentially confuse viewers as well as imply that *Sherlock*'s world is timeless. Active hyperlinks join various blog entries, including entries on the special cases John has published, and comments grouped by fictional commentors; the inclusion of hyperlinks gives users the impression of interacting with the site by allowing choice in how and in what order the threads are read. At present, the blog contains five embedded videos

Exclusive and Inclusive World Building   **49**

("Hello Boys," March 16; "Actually, Happy New Year," January 1; "Untitled," June 16; "The Empty Hearse," November 7; and "The Sign of Three," August 11), helping to reinforce the impression that the show, its characters, and its world are real. The video filed under "Untitled," from the June 16 post, for example, looks like a real clip from the BBC about Sherlock's alleged suicide. Using actual BBC sets, logos, and commentators, the video reveals that Sherlock had fabricated the existence of James Moriarty, in reality an actor named Richard Brook, to cover up the many crimes he'd committed. In a pièce de résistance of metarealism, the broadcaster concludes that John's blog "which made Sherlock famous, was revealed to be nothing more than a work of fiction" ("Untitled")—which, of course, it is.

Much like Doyle's original stories, which often referenced unsolved or undisclosed cases such as "The Giant Rat of Sumatra" (an oblique reference to which is made in "The Empty Hearse," S3E1), *Sherlock* makes similar use of unexplained timeline gaps, references, and cases during episodes, all of which contribute to the show's greater verisimilitude. One way of using transmedia sites like John Watson's blog is to fill in those gaps and flesh out the world online. John's blog entries provide prequels to the show's main events, such as the December 15 entry "Nothing," which refers to John's therapist's request that he write a blog to deal with his PTSD and predates the start of the show; audiences could also read the November 5 post, "Many Happy Returns," and the companion online mini-webisode of the same title as prequels to season three. The show also incorporates various interquels (narrative events that occur between existing episodes in a series) and intraquels (a sequence that occurs during a gap within a single episode) (Wolf 207).[15] Interquels can be interwoven directly into the main narrative or merely tangential; they can fill in character backgrounds (for example, Molly Hooper's blog and Connie Prince's website) or develop new characters—such as John Watson's original fan character, Jacob Sowersby (see the comments section and January 1 video entry). John's blog frequently uses interquels between seasons, in particular, to fill the audience in on what the characters have been doing during the show's two-year hiatuses. For instance, at the beginning of season two in "A Scandal in Belgravia," the audience sees John sitting at his desk typing at his laptop as Sherlock stands across from him sipping coffee. Centered on screen above the characters' heads is the text of John's blog posting from May 30 entitled, "Life Goes On." The viewer can then go to the web and open up John's blog entry of the same date to read about the cases covered since the show was last on the air:

> Time to write up a few notes. I'm going to tell you about a couple of the smaller cases we've been involved in. What really happened on the Tilly Briggs pleasure cruise. Then there was that really odd case with the melting laptop and the time Sherlock stole a bus. Just another typical week at 221b Baker Street! (Lidster)

The reader here learns of at least one new (interquel) case, the "Tilly Briggs Cruise of Terror" (included on the blog but never mentioned on the show) and thus is given the illusion that the show's world exists beyond our television screens. By using interquels to expand the world beyond the screen, the BBC *Sherlock* world gains greater verisimilitude as a whole.[16]

A bit less common, intraquels fill gaps within a single episode or season (Wolf 208). These are incredibly handy, especially in a show that often deals with several mysteries in a single episode. Even a ninety-minute episode does not provide time enough to cover six mysteries, such as those in "The Great Game" (S1E3), for example, let alone the litany of cases Sherlock and John solve at the beginning of "A Scandal in Belgravia" (S2E1), the rash of cases Sherlock includes in his best man's speech in "The Sign of Three" (S3E2), or the even briefer excerpts at the beginning of "The Six Thatchers" (S4E1), so *Sherlock* makes even more effective use of the intraquels on John's blog as the seasons go on. For instance, in "A Scandal in Belgravia," we see the beginnings of several cases, but except for one, all are relegated to John's blog for development. In one episode, "The Geek Interpreter," the audience gets to see three young men seated in Sherlock and John's flat as they begin to explain their problem: Chris Melas and his friends had created a website analyzing a comic book series, *Kratides*, and they had realized that the material in the comics was coming true in real life. Sherlock decides to take the case, and the next thing the audience sees is John typing the entry into his blog: "The Personal Blog of Dr. John H. Watson. The Geek Interpreter. Three young men came to Baker St claim . . ." (Lidster). It is only when the viewer goes to the blog that she can get the full details of Chris's case, his suspicions, and how Sherlock solved the mystery. To further build on the verisimilitude, John ends "The Geek Interpreter" post by pointing readers to other social media to attest to the truthfulness of his story: "You may have read about the comic's demise on Twitter,

Facebook or Google+" (Lidster). The blog entries also give the audience a better sense of John's voice as well as what happens with Sherlock "when the cameras are off," so to speak. By developing prequels, interquels, and intraquels, Joe Lidster and *Sherlock* use transmedia platforms to further develop the world of the show, something especially important given the sporadic showing of *Sherlock* (only three ninety-minute episodes every eighteen to twenty-four months). Viewers can read about the goings on at 221b Baker Street, both between seasons and during episodes, and see how the world is being created, but these formats exclude them from participating in, interacting or actively engaging with, or changing the content and direction of the show, its characters, or its world.

Participation versus Interactivity: Audience Assumptions

For some critics, transmedia worlds stimulate deeper audience engagement and immersion because they integrate audience participation and interaction (Wolf 13; Jenkins, *Convergence* 95–96; Hutcheon 135). The debate over the importance of audience participation versus interactivity dates back to traditional audience reception research from the 1970s and 1980s (Abercrombie and Longhurst, Fiske)—Martin Ericsson even argues that it goes back all the way to early modernity and the origins of Western conceptions of the artist's relationship to the audience (Ericsson). The terms *interactivity* and *participation* are often used interchangeably in transmedia scholarship; however, the two provide very different experiences. Jenkins tries to articulate the differences between the two in his "Transmedia 202" blog post, but Mark Wolf's *Building Imaginary Worlds* provides a clearer explanation: "Interactivity, which is made up of choices, splits narrative threads into alternative story lines, each of which can be followed, depending on how decisions are made" (220). While the variety of choices and the act of choosing provide users with the illusion of infinite possibility and perhaps, Wolf argues, a greater sense of verisimilitude (221), the choices have been predetermined by the creator(s) and the technological design. The user has the agency to choose what direction the narrative will take, but the directions themselves have been preprogrammed into the world.[17] This seems to be diametrically opposed to the actual definition of "to interact," which, according to the *Oxford English Dictionary* (*OED*), means "to act *reciprocally*, to act on each other." Interaction, by this definition, is a two-way process. Yes, the user can make decisions that affect how the game or narrative will proceed; as a result, however, the game should in some way react or respond to the player. New storylines, characters, attributes, or challenges should result from the player's interaction. In the example of John Watson's blog, the website gives the appearance of allowing fans to interact more directly with the character's purported personal webpage, but all the user actually can do is to choose among predetermined paths.[18]

"Interact"—with its emphasis on reciprocity, mutual interaction, decision making, and so on—sounds suspiciously like the way many critics define participatory culture. To be fair, the *OED* defines "participatory" as "characterized by, relating to, or involving participation; (of a form of art or entertainment) that allows members of the general public to take part." So how is "to take part" different from "to act reciprocally"? Participating in a transmedia world, in this sense, implies joining in or immersing oneself in something that already exists and is complete. Such a definition would imply less control or influence over the narrative in a participatory fiction than an interactive one. For critics like Wolf, Jenkins, and Ericsson, however, participatory narratives are much more open-ended and collaborative than interactive ones. Participatory worlds are more "under the control of media consumers," Jenkins argues, and they allow users to "make permanent changes that result in canonical additions to the world" (Jenkins, "Transmedia 202"; Wolf 281). But the question remains: Whose canon? Are participants permanently changing the authorized canon of the show, the one created and maintained by the producers? Or are they affecting the fan-produced and maintained fanon, which often extends, refocuses, or challenges the established fictional world? While fans may provide alternatives to the canon, most producers preclude audience influence in the writing and creation of their work. Even though many producers want to label their work, particularly paratexts and extensions, such as video games, apps, websites, and so on, as interactive and/or participatory, the fictional world's creators still maintain primary control over the world.

Part of the confusion over interactive and participatory worlds perhaps comes from the false delineation between the two.[19] Transmedia worlds, by definition, are large and virtually without boundaries; many include a variety of narrative threads, media forms, and structures, including both interactive and participatory elements. A single world can include participatory fanfiction along with interactive games. The assumption is that participatory fictions are somehow better, more immersive, and more engaging than interactive texts simply because they are participatory.[20] Noninteractive transmedia, however—media that seemingly exclude users from participating in world building or making permanent changes to the canon—are just as powerful in establishing hyper-diegesis and building fan engagement with the fictional world.

John Watson's Blog and Exclusive Transmedia

John Watson's blog helps create the illusion that *Sherlock*'s characters and world are consistent, coherent, and complete by presenting a realistic yet closed off digital view inside the workings of 221b Baker Street. Although the blog seems interactive in its design, viewers are actually presented with the simulation of a blog, one that is sealed off from any outside fan interference or revision. Like most blogs, John's has a side bar with an "About Me" section giving his background, hyperlinks to major cases he has written up, and a list of commenters on the blog (an unusual blog feature). Unlike most real blogs, however, these features are not interactive. Clicking on John's "My Photos" section to see additional examples quickly reveals that the link is not active. At least one blog post includes additional pictures ("26th April"), but the blog contains no other additional photos, even though the blog format raises this expectation. Nor can fans add pictures of the characters or screenshots from the show to build on John's digital archive. In a typical blog, readers can add personal comments and reactions to different images or particular blogs posts; however, even though John's blog includes comments for each of the posts, these entries are now closed to the fan viewer. For instance, when the reader clicks to read "The Empty Hearse" post of November 7, she sees thirty comments in the comment section. Canonical characters, including Sherlock, John, Mrs. Hudson, and Mike Stamford, along with several unknown original characters (theimprobableone, Dame Latif, Donna Stavely, anonymous), respond to Sherlock's return from the dead and the truth about Moriarty's identity. In addition to using major characters and unknowns, the comment sections make effective use of additional canonical characters mentioned only in passing in the show: examples include John's alcoholic sister, Harry, and "Stella and Ted" from the telegrams sequence in "The Sign of Three," and all further contribute to the realism of the *Sherlock* world.

While the photos and comments features give John's blog the appearance of interactivity, it remains an appearance only.[21] Blog users cannot click anywhere to add comments; there is no way to find out more about specific commenters. Arguably, this detracts from the blog's persuasiveness and effectiveness as a transmedia object; however, an exclusive system allows the show's creators to build a consistent and coherent world that seems complete on its own, without audience interaction and participation. Rather than weakening the blog's verisimilitude and world, the exclusiveness of the locked photos and comments reinforces it.

Sherlock: The Network: Key Features, World Building, and Verisimilitude

In contrast to the exclusivity of John Watson's blog, the app Sherlock: The Network released in January 2014 makes extensive efforts to be as inclusive as possible. Developed by the award-winning firm the Project Factory for Hartswood Studios, the interactive game comprises ten cases that place the user directly in the world of *Sherlock*'s London. As a member of Sherlock's homeless network, users navigate Sherlock's London by foot, tube, or taxi (the last two of which are presented as problem-solving games). Along the way, players earn money, accumulate valuable tools, and gather clues to help them solve the various crimes Sherlock assigns them. Each game culminates in a scene in the player's "mind palace," where she must put the various clues together to solve the crime. The game includes fifteen minutes of exclusive footage of Benedict Cumberbatch, Martin Freeman, and Mark Gatiss reprising their roles from the television show, additional black-and-white recut scenes from the series, and several audio files and mobile phone text messages from the protagonists and original characters. Although some critics argue that video games are not narratives (Jesper Juul, quoted in Ryan and Thon 11), others argue that the format provides a level of "spatial storytelling" that allows users to "extend" the narrative experience to "virtual representations of the storyworld" where they can "enact [their] most basic relationship to the world" (Mittell, "Strategies" 260; Murray 143). By participating in the virtual story space of Sherlock: The Network, users gain the experience of participating in, and contributing to, *Sherlock*'s world.

Sherlock: The Network is clearly participatory; users must make decisions about how to move through the city, must actively seek out clues at crime scenes, and must solve puzzles by moving materials around on the screen. For some, participation in a video game or app makes the world seem more real than games lacking such activity; players have the ability "to act within [the world] rather than just observe it" (Wolf 221), unlike their positions vis-à-vis John Watson's noninteractive blog. As a result, some critics and users argue that Sherlock: The Network is more immersive than John Watson's blog because acting within the game can give players the illusion that they are *participating* in the world as co-creators. Although the app appears to be participatory, however, users cannot change the direction of the narrative or the outcome of the cases; all paths are predetermined by the programmers, and users can only make decisions within set parameters. The game, like John's blog, remains a corporately devised and controlled world that may be participatory but that remains closed to change or adaptation.

Both the webpage and the app for Sherlock: The Network establish from the outset that BBC *Sherlock*'s London is key to the player's immersive experience. The main image on the game's website evokes the title credits of the television show, framed by Benedict Cumberbatch's profile and the now iconic *Sherlock* London skyline. The website's tagline—"Immerse yourself in the world of Sherlock Holmes" (the Project Factory)—reinforces audience expectations for contemporary transmedia outlets: that the ensuing experience will be both imaginatively engrossing and intellectually stimulating, that it will place them within the environment of the show as well as (re)creating the world of the show and all that goes with it. The app developers accomplish this in two ways: by making navigating London a specific task within the game and by using iconic symbols, images, and tropes from both the real and the transmedia world.

The main tool of the game is the method of transportation used to navigate the city. Each time the participant is given a task by Sherlock, she must decide whether to walk or travel by Underground or London taxi. The only significant impact of the decision is how much time the user will need to travel, which can affect the final score. The user can pinpoint her location in relation to specific, real-world London locations, many of which are identified in the television show itself: Marylebone Road near Baker Street, real London Underground stations and Tube lines (Bank and Farringdon), and shots of real London streets. Having users navigate the streets and underground lines of the real world highlights the role spatial storytelling plays in the *Sherlock* world. "Tie-in games that fans seem to embrace the most," Jason Mittell argues, are those which "re-create their television universes with vivid and immersive storyworlds" ("Strategies" 260). This kind of "commodity braiding" interconnects the televisual world with an entire range of commodities audiences can purchase in their own lives (games, props, clothing, tie-in novels), further cementing the connection between audience participation and engagement with the world (Freeman, "The Wonderful Game of Oz" 47).[22] Navigating *Sherlock*'s London is one way fans can enact the world of their favorite cult show and, as a result, become closer to the characters and more immersed in the fictional world (Murray 143).

The physical geographic world need not always be (re)presented photo-realistically for it to feel immersive for users. Even though they are clearly illustrations, London icons like the Tube symbol and the famous black taxi in the screenshots further ground the player's immersion in *Sherlock*'s world through their semiotic symbolism. The London Underground symbol is as much of an iconic symbol for London as the deerstalker cap is for Sherlock Holmes; both act as figurative shortcuts that imbue a specific symbol with a surplus of meaning. Similarly, even though the archetypal black taxi cabs are not restricted to the London streets but are available throughout the UK, they are frequently identified with the city's urban environments and with Sherlock, in particular, since John and Sherlock frequently use black cabs to visit clients, search for clues, and generally move about the city. Navigating and recreating *Sherlock*'s world works both at the physical and the semiotic levels.

Sherlock: The Network, in addition to recreating *Sherlock*'s fictional world through its navigational system, also immerses users in it by using actual sets and screenshots from the show in some game applications. For instance, in a few situations the player must identify key clues located in 221b Baker Street itself, with the app using screenshots of the show's interior sets to place the user within the sphere of the actual TV show. Panning around the room the user can see Sherlock's music stand with his latest composition, the famous wallpaper with the (barely) highlighted yellow smiley face, and more. In other challenges, such as the audio descrambler game, the sound bite is framed against a blurred out black and white background of Sherlock's figure at the top of St. Bart's Hospital, as seen at the end of "The Reichenbach Fall" (S2E3). Even though the clue

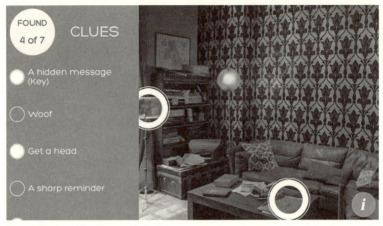

Clues (Sherlock: The Network)

does not directly relate to this particular scene or episode, by framing the new case within the context of actual imagery from and the musical soundtrack of the show, the viewer experiences a greater sense of urgency and involvement with Sherlock's life and cases. Using readily recognizable visual icons from *Sherlock*'s world—London streets, black taxis, the Underground, the 221b set—immerses app users in *Sherlock*'s world in ways John's blog, given its hermetically sealed, noninteractive framework, does not.

Sherlock: The Network and Inclusive Transmedia

The promotional website for Sherlock: The Network works diligently to assure users that the app provides the kind of participatory, immersive experience they have been conditioned to expect in transmedia storytelling. Rather than describing their clients as players, for example, the website cleverly describes them as participants. By labeling them as participants, the designers clearly intend to indicate that audience members are actively engaged with events in the game and with creating the game world (although, of course, this isn't accurate); participants are thus given the impression of control, verisimilitude, and inclusion. To reinforce the inclusive, participatory element, the app frames the participant as an actual member of Sherlock's homeless network, a concept that traces back to Sir Arthur Conan Doyle's original creation of Sherlock Holmes's scrappy gang of "street Arabs," "the Baker Street Irregulars," in his first two novellas, *A Study in Scarlet* (1887) and *The Sign of the Four* (1889). The app website strengthens participants' desire to join the network by reinforcing Sherlock's need for the particular participant's talents. Proclamations that "Sherlock Holmes has a message *for you. He wants you* to help him solve his latest case" posit the participant as an important, unique member of Sherlock's crew. Use of second person statements, such as "Someone close to Sherlock is in trouble and *he needs you* to join his trusted network" (Sherlock: The Network; emphases added), reinforces the participant's sense of occupying a special place inside the network; Sherlock needs YOU, not some unidentified gamer. *You* are someone Sherlock trusts when those closest to him are in danger.

In addition to making participants feel needed and special, Sherlock: The Network uses various forms of social media to include the participant in the action of the game and the world of the show, specifically text messaging and voicemail. Since the app was originally designed for iPhones (and iPads), the developers brilliantly invoke the device's definitive characteristics to make the game more believable and immersive. Key to the main premise underlying Sherlock: The Network is that participants communicate with Sherlock and solve crimes using their mobile phones. To solidify that connection, the developers frequently employ text messages from the major characters (Sherlock, John, Mycroft, and Molly) to relay important clues and information. The user is notified of an incoming text message by the appearance of the character's image at the bottom right of the screen.[23] Clicking on the notification takes the user to the text message. While the format does not provide a particularly realistic image of a text message, the impression that the participant is receiving texts from John, for instance, can help her feel she is really part of Sherlock's crime-solving world.

For even greater verisimilitude, the app also includes voicemail messages from major characters. During key fact-finding scenes in each case, the participant may receive audio voicemail recordings from Sherlock, John, and even Mycroft, in voicings supplied by Benedict Cumberbatch, Martin Freeman, and Mark Gatiss, respectively. The system is similar to that of the text messages; after clicking on the notification, the participant is taken directly to an audio file to hear the appropriate actor relaying the message. Participants can listen to the audio recording, replay it, or read a transcript of the message. Users never know when they might "get the

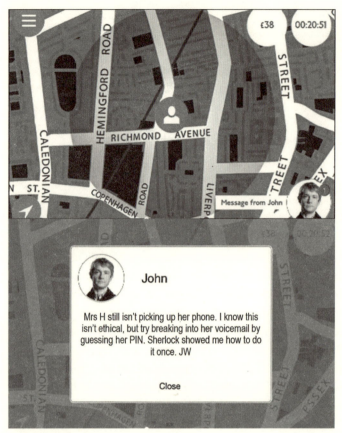

John text message (Sherlock: The Network)

call" from Sherlock during the game, so they must constantly be on alert for incoming messages. By using the actors' images and voices, players get the sense of being in direct communication with the show's characters. Thus, Sherlock: The Network compounds the sense of realism created for *Sherlock*'s world by layering levels of interaction: using a mobile phone device, invoking the genre conventions of the mobile phone itself through text messaging and voicemails, and using the images and actual voices of the actors playing their main roles on the show. Much like the new BBC editions of Arthur Conan Doyle's Sherlock Holmes novels with Cumberbatch and Freeman on the covers as Holmes and Watson, Sherlock: The Network reinforces the idea that the actors *are* the characters; character and actor become interchangeable, something that becomes increasingly both interesting and problematic as we explore fanfiction genres such as slash and RPF. All of these factors combine to reinforce the audience's perception of being immersed in *Sherlock*'s world.

Connecting all of these elements—using second person pronouns in the advertising material, employing the visual iconography of the show and of London, invoking mobile phone conventions such as text messaging and voicemail alerts—is Donald Horton and R. Richard Wohl's theoretical concept of parasocial relationships. First published in 1956, "Mass Communication and Para-Social Interaction: Observations on Intimacy at a Distance" was foundational for television and celebrity studies. Originally analyzing television personalities in 1950s game and variety shows, Horton and Wohl posited that when a television figure directly faces and speaks to the camera (what Horton and Wohl term "direct address"), the audience feels as if the television personality is "conversing personally and privately" with them, as if they had a personal relationship. The audience is thus "subtly insinuated into the program's action and internal social relationships and, by dint of this staging, is ambiguously transformed into a group which observes and participates in the show by turns." Like our earlier definition of interactivity, this "simulacrum of conversational give and take" is "one-sided, controlled by the performer, and not susceptible of mutual development" (Horton and Wohl). Horton and Wohl see the audience as participating in the world by creatively imagining they are part of the show's world and have somehow been singled out by the lead to be part of his inner circle. Of course, this perceived relationship is an illusion; more important is the method by which the TV personality creates feelings of intimacy, authenticity, and inclusion among performer, audience, and world (Bennett 33).

Sherlock: The Network frequently uses direct address and invokes parasocial relationships through its use of voicemail and video, to facilitate the participants' feelings of inclusion in the fictional world. As soon as the player completes the user profile and begins the game, she receives a direct address video from Cumberbatch's Sherlock explaining the homeless network arrangement. Apparently at home at 221b Baker Street, he glances up from his microscope and seems to look right into the user's eyes as he addresses the camera:

Sherlock's opening video (Sherlock: The Network)

[Sniffs] So, you want to be in the homeless network. Hmm. . . .
Clearly, you look the part. [Sniffs] And . . . yep. Now, your duties:
there are places that I, thanks to my notoriety and refined sense of
smell, cannot go that you can inhabit. You, my fetid friend, are—for
all practical purposes—invisible. . . . [*Shouts offscreen*] Mrs. Hudson,
where are my spare mobile phones? I'm going to give you a phone.
That's how we'll stay in touch. So keep an eye out; there's no shortage
of crime out there if you don't mind getting your hands dirty which,
clearly, you don't. You might be successful. Off you go. (Sherlock: The
Network)

Sherlock, by looking directly into the camera, makes the player feel like
she is inside 221b Baker Street with Sherlock Holmes himself. Sherlock
also invokes other senses in this early scene, in this case smell, which, in
addition to later uses of sight and sound helps convey greater authenticity
to the world. In addition, Sherlock's audible sniff contributes to the illusion that the player really has been living on the streets for a substantial
period of time, reinforcing as well the character she is supposed to play.
(Some audiences may also read Sherlock's dismissive sniff as disparag-
ing to fans, however, which serves to further divide corporately devised
transmedial extensions and those created by fans themselves.) By shout-
ing offscreen for Mrs. Hudson, the participant also gets the sense that the
world of 221b Baker Street extends beyond the visible boundaries—that
the building has two other floors, that Mrs. Hudson lives in a flat down-
stairs, and that London is right outside the window. Ultimately, Sherlock,
in the opening scene, clearly invites the player into his world to perform

as an active member of his homeless network, to actively participate in the navigation of that world.

While Sherlock's use of direct address in the game is the most effective, both Mycroft and John use it in key scenes to guide the user with clues and insights. Mycroft is relatively passive in his ubiquitous black sedan; John, by contrast, is the most active character in the game and is often seen in action out in the field. During one case, the player catches up with John after the two have chased after a criminal; in another, John is talking to the player outside a container warehouse when gunshots are heard. John's camera angle immediately shifts to the ground, as if he is running with his camera phone pointed downward, toward the injured person. Once there, John proceeds to give CPR while the camera is still running nearby, almost as if the player herself had been shot. Such innovative uses of direct address make the participant feel like she is talking with John in person as she actively participates in chases and dangerous situations with him and other main characters. The app's interactive features, including the direct address elements (video, voicemail, and text messaging), all work to create and reinforce the world originally established within the parameters of the television show (or, one could argue, in Sir Arthur Conan Doyle's original nineteenth-century Sherlock Holmes stories). Although Sherlock: The Network constantly works to include the player in the world of the show, the world itself remains closed to any player-initiated change, revision, or challenge. Like John's blog, the tie-in game appears, on the surface, to be a diegetic extension that encourages fan participation and contribution, thus creating an immersive and engaging experience, but it also reinforces the impression that the world itself remains the design and under the control of the showrunners and producers.

Conclusion

Sherlock's clearly identifiable features—the 221b set, the iconic London skyline, Sherlock's Spencer Hart suits, Mycroft's black sedans—create a canon within which the showrunners, transmedia creators, and game designers work. The television show builds on and extends the world Arthur Conan Doyle created in his nineteenth-century Sherlock Holmes stories, updating that world with twentieth-century settings, technology, and characters, and both these sets of parameters limit the amount of play, interactivity, and participatory elements available to fans engaging with corporately devised transmedia extensions. While the show's producers work to extend the TV show's world through different media, such as websites, tie-in novels, merchandizing, and video games, each feature still works within the parameters established by the show's original canon. Designers can imagine parallel storylines, interquels, intraquels, and even original characters, but they do not and cannot change the basic elements of the fictional world. For truly participatory transmedia extensions, ones "that result in canonical additions to the world" (Jenkins, "Transmedia 202"), one must look to fans and fanfiction. Through their writing, fans invoke the already established corporate world of the show, but they also explore genre and characterization changes that both radically challenge and reinforce the show's world. The remainder of this book will explore the ways in which fans remain faithful to, revise, and challenge *Sherlock*'s world and characterizations through media- and genre-based fan writing.

CHAPTER TWO
A CASE OF IDENTITY
Role Playing, Social Media, and the BBC's *Sherlock*

Here we shift away from closed corporate models of world building to open fan-produced texts. Looking at Facebook, Tumblr, and Twitter, we begin to explore the differences between corporate world building and fan world building by analyzing the ways in which fans use role playing to explore and reinforce *Sherlock*'s canon. While *Sherlock*'s producers are invested in creating, maintaining, and preserving a particular, identifiable, marketable version of *Sherlock*'s world, fans are drawn both to reproducing and reimmersing themselves in that original world and to challenging it in new and innovative ways. Corporately devised worlds are perhaps necessarily closed to fans' active participation, while fanfiction and online role-playing narratives invite audiences to make changes to and interventions in the canon that result in alternative points of view, narrative arcs, characterization, and settings—that is, in a parallel and intersecting fanon that depends on, and diverges from, the show's original canon. Viewed together, both corporate and fan extensions combine to create the transmedial world we know. As Cornel Sandvoss explains, critics and fans alike need to reimagine texts as "frames of reliable meanings that span across single or multiple communicative acts, including visual, sound-based, and written communication," including distinctions between authorized and unauthorized additions to the canon. Once we "remove authorship as the essence of textuality," Sandvoss continues, "it is now not by the producer but by the reader that the boundaries of texts are set" (Sandvoss 22). Moving from the producer's to the reader's authority signifies a momentous shift in cultural capital, literary authority, and literary value, and online role-playing narratives provide crucial insight into how fans actively (re)create fandom worlds in their writing.

Canon, Compliance, and Fidelity

As discussed in the introduction, what defines fanfiction is its foundational relationship to the source text's canon and its emphasis on character. Fanfictions adopt the established characters, settings, and major plotlines of an established fictional world and transform them in a variety of ways, including but not limited to expanding established storylines and character arcs, shifting points of view, creating new original characters, and/or placing the established characters in different settings or worlds. As Hellekson and Busse explain in the introduction to *Fan Fiction and Fan Communities in the Age of the Internet*: "The community of fans creates a communal (albeit contentious and contradictory) interpretation [of the source text] in which a large number of potential meanings, directions, and outcomes co-reside" (7). Fanfiction's dependence upon an identifiable connection to the storyworld suggests that canon compliance is essential to analyzing fan writing.

Canon compliance refers to fanfiction's adherence to the principal tenets and canonical features found in the source text or world; stories must reproduce identifiable characters, settings, and formal elements from the source world, whether through the corporately devised canon or through community-based fanon beliefs and tropes, or risk losing readers and/or being criticized for creating unrealistic or unbelievable versions of the world's main elements. Like other literary and media adaptations, fanfiction depends on its audience's familiarity with the source text; it is inherently dialogic and thus requires a level of intertextuality largely absent from other literary forms. Fanfics, like adaptations, are constructed of "mosaics of citations that are visible and invisible, heard and silent," and this "conceptual flipping back and forth between the work we know and the work we are experiencing" creates a form of "interpretive doubling" whereby the author and reader experience the world and its (re)creation simultaneously (Hutcheon 21, 139). Although fanfics don't profit from the economic protections and benefits accorded authorized literary and media adaptations, both include a *reciprocal* relationship between the source text and the adapted or fan text: the reader flips back and forth between the work we know and the adaptation.

Not all audiences encounter an adaptation *as* an adaptation, however; the adaptation may represent their first introduction to the content. Some fans experience a fictional world through the fan text first and only return to the original source text after having already experienced the transformed world. This constant refiltering of original and adaptation, depending on the order in which the fan enters the world, changes how audiences experience each incarnation. For some critics, "fans' understanding of the source is always already filtered through the interpretations and characterizations existing in the fantext" (Hellekson and Busse, "Introduction" 7). Even though a fan may encounter a specific fictional world for the first time through a specific fan text, however, the underlying world consistency of that fanfic both comes from and is influenced by the original source. Thus, at some level, fanfic's interpretive doubling depends on the audience's prior knowledge of the source text and their ability to recognize references and citations to that source world when encountered in a new context. Based on these conditions, canon compliance seems to be a foundation of and integral to all fanfiction.

Faithfulness, or fidelity, to the source text has been a hot topic in adaptation studies generally, and it raises important questions about canon compliance, immersion, and world building for fanfiction as well. First introduced in George Bluestone's still influential *Novels into Film* (1957), fidelity studies focuses on a unidirectional transition from source text to film (or other media), with the literary source text always retaining more cultural capital than the adaptation acquires. This is a derivative model of mediation that sees the source as somehow pure, untainted, and unaffected by the process of adaptation, while the adaptation itself is seen as a cultural and artistic derivative of the original source. In fandom, this assumption is repeated in the prioritization given the authorized, corporate world over fans' unauthorized appropriation. The concept of "textual poaching" as explored by both Michel de Certeau and Henry Jenkins reinforces the belief that the professional world is superior to the fan world and subsequently deserves protection by the legal trappings of trademarks, licensing, copyright law, and capitalism. In this hierarchical model, the source text is always at the pinnacle of artistic achievement, while any and all adaptations fall lower on the scale of literary and generic value.[1] In the fidelity model, the goal or purpose of adaptation is to identify fiction's essence or spirit and then reproduce it in a new medium, usually film

(Albrecht-Crane and Cutchins 11–12; Andrew 31). As a result, most adaptations are assessed on how well they recreate the original source text's essence in the new version—that is, by how faithful the adaptation is to the source text.

Over the past few decades, however, many scholars have begun to dispute the place of fidelity as the primary evaluative tool in adaptation studies. Similar to Jason Mittell's arguments against genre studies, film critics such as Robert Stam have argued that fidelity is problematically essentialist; at heart, it "assumes that a novel 'contains' an extractable 'essence,' a kind of 'heart of the artichoke' hidden 'underneath' the surface" (Stam 57). Rather, "no such transferable core" exists, only an assortment of "verbal signals that can generate a plethora of possible readings" (Stam 57). Therefore, artists, critics, and audiences are forced to ask what a text is supposedly faithful *to*: Is it some undefinable essence? Is it a basic narrative structure? Or merely the raw material that makes up the source as a whole? (Cardwell 60). "Fidelity to what?" is a particularly rich question when applied to *Sherlock*.[2]

From the beginning, *Sherlock* was clearly identified as an adaptation of Sir Arthur Conan Doyle's late nineteenth-century Sherlock Holmes stories. Steven Moffat and Mark Gatiss have been immensely careful about acknowledging the source texts, and they made it clear from season one that their work is an appropriation of Sherlock Holmes rather than a literal adaptation. Like French pastiche, appropriations comprise "a medley of references, a composition made up of fragments pieced together" (Sanders 5). References to the source text may be obscured or embedded in the new product and only visible to audiences with specialized knowledge. In the credits for the first season, Moffat and Gatiss simultaneously undermine and invoke the authority of Sherlock Holmes's literary father (Arthur Conan Doyle) by claiming that their *Sherlock* is based on Doyle's *character*, not on specific *stories*. "Based on" implies that *Sherlock* takes the Doyle canon as a springboard, a place from which to start. The episodes' credits remind viewers that each episode is authored (in the Foucauldian sense of the word) by individual writers (Moffat, Gatiss, and Steve Thompson), and Moffat and Gatiss are also listed as the show's cocreators in each episode's credits. By asserting their literal authority over *Sherlock*'s stories—and success—Moffat, Gatiss, and Thompson are free to use whatever canonical elements they like to create something new.

They have to adhere to Sherlock Holmes's world, but they need not necessarily be wholeheartedly faithful to it.

Even though several indicators alert audiences that this is an appropriation of Sherlock Holmes, Moffat and Gatiss seem to go out of their way to credit Arthur Conan Doyle for *Sherlock*'s success. In an interview with Digital Spy, Mark Gatiss clarified: "I think it's worth saying, first of all, this series is credited as being created by Steve [Moffat] and myself. Obviously, it's Arthur Conan Doyle's genius which is behind it" (Digital Spy). Such oscillation between intertextuality and fidelity highlights the seemingly conflicted attitudes that Moffat and Gatiss have toward adaptation and appropriation. Much of the original press about the show's faithfulness to Doyle's canon seemed to be the result of an anticipated backlash from Sherlockian audiences who, it was anticipated, might fear that the show's modern setting would dilute its authenticity. For instance, the original press packs emphasized *Sherlock*'s fidelity to the original stories as well as to later film and television adaptations (Rixon 168), and many of the preliminary reviews proclaimed the show was "truer to the spirit and heart of the original Canon than other adaptations" (Takenaka 20–21). Sue Vertue, head producer for Hartswood Studios, used similar language, claiming that "the whole soul of it is the same and true to the original Sherlock Holmes stories" (Ward). Finally, Steven Moffat, perhaps the most public face of the writers behind the show, claimed that *Sherlock* was, at heart, a faithful adaptation of Arthur Conan Doyle's hero, arguing, "We've really been quite faithful in a way to lots of the ingredients in those stories" (BBC One, "Steven Moffat and Mark Gatiss").[3]

With so many early claims for appropriation in season one, it was a surprise to see that the credits for *Sherlock*'s second season shifted away from the appropriative phrasing "based on Sir Arthur Conan Doyle's Sherlock Holmes" to the much more specific, adaptation-evoking "Based on the Works of Sir Arthur Conan Doyle."[4] Unlike the first season, where the writers advocated for their right to update and change the original stories, these credits literally invoke the authorial power of the original source text. Interestingly, as Moffat and Gatiss created more episodes, they seemed to become more faithful to the original Doyle canon. Several factors illustrate the adaptive turn in seasons two and three: the major character names and plot points of each episode follow the trajectories indicated in the original stories, and virtually all of the episode titles directly reference specific story titles from the Doyle canon.[5] Season three seems to take more liberties with plot than season two, however. For instance, while "The Empty Hearse" is, essentially, the story of Sherlock's return and includes several references to Doyle's "Empty House" story, "The Sign of Three" is a much looser adaptation of Doyle's *Sign of the Four*.[6] Similarly, although the final episode in season three, "His Last Vow," clearly refers to Doyle's "His Last Bow," the actual plot of the episode clearly follows Doyle's story, "Charles Augustus Milverton." Season four followed a pattern similar to that of season three, with episode titles clearly playing on Doyle stories ("The Six Thatchers," "The Lying Detective," and the mysterious "The Final Problem," which has the same title as Doyle's story of Holmes's meeting with the nefarious Professor Moriarty and his fall, allegedly to his death, at the Reichenbach Falls, a story already adapted by Moffat and Gatiss in 2012's S2E3 cliffhanger, "The Reichenbach Fall").

Even with the various nods to Doyle's literary authority, *Sherlock*'s creators constantly undermine their own professions of fidelity. Yes, producer Sue Vertue claims that *Sherlock* is "the same and true to the original Sherlock Holmes stories" and then adds "*but* it has a modern twist" (Ward, emphasis added). Steven Moffat argues that the show is "quite faithful" in how it incorporates the original stories into the show, but then adds the caveat that it is "using them in new ways" (BBC One, "Steven Moffat and Mark Gatiss"). Both Moffat and Gatiss have commented frequently that their creation is influenced not only by Doyle's original stories, but also by other film adaptations and pastiches such as the modernized Basil Rathbone films of the 1940s and, significantly, Billy Wilder's 1970 incarnation, *The Private Life of Sherlock Holmes*. Doyle's original fifty-six short stories and four novellas weren't the only things up for grabs: "Everything was canonical," cowriter and co-creator Mark Gatiss claimed in his commentary on the "A Study in Pink" DVD. "Every version. We're not just drawing on the stories but the Rathbone films, Jeremy Brett . . ." (*Sherlock: Season One*, "Commentary to 'A Study in Pink,'").[7] Sherlock's bullet-drilled smiley face in "The Reichenbach Fall" harkens back to the similarly created "V. R." (for Victoria Regina) noted in Doyle's "Musgrave Ritual." Other scenes and mannerisms closely model Sidney Paget's original illustrations for *The Stand Magazine*. Many of the plot elements from season two's "A Scandal in Belgravia" seem based on Gabrielle Valladon's character in Wilder's *Private Life of Sherlock Holmes*, and Mary Watson's alias, "Gabrielle Ashdown," in season four references an alias used by Holmes in Wilder's film. In another example, one scene from "The Reichenbach Fall" was modeled on a strikingly similar sequence in *The Woman in Green* (1945; directed by Roy William Neill) with Basil Rathbone as Holmes. The scene immediately following Moriarty's acquittal in "The Reichenbach Fall" shows Moriarty proceeding to 221b Baker Street and breaking into the building. As he ascends the stairs, Sherlock's violin playing pauses then restarts, causing Moriarty to halt on the stairs, worried that Holmes has heard his approach. By basing their own shots and mise-en-scène on other adaptations, Moffat and Gatiss effectively widen the canonical realm at the same time that they reinforce it. By claiming "everything was canonical," they are able to argue that every appropriation is also an adaptation: if every version of Sherlock Holmes is a potential source text, then no matter how Moffat and Gatiss assemble their version, it can potentially be faithful to another version previously in existence. The showrunners' seeming openness to the Sherlockian canon places the show within a continuum of adaptations and appropriations, ranging from early nineteenth-century pastiche to Edith Meisner's 1930s radio dramas to contemporary film, television, and fanfictions.

Ultimately, Moffat and Gatiss argue that their philosophy of adaptation and appropriation is about finding equivalents. Moffat recalled:

> I remember Mark thinking, he [John Watson] wouldn't write a journal now; he wouldn't write memoirs. He'd write a blog. . . . And he wouldn't have teams of homeless children; he'd have homeless people on the streets selling *The Big Issue*. In a way, it allows you to see the stories in the way the original reader would have read them . . . . (Ward)

In a sense, Moffat seems to be arguing that updating *Sherlock* and appropriating key elements from the main stories in the end makes them even *more* faithful to the original texts; the creators' bricolage approach to the canon allows contemporary audiences to enjoy approximately the same position of the material as Doyle's original audience had. These canonical equivalents all combine to create a particularly Sherlockian canon that then gets absorbed, reproduced, and transformed through contemporary fanfiction.

Understanding *Sherlock*'s creators' complicated relationship to the

Sherlock Holmes canon is integral to grounding fanfiction's investment and participation in that world. Moffat and Gatiss's allegiance to the authority of Sir Arthur Conan Doyle illustrates a particularly strict adherence to the notion of canon and copyright. Even though their show is clearly an appropriation and reenvisioning of Doyle's characters, Moffat and Gatiss remind their audiences and critics that Doyle *owns* Sherlock Holmes and his world. This sense of ownership, then, becomes integral to the writers' own relationship to fanfiction. As we saw in discussing *Sherlock*'s transmedia extensions in the previous chapter, *Sherlock*'s corporate world building tends to be closed off to fans and general audiences; fans can read John's blog but they can't comment on it. They can watch and listen as Sherlock speaks to them in Sherlock: The Network, but they can't respond.

It's surprising to many fans, then, that both Moffat and Gatiss define themselves as fanboys. Both Moffat and Gatiss began working in television based on their abilities to write using other people's voices and worlds, Moffat as a contract writer for *Doctor Who* under Russel T. Davies and Gatiss as the author of a *Doctor Who* tie-in novel. What differentiates their work from fanfiction is money. Writing and publishing adaptations and appropriations such as *Sherlock* carries particular cultural and legal protections; writers publish under their own names (to much fanfare) and their work is copyrighted and protected from plagiarism and illegal appropriation. Fan writing, on the other hand, relies on fan labor—that is, *free labor*—with no protections, copyright, public accolades, or monetary reward for the effort. The tension between paid professional adaptation work and unpaid amateur (that is, unauthorized) fan work is a recurring topic in contemporary fan studies, particularly in light of E. L. James's successful fanfic publication, *Fifty Shades of Grey.* These debates between authorized and unauthorized writing and between canonically compliant texts and unfaithful renditions exist within fandom, too, and they are often sites of heated debate over the nature of world building, characterization, and realism.

Online Sherlockian Worlds: Role Playing and Fanfiction

As what has been termed the most frequently represented literary character of all time, it is perhaps no wonder that Sherlock Holmes's cult status is alive and well on numerous contemporary social media sites. With several different sites and formats available, fans have many choices regarding how they interact with their favorite shows, its characters and storyworld, and recent studies such as Janet Murray's *Inventing the Medium: Principles of Interaction Design as a Cultural Practice* (2011) and Louisa Stein's "'This Dratted Thing': Fannish Storytelling through New Media" (2006) illustrate different ways the format of a particular media site can influence the content or genre of the products created there. While Murray's book explores the relationship between form and content from a design interface perspective, Stein approaches the issue in terms of literary genre. Her claim that "genre . . . functions in a similar way to canon and fantext in terms of restriction and impetus: shared understandings of generic codes and tropes contribute story possibilities and yet also limit the ranges of types of stories told" (Stein 248) raises important questions about the relationship between social media platforms and fanfiction genres. For instance, are the collaborative narratives on social media sites fanfiction or role-playing games? How can the two be distinguished? What distinguishes storytelling in one social media site from that on another?

Stein and Kristina Busse conclude that "fannish role-playing games cannot be explained in terms of narrative alone, nor can they be easily classified as games" ("Limit Play" 204). They view these works as interactive, performative character collaborations heralding a new transmedia artistic form hitherto unexplored. Outside of live-action role play (LARP) and cosplay, narrative-based role-playing games (what I am calling role-playing narratives or RPNs) provide a revealing entry point for analyzing how fans enact fandom through literary practices like fanfiction. While Sherlock: The Network allowed fans to play the role of a fictional character within the producers' corporately controlled transmedia world, narrative RPGs and fanfiction give audiences the power to change the narrative structure, themes, and characters of the show—while still remaining consistent with the world. In both RPNs and other fanfiction, the syntax and vocabulary (both literal and metaphorical) from the source text provide the framework structuring the narrative. In terms of *Sherlock*, this can range from aspects such as the setting of 221b Baker Street or the physical appearance of the characters (dictated by the actors cast to play the television roles) to characters' dialogue phrasing and speech patterns. To build a convincing world, RPN and fanfiction characters must speak like their source characters, they must interact with other characters from the show in textually appropriate ways, and they must respond to new situations in ways that are consistent with their televisual counterparts. For many, compliance with the source text, measured in terms of a "collective creation of belief" (Pearce 20) remains the most important element of both fanfiction and online role-playing narratives.[8]

So far, little research has been published on the intersections between fanfiction, role-playing games, and social media genres and platforms. Makers of role-playing games have had to carve out a niche from historic understandings of tabletop role-playing games, text-based multiuser domains, and the hugely popular massive multiplayer online role-playing games (MMORPGs). At heart, role-playing games are interactive and experiential storytelling games. Beyond that, however, RPG scholars such as Sarah Lynne Bowman have strict rules for defining the genre: the game must establish a sense of community through "ritualized, shared storytelling"; it must include "some form of game system," including problem-solving tasks; and players must be required to "alter their primary sense of identity by developing an 'alternate Self'" (Bowman 11–12). Bowman's definition, clearly based on traditional live-action role-playing games such as Dungeons & Dragons, also requires a guide or game master who is in control of the overall narrative arc and responsible for conflict resolution (Bowman 12). Bowman's game characteristics, while essential in defining and analyzing the parameters of LARPs and perhaps MMORPGs, don't always make sense for the type of fictional role playing that I describe here, which is why I propose the term "role-playing narratives" as a distinct genre separate from, but connected to, more familiar RPG practices and conventions.

A key element of role-playing narratives missing from Bowman's description of RPGs is the emphasis on temporality. LARP games, in particular, are situated within a finite moment in time. Their actions, story arcs, and resolutions are ephemeral; once the game is over, no physical evidence remains of its existence, other than in the players' minds. One fascinating element that online role-playing narratives can add, then, is the possibility of experiencing and/or witnessing a role play *after* it has been completed. At the same time, however, the emphasis on Facebook, Twitter, and Tumblr is on immediacy, which can often cause significant reading comprehension and coherence issues. Both Twitter and Tumblr, for example, share their most recent information first, meaning that all role-playing dialogues run backward, thus requiring the reader to scroll from the bottom of the screen up. This makes following a narrative arc after the fact challenging, as is evident in this discussion between Mycroft Holmes and M-holmes on Tumblr:

> RICHARDBROOKONLINE: You're old news, Holmes, you just don't see it yet. Goodnight. *Leaves the house, whistling as I do*
> MYCROFT: Egotism is the anesthetic that dulls the pain of stupidity. MLH
> RICHARDBROOKONLINE: *Stops* Is that supposed to get a rise?
> MYCROFT: Just a thought, James, just a thought. *Chuckles* On your way, boy. I have adults to play with.
> RICHARDBROOKONLINE: I was bored. Waste of time. *makes for the door*
> MYCROFT: *Smirks* You must stop quoting your father, James. (M-holmes)

Having the narrative run backward interferes with the coherence of the world—one of the basic tenets of RPGs—and forces readers to reorient their reading strategies, possibly alienating them. In contrast, Facebook's commenting feature allows a role player to post a prompt to which other player/characters can reply, thus creating an embedded linear story; however, if a storyline goes beyond the original status update, it becomes difficult to follow. On the other hand, fanfic readers may initially encounter a text days, months, even years after its original posting and still have no trouble following the characters or storyline.[9]

In addition to temporality, Heather Osborne's essay, "Performing Self, Performing Character: Exploring Gender Performativity in Online Role-Playing Games" (2012), provides even finer distinctions between the different forms of role-playing games. For Osborne, RPGs emphasize performance, collaboration, characterization, narrative, and game play, all on equal footing. She differentiates between narrative RPGs—that is, games that "rely on the players' mutual suspension of disbelief to define the extent of the shared world"—and MMORPGs that rely on computer software to create the game world (Osborne 1.1). Role-playing narratives, specifically, are text based; rely on improvisational written description, action, internal monologue, and/or dialogue; and do not require any specific computer software, knowledge of commands, or computer-generated worlds (Osborne 2.4, 2.6). While MMORPGs prescribe character types (dwarf, wizard, troll, and so on) players are still allowed to define their character's personality traits and many physical characteristics. In contrast, fanfiction and RPNs come with preset lists of characters, behaviors, geographic locations, and situations originating in the source text, film, or television show, all of which are clearly based on the source text's canon. As a result, one way to evaluate fanfic RPNs is to gauge their faithfulness to the source text; in addition, they can be assessed according to how creatively and skillfully the fan made the text her own.

Some fan writers seem to differentiate more between their personal identities and actions and those of the canonical fictional characters they write about. Rather than seeing their creations as representatives of themselves, as RPG gamers do, fanfic authors distance themselves from their creations and write about other characters. In fact, they often distrust fanfic characters who seem too similar to another gamer in interests, needs, and personality. These *Mary Sue* characters (a term used to label an idealized original female character loosely modeled on the author) have traditionally been vilified in many fandoms for violating the tenets of the world and for "bastardizing the canon universe of the original text by shifting the narrative fulcrum from the primary characters to a new, unrecognized character" (Bonnstetter and Ott 350). "Mary Sue shifts the main focus from the media characters readers want to read about" (Pfleiger, quoted in Bonnstetter and Ott 363). Instead of writing fictional representations of themselves (as gamers do with their avatars), fanfic authors are invested in developing canonical characters already established in the source text.

This blurring between an RPN character as self (that is, as a personal avatar) versus RPN as fictional character became a major point of contention on a particular Facebook RPN account for Shock Holmes. Over a period of several months in 2013, Shock declared the page was *not* a collaborative role-play page (even though it was named after Holmes's character and the profile picture was a photo of Benedict Cumberbatch as Sherlock). On April 29, 2013, in particular, Shock wrote, "We post what WE like. We DO NOT post endlessly lame discussions involving the repetition of the *Sherlock*'s dialogue. We do not role play. We do not sit around all day moaning about when the next season is coming. WE HAVE LIVES IN BETWEEN SHERLOCK EPISODES AND WE FILL THOSE LIVES WITH

FABULOSITY." At the same time the author(s) denied any responsibility to their audience or fidelity to the BBC *Sherlock* world, they simultaneously invoked Cumberbatch's authority later in the same status update: "If you think Benedict Cumberbatch looks twice at a woman who isn't a Fashion Goddess think again." Clearly, audiences believed, seeing the profile pic and character name, this was a role-play page, yet its creators denied this was their motivation. Such dissonance between creator and audience illustrates the difficulties of making sweeping generalizations about intention, audience, and pleasure.

Gaps

One effective way online RPNs establish *Sherlock*'s world and consistent characterization is through the use of textual gaps. Textual gaps refer to status updates that occur in a contextual vacuum, providing the audience with little to no guidance as to their meaning or reference. Such postings are simultaneously in character yet out of context, prompting the audience to fill in gaps in the storyline. Gaps not only engage the reader in active construction of the world; they also create the illusion of lives lived beyond the role play itself. Facebook status updates like Sherlock Hollmes's ". . . No. It really wouldn't" force the viewer to imagine an entire world outside the role play (Hollmes, February 4, 2012). Audiences must ask themselves: Who is Hollmes speaking to? What question or comment is he responding to? What does "it" refer to? What was his interlocutor's prompt? All of these questions imply an interaction between Hollmes and another character happening offscreen. The reader is only catching a glimpse of the action; the less is revealed, the more behind the scenes activity is implied. The implication is that the storyline and action continue offscreen, *even when the audience is not observing or participating in it.* In the end, the RPN appears more realistic because of what is *not* said rather than what *is*. Holmes and Watson become more believable as real characters because their characters imply a life lived beyond the screen. Textual gaps extend this verisimilitude, or semblance of realism, first to the role play itself, and then beyond its constructed boundaries. The world of the show, then, is both within the role play itself and beyond it in the imaginary spaces of the reader's mind. The infinite diversity of storylines fulfills viewers' need to consume more of the text outside the limiting boundaries of the original source.

The previous chapter's discussion on interquels and intraquels in corporate transmedia storytelling indicated that both the act of world building and the act of reading involve participants using their imaginations to fill narrative gaps in the storyworld. As reader response theorists Roman Ingarden and Wolfgang Iser observe, literary texts (as well as other artistic forms) are incomplete until a reader encounters, internalizes, and interprets them. In this process, the reader actualizes the text by filling in gaps with personal knowledge and experiences, including prior knowledge of the fictional world. According to Iser:

> Blanks and negations denote the missing links and the virtual themes along the syntagmatic and paradigmatic axes of the text. They make it possible for the fundamental asymmetry between text and reader to be balanced out, for they initiate an interaction whereby the hollow form of the text is filled by the mental images of the reader. In this way, text and reader begin to converge, and the reader can experience an unfamiliar reality under conditions that are not determined by his own disposition. Blanks and negations increase the density of fictional texts. (Iser, *Act* 225–26)

The reader is thus as active in constructing the text as is the writer, and each reading experience becomes a transaction between the unique text and the reader in a specific moment in time.[10]

Iser's theories about reading literary texts seem particularly prescient with regard to online world building. In *The Implied Reader: Patterns of Communication in Prose Fiction from Bunyan to Beckett* (1974), Iser states:

> The literary text activates our own faculties, enabling us to recreate the world it presents. The product of this creative activity is what we might call the virtual dimension of the text, which endows it with its reality. This virtual dimension is not the text itself, nor is it the imagination of the reader: it is the coming together of text and imagination. (279)

That is, the literary text's indeterminacies activate readers' minds, enabling us to recreate the fictional world there. In RPNs and other fanfiction, any events we imagine happening in the gaps of the story are influenced by what we already know about the character and canon from both the source text and the role player's previous activities. It is this oscillating "anticipation" and "retrospection" (Iser, *Implied Reader* 280)—looking forward to predict new storylines, new action, new character development, while at the same time looking back at the storylines that came before, back to the TV show, to Arthur Conan Doyle's source texts—that become the theatre in which role player and audience interact, reinforcing the worldness of both the show and role play.[11]

Such interactivity, while a defining characteristic of RPGs, can also cause significant disruptions to online narrative storytelling. While some crack!fic role playing may welcome alternative voices in the middle of an RPN, Twitter and Tumblr's interfaces do not allow users to control when new updates enter their newsfeeds. On both sites, members follow multiple users at a time, making it impossible to isolate a single group of postings. Postings are organized into a single coherent newsfeed, the order of which is dictated by timeliness, thus two characters in the middle of a role play risk being interrupted by incoming news. One such Twitter role play between Sherlock@Cumberholmes and John Watson@Doctor_Wat was interrupted by off-topic updates from Benedict Cumberbatch@Cumberbitches.

The more people an individual follows, the greater the likelihood that an RPN will be interrupted. This is similarly multiplied when the role play contains more than two characters at a time. The greater the number of tweets or posts per minute, the harder it is to follow a narrative. Traditional fanfiction, by contrast, is generally posted in completed units and does not allow readers to interrupt the narrative arc or interject commentary in the middle of the story. Fans can read one-shots (short stories with the entire action included in one episode), works in progress, or multichapter novellas, but all commentary is relegated to the comments section. While they can comment on each individual installment, they cannot interject their own feedback or ideas into the middle of a description, dialogue, or scene. RPN interruptions highlight the temporality of such narratives and the risks of the open text: when texts are truly open to audiences, authors provide opportunities for readers and participants to change the story and potentially to derail their intended storyline.

While Twitter and Tumblr automatically interject new updates within users' newsfeeds, thus potentially interrupting an RPN narrative, Facebook suffers from similar liabilities—not necessarily from an interface design standpoint, but in users' ability to participate in other RPNs without their creators' express permission. For instance, in the following Facebook

Twitter exchange (@Cumberbitches, Twitter)

role-play excerpt, John Watson finds himself making tea for too many of the wrong Sherlocks:

> JOHN Watson: Tea. Lots of it.
> SHER-LOCK Holme: Well I shall have a cup John!
> ŠHERLOCK Holmes: I'll have milk and three sugars.
> JOHN Watson: I am the one who's got a cold. In all fairness you should be making me tea.
> SHER-LOCK Holme: Fine!! But only if I can smoke!!
> ŠHERLOCK Holmes: It's a mild cold, just the sniffles. So of course you should be the one to make the tea.
> JOHN Watson: Oh, cheers. Very nice.
> ŠHERLOCK Holmes: Who said I was nice? If you'd like I could try my hand at this 'nice' business. But I'd have to warn you, the last time was disasterous. [*Sic.*]

JOHN Watson: If you can manage until I am well again that would be great.

SHER-LOCK Holme: *chuckles and makes them all tea* here you go

. . . . . .*he then lights up smirking* (John Watson, February 14, 2012)

What is most ironic about this example is that neither of these Sherlock Holmes role players is the one from this pairing (John Watson/Sherley Holmes). By engaging in a RPN, a character opens herself up for communication with other role players as well as additional fans. When other participants step in and invade the constructed world of the role play, then the boundaries of the world become permeable, making the enterprise less faithful to the source text. Corporate world building, by contrast, keeps the canon and world of the show closed off from audiences and other users who might want to change the focus of the story. Without an author's note or other clarifying data, RPN audiences cannot tell whether such activity disturbs the RPN's narrative arc and the consistency of the fictional world or if it is welcome (for example, as crack!fic).[12] In a role-playing narrative, however, such participation may be unwelcome—even though this openness is how the role players became involved in the first place.

In response to the aforementioned scenario, John Watson posted an administrative note on his page asking other fans and characters not to interrupt ongoing role plays:

//I'd just like to say a few words to anyone who'd like to read them. If you could do these favour [sic] for us, both me and Sherley would be very grateful.

1. When going through the picture in either my or Sherlock's galleries, please don't "like" each picture separately. Instead, "like" the gallery itself. It's fine to "like" 2 or 5 or 7 pictures, but when log on to 15+ notes . . . Well, I am sure you understand why we would prefer 1 note to 15.

2. We love getting feedback from you guys. It's lovely to see that you enjoy this as much as we do. However, please don't leave comments in the middle of an ongoing rp. If you have something to say, please do so on our wall instead. This makes it so much easier and neater both for me and Sherlock and others who read the rp. Especially considering I edit and post the rps on tumblr

and if I have to work around a comment in the middle of the rp it's suddenly a lot more work and a lot less fun than it ought to be.

Thank you for reading. (John Watson, February 14, 2012)

According to these players, interruptions make the RP "much less fun than it ought to be," and as a result they feel compelled to preserve their fictional world by policing its boundaries, similar to the ways corporations such as the BBC and Hartswood Studios police their worlds. While some traditional fanfic seems to allow for canonical inconsistencies (examples include crack!fic and AUs, among others) most online RPNs seem to reinforce the "coherence, completeness, and consistency within the world's environment, aesthetics, and rules" (Pearce 20). From the players' perspective, RPNs are dependent on other role players to survive. At heart a collective activity, role playing cannot function without other participants. From an audience perspective, however, when other characters, fans, and/or readers break through the constructed boundaries of the world, writers/gamers risk working at cross-purposes to one another. If the world isn't believable, fans won't read about it. If it is too believable, they will want to be part of it. In such interactions, every reader becomes a potential participant, raising important questions regarding genre and audience in online communities.

Worldness and Internal Consistency

Another important element of worldness is the internal consistency within each fandom role-play narrative. While traditional fanfic authors can publish multiple stories under the same pseudonym, each has its own title, can be found by an individual hyperlink, and has its own distinct header, genre conventions, and tags. Publishing multiple fan narratives within a single role-play account, however, can confuse readers and risks alienating them from the fictional world. Some critics, such as like Stein and Busse, argue that this episodic nature defines all role-playing games: "Rather than presenting a linear, holistic narrative, the saga is communicated in fragments, through posts and comment conversations, and sometimes through the added dimensions of hyperlinks to online images, articles, and other journals" (Stein and Busse 204). Although Facebook RPNs appear, on the surface, to be fragmented and episodic, however, they are still all centrally located on a single character's or group of characters' Facebook pages; in addition, most of these RPNs consist of characters responding to one another's status updates, so the storylines are embedded within a linear narrative (sometimes inverted, if presented through multiple status updates). "What holds a distributed narrative together, what unites the disparate elements," Paul Booth agrees, "is the desire for narrative unity" ("Rereading Fandom" 520). Constantly shifting between the original world of *Sherlock* and the many alternative storylines and universes has the potential to disrupt both narrative unity and the world.

One such example of world/narrative inconsistency occurred in the Facebook RPN between Sherley Holmes and John Watson in February 2012. Within three short months, the role players introduced and abandoned three different storylines, all from drastically different crossover worlds disconnected from *Sherlock*: Sentinel-Guide (based on a Canadian television show that aired from 1996 to 1999), Hogwarts (based on the *Harry Potter* universe), and *Game of Thrones*, George R. R. Martin's fantasy novels and the current HBO TV series. If successful world building depends on coherence, completeness, and consistency, then each additional storyline within a single account potentially weakens the worldness of the role play and its connection to the source text, thus depriving the audience of the narrative excess and pleasure that role playing can provide. Sherley Holmes, one of the role players in the aforementioned example, worried that too much world jumping in such a short time might cause the audience to miss the world (*Sherlock*) that drew them to the role play in the first place.

An emphasis on worldness doesn't necessarily mean fans can't use their creativity to imagine new and unique scenes, emotions, and relationships for their favorite characters, however. As long as the reader is reassured that the writers are "maintaining the source text as discursive referent" (Stein and Busse 196)—that is, that the world itself still acts as center, as the thing all genres define themselves *against*—then, even though the narrative may stray significantly from the source text, the original still imposes limits on how the role players may be expected to act in character and requires them to conform to these expectations.[13] The most popular fanfiction and RPN genre, for example, is slash, and it seems similarly inconsistent with the world of the BBC's *Sherlock*. The show consistently plays with its audience's contemporary expectations regarding Sherlock and John's close friendship, including several hints and jokes as to their supposed homoerotic connection. Often accused of "queer baiting,"[14] the show's writers constantly blur the boundaries between the characters' homosocial and homoerotic relationship. Traditional fanfiction's obsession with slash pairings is examined in chapter 3, but slash is one area where role players seize on a subtext from the show and turn it into a kind of role-play fantasy that may or may not reinforce *Sherlock*'s world. Working within common canonical situations to create a sexual relationship between Sherlock and John, the Facebook RPN Sherley Holmes/John Watson satisfies fans' craving for a homosexual relationship that is both supported by and simultaneously outside or beyond the canon. In the following example, the two are portrayed naked, snuggling together in bed:

> *The room is dark when John wakes up. Taking a deep breath, he yawns, lifting his head from the pillow slightly. It takes him a few seconds to gather his surroundings. When he does, John freezes. In his sleep John had snuggled up next to Sherlock, his arms wrapped around his chest in a solid embrace. And they were spooning. John can feel himself blush. Not wanting to wake Sherlock he lies still. This was surprisingly nice. John closes his eyes and smells Sherlock's hair, feeling the warmth of his body pressed against his. It's only when he realizes Sherlock is naked John gets the willpower to pull away, a blush spreading across his cheeks.* Sherlock? (John Watson >Sherley Holmes February 8, 2012)

Most fans recognize that no real textual evidence supports a homosexual relationship between Sherlock and John in Doyle's stories, and while the BBC production constantly draws attention to and plays with the idea, no evidence in the series (as yet) suggests anything more than a close friendship.[15] Online *Sherlock* RPNs like those on Facebook, Twitter, and Tumblr clearly rely on the worldness of the show in the sense that their characters are obviously based on the BBC incarnations; however, they simultaneously alter that world by placing the main characters in a relationship not found in any of the original source texts, thus altering the very world they seek to recreate. This does not keep fans from making a m/m relationship between Sherlock and John the most prevalent fantasy pervading fanfiction. Having the characters in a relationship that is publicly a friendship and privately a romance need not violate canon compliance;

in fact, it may underscore fans' sense of the realism of such duality. Fan investment in and faithfulness to the world of the show are thus more complex than merely reproducing storylines and dialogue from individual episodes. Fanfiction and online RPNs such as those discussed here offer a glimpse behind the scenes into a world both persuasively real and at the same time unknown and/or hidden.

Digital Verisimilitude and Technological Limitations

In addition to general worldness and characterization, online RPNs add additional layers of realism through the inclusion of realistic digital media and artifacts available on particular digital social media platforms. Postings from role-playing characters, with thumbnail images of the actors who portray the characters on-screen, allow writers and readers to enter into a fantasy world in which they can watch their beloved characters interact in real time. On March 22, 2012, for example, John Watson posted to Sherlock's wall what looks like the transcript of an email. John follows the formatting of a real email, including the email addresses of both participants, a relevant subject line, and a realistic looking grocery list. Such attention to detail—as well as to additional media forms—works to reinforce the idea that these characters are living real lives outside the show. They have email accounts, buy groceries, take trips. While limited somewhat by the interface design of Facebook, Sherlock Hollmes and John Watson are clearly playing with fans' concepts of simulacra and simulation; by copying actual email formatting, the role players simulate a realism that doesn't actually exist. Such attention to detail blurs the boundary between the real and the imaginary, reinforcing the fantasy of the role-playing world.

While Facebook provides extensive opportunities for narrative world building, Tumblr's primarily visual format provides an added dimension of verisimilitude. In her history and analysis of Tumblr's impact on fan studies, Louisa Stein notes that, from its inception in 2007, Tumblr "offered users the ability to share visual images, still and moving, combined with limited text, in what seemed like a fresh aesthetic, although in truth it had evolved from prior platforms Projectionist and Anarchia" (Stein, "Tumblr" 87). The previous email modeled status update is somewhat hindered by Facebook's interface design; even though it is essentially formatted correctly, it doesn't look like a real email. Conversely, Tumblr

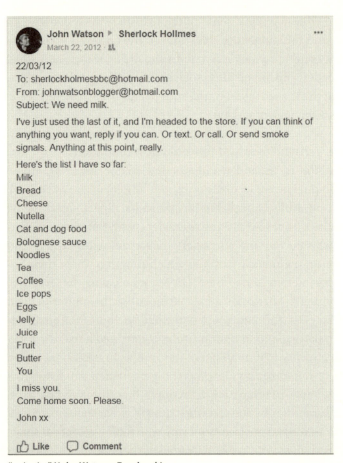

"22/03/12" (John Watson, Facebook)

blogs like textsfromjohnandsherlock.tumblr.com have experimented with digital artifacts like images of Sherlock's handwritten journal. Digital images and document design allow writers to work around interface limitations in ways that not only create more storytelling freedom but also provide greater verisimilitude for the audience.[16] Text can be impersonal, but a real document in Sherlock's handwriting collapses the gap between fiction and reality. Such artifacts sustain and promote the illusion that Sherlock is a real person; he has a journal, this is his handwriting, he is out solving a case with John and Lestrade. The closer the artifacts approximate the real in appearance and content, the more closely the RPN reinforces the world of the show.

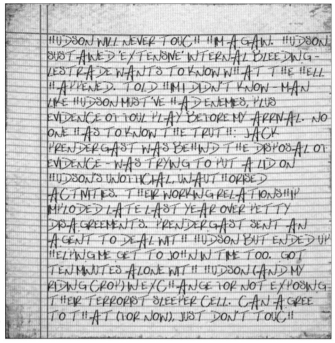

HUDSON WILL NEVER TOUCH HIM AGAIN. HUDSON
JUST HAD 'EXTENSIVE' INTERNAL BLEEDING -
LESTRADE WANTS TO KNOW WHAT THE HELL
HAPPENED. TOLD HIM DIDN'T KNOW - MAN
LIKE HUDSON MUST'VE HAD ENEMIES, PLUS
EVIDENCE OF FOUL PLAY BEFORE MY ARRIVAL. NO
ONE HAS TO KNOW THE TRUTH: JACK
PRENDERGAST WAS BEHIND THE DISPOSAL OF
EVIDENCE - WAS TRYING TO PUT A LID ON
HUDSON'S UNOFFICIAL, UNAUTHORISED
ACTIVITIES. THEIR WORKING RELATIONSHIP
IMPLODED LATE LAST YEAR OVER PETTY
DISAGREEMENTS. PRENDERGAST SENT AN
AGENT TO DEAL WITH HUDSON BUT ENDED UP
HELPING ME GET TO JOHN IN TIME TOO. GOT
TEN MINUTES ALONE WITH HUDSON (AND MY
RIDING CROP) IN EXCHANGE FOR NOT EXPOSING
THEIR TERRORIST SLEEPER CELL. CAN AGREE
TO THAT (FOR NOW). JUST DON'T TOUCH

"Hudson will never touch him again" (textsfromjohnandsherlock, Tumblr)

Textsfromjohnandsherlock also incorporates other digital artifacts, including photoshopped screen captures of imaginary texts between the two characters, implying a more realistic, real-time dialogue. The blog's authors, Seth and Chel, use the role play to respond to and play with fan expectations and fantasies around the show, especially with regard to slash. Textsfromjohnandsherlock toys with the BBC *Sherlock* source text in several ways. First, it plays with the question of whether Sherlock and John are in a romantic relationship. Second, it simultaneously builds on fans' fantasies (supported by copious fanfictions) that the men indeed are in a sexual relationship, teasing that they, unlike the real show, are willing to give readers what they want—only to pull back at the last minute. This teasing creates a level of anticipation in the audience, keeping them believing they are on the brink of having their fantasies fulfilled; fans are frequently reminded of their desire, but textsfromjohnandsherlock didn't fulfill these expectations until late 2013, when the two characters confirmed they had consummated their sexual relationship, thus fulfilling many fans'

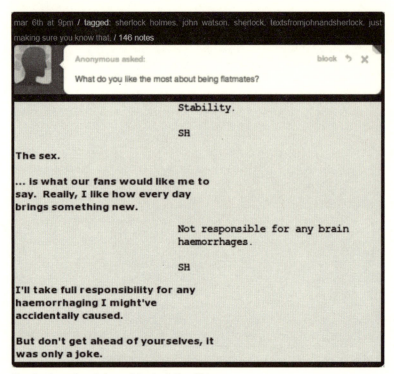

March 6 (textsfromjohnandsherlock, Tumblr)

homoerotic fantasies about the show's main characters. Lastly, the blog calls attention to the slippage between the RPN and the show's characters by referring to what their fans want. The role play makes it impossible for the audience to tell which fans the characters are referring to: fans of the BBC's Sherlock and John or fans of Seth and Chel's role-play characters. This blurring between source text and fan production provides exactly the kind of frisson fans love and adaptation studies explore. Textsfromjohn-andsherlock deliberately plays on this interpretive doubling by toying with the boundaries between source text and role play, between reality and fiction, and thereby reinforces the verisimilitude and world of the show without necessarily being faithful to it.

While Facebook and Tumblr allow fans to create hyper-realistic role-play narratives, they come with their own technological limitations. Each format has particular characteristics and idiosyncrasies, and fans choose the specific social media platform that best meets the needs of their creation and fan communities (Stein, "Tumblr" 86). As Stein explains, "Each interface used by fans develops and maintains its own community norms, expectations, and limits of code and culture. In some cases, fans will use a given interface in a way consistent with its officially stated intent. In other instances, fans use interfaces in unintended, negotiative, and even resistant ways" ("Tumblr" 86). All formats, however, share an inherent temporality. While Tumblr provides an archive in which researchers and fans can look up older postings, Twitter initially deleted any tweet more than three weeks old. Facebook, with its timeline and relatively easy linear access to older posts, seems to be the easiest interface to use for RPNs, but that ease of access may be short-lived. In early 2011, industry analysts, bloggers, and online role players reported that Facebook planned to ban role players from the site (Applegate, "Facebook"), perhaps by targeting individuals initially using the "Verified Official Role Player" tag on their pages, like the one found on Shock Holmes's (originally sherlock holmes-bbc) info page (Shock Holmes, October 27, 2011).[17] By the end of 2011, many users claimed their role-play accounts had been disabled by the company (Applegate, "Facebook," comments).[18] Similarly, recent Facebook policy regarding profile names have precluded multiple characters with the exact same name spellings, making it both easier to create characters and more difficult for Facebook to track them down. On September 22, 2012, for example, Facebook RPN pairing Sherley Holmes/John Watson both asked current readers to unfriend them due to fears their accounts were going to be disabled:

> I have a sad question to ask you guys; Since the probably of fb shutting down my account is much bigger now that I have over 1000 fb friends, I will kindly ask those who are not following my posts to unfriend me. No hard feelings. I will look at it as a favour from your side =). (Sherley Holmes, September 22, 2012)

One might speculate whether such strategies are part of a corporate world building strategy to contain intellectual property and keep control of the canon out of fans' hands. Each platform's technological profile puts restrictions on how fans can use (and exploit) the genre conventions to tell stories. In this sense, the structural limitations imposed by social media sites created by corporate entities and motivated by profit rather than by community perform similarly to the BBC network and *Sherlock*'s creators.

Corporations install boundaries to control what fans can and cannot do with the world. The consequences of such actions for role players, fans, and researchers are unknown. The ephemeral nature of social media sites not only highlights the rapidly changing genres of fanfiction and RPNs, it also highlights the urgency for fans and scholars alike to engage with and capture these narratives of play before they are gone.

While most current research on RPGs seems to focus on identity formation, community, and the game elements of play, I want to bring more nuance to examining the differences between role-playing games and role-playing narratives to highlight the formative roles that canon and world building play in online fanfiction. RPNs allow fans to enact the *Sherlock* world by deliberately inhabiting the lives and voices of the show's original characters. Individual narrative role plays and characterizations are often critiqued by fans for their (in)ability to recreate and remain faithful to the syntax and worldness of the original source. Many fan extensions remain compliant with the canonical world, while others view fanfic as a resistant activity—a form of noncompliance—and begin changing the very elements that drew them to the world in the first place. Small changes can lead to wider and wider violations of canon until authors risk alienating their audiences and losing any explicit or implicit connection to the original source text.

CHAPTER THREE

QUEERING *SHERLOCK'S* WORLD
Slash, Fanfiction, and (Non)Compliance in World Building

In her essay, "Writing Bodies in Space: Media Fan Fiction as Theatrical Performance," Francesca Coppa argues for a performative analysis of fanfiction. Building on Barthes's ideas of the performative writerly text, Coppa maintains that fanfiction is a writer's way to make literary characters act within the framework(s) of different genres (230). In RPN fanfiction, we saw fans literally embodying the fictional characters they are composing, enacting the character's first-person voice and experiences. In slash fiction,[1] writers make same-sex fictional characters perform according to romantic and erotic behaviors, tropes, and storylines.[2] Sexual identity is an integral element of both real individuals' and fictional characters' selfhoods, so changing such a fundamental part of that identity would seem to be a major violation of the foundation laws, parameters, and characteristics of the fictional world.[3] Yet characters in slash fiction remain compliant with the original fictional world because they remain consistent in their characterization, traits, and mannerisms.

Not all slash fics include explicit (homo)sexual acts, but such acts are a primary element of some of the most popular fics on the internet. Sex can occur in the context of an emotional relationship or strictly in a sex-for-sex's-sake scenario, as seen in PWP (Plot? What Plot?) stories consisting of single, stand-alone sexual encounters. In PWP stories, sex is "lingered over as a sex scene, a difference evident in the timing of the narration, where time is both condensed and extended to mimic the representative structures of pornography" (Driscoll 86). In longer erotic slash narratives, however, "the 15,000 word build-up to a sex scene is as much part of the erotic reading experience as the actual sex scene itself" (Jung). For some critics and readers, slash becomes a form of feminized pornography that highlights and validates women's sexual identities and desires.[4]

Let's look at slash from a literary perspective: as an exploration of queerness, characterization, identity, and world building. Slash is often analyzed in isolation rather than as "a node in a web, a part of an often complex intertextual sequence," one with "a close and running relationship with (at least) one other text" (Green et al., quoted in Stasi 116, 119). Effective slash fiction shows several similarities to the main definitions of world building: "a plausible and logical plot; effective and accurate use of language and style (particularly with the speaking characteristics of the main characters); consistent characterization (particularly adhering to 'canon' in non-AU worlds); verisimilitude achieved through research; and editing" (Bury 100).

Why Write Slash?

One of the most popular research questions in fan studies inquires into the motivation behind straight women's interest in, and contribution to, slash fiction about male characters. Looking back over the substantial history of slash fanfiction, published primarily since the mid-1980s, reveals three major answers: slash is a feminist act, women readers both desire and identify with the male protagonists in the slash relationship, and slash rejects traditional gender and heteronormative behaviors. For scholars in the first group (Penley, Kustritz, Booth, Scodari, Salmon and Symon, and Lamb and Veith), slash represents a liberatory act that subverts patriarchy by transforming the traditional gender roles and romantic relationships found in most narrative plots into potentially gender-neutral relationships based on equality (Kustritz, "Slashing" 379; Booth, *Digital Fandom* 72). Constance Penley sees slash as a "guerilla act" that "retools" modern-day masculinity ("Brownian Motion" 155). Slash can also be seen as a feminist response to the antipornography debates of the 1980s. Joanna Russ's famous 1985 article, "Pornography by Women, for Women, with Love," argued that most slash focused on male/male relationships (rather than on female/female or even heterosexual relationships) because no one could imagine men and women having the same kind of equal, complex, or gender-ambiguous relationship or the same level of intimate commitment that readers could accept between two men (Russ 84). Such sexually explicit content can be seen as a metaphor for women's desire for romantic and sexual relationships between equals (Lamb and Veith 238). In a more problematic vein, evolutionary biologists like Catherine Salmon and Don Symon claim that women's biology dictates that women want nurturing relationships and monogamy rather than sex; thus, erotic fiction such as romantic slash emphasizes emotional connection over sexual explicitness (99). While some feminist critics worry about the potentially essentialist elements inherent in evolutionary biological arguments, all of the noted critics clearly identify feminist patterns and motivations behind why fans write and readers read slash fiction.

The second approach, which sees the appeal of slash in identification and desire, finds its roots in psychoanalytic theory and the work of film critic Laura Mulvey. In her revolutionary essay "Visual Pleasure and Narrative Cinema" (1975), Mulvey argues that watching a film puts the audience in the same position as the (typically male) protagonist. The viewer thus engages in the voyeuristic activity of objectifying and fetishizing female bodies through the literal lens of the camera and the metaphoric gaze of the male protagonist and director. By replacing the female sex object with a man, feminist critics such as Constance Penley argue, slash portrays a sexual relationship between equals (two men) while allowing women to identify with and "have (as sexual objects) either or both" of the characters (Penley, "Feminism" 314).[5] Busse implies that such exchanges can turn fandom into a "queer female space" ("My Life" 208), which leads us to our final theme: the rejection of traditional gender and heterosexual norms.

Some critics, such as Henry Jenkins (drawing on the work of Eve Sedgwick), see slash as ultimately concerned with contemporary conflicts within masculinity; they argue that slash is a response to the media's construction of male sexuality in television, film, and pornography (194) and that it opens the way for "the realization of homosocial desires" by throwing cultural ideas about masculinity into crisis (Jenkins, *Textual Poachers* 194, 210). But focusing solely on gender norms, and on masculinity in particular, risks privileging patriarchy and masculinity above other gendered behaviors. For Elizabeth Woledge, for example, slash is less about gender than it is about the "nature of the relationship" between the (predominantly male) characters; she argues that "intimacy, not sexual union, is the defining feature" of slash (105). These examples, however, run the same risk of essentializing male and female gender norms and desires as do the psychoanalytic examples. Because the majority of slash partnerships are male/male rather than female/female, traditionally masculine behaviors, values, bodies, sexualities, and general experiences remain the dominant norm in contemporary Western society. The rise of female/female slash fanfiction over the past few years potentially highlights the increase in the number of popular, strong women protagonists dominating contemporary media (for example, in *Xena*, *Once Upon a Time*, *Rizzoli and Isles*, and others) and a growing interest in and validation of women's identities, sexualities, and experiences.

Critics such as Rhiannon Bury, Susanne Jung, and Sara Gwenllian Jones similarly highlight the shift from gender-focused analyses of slash to critiques of heterosexuality and heteronormativity. For Bury, making connections with other women readers and writers writing about male relationships is "less a rejection of gender norms than a rejection of heterosexual norms" (Bury 13). Jung and Jones both worry that reading slash as resistant to dominant gender norms potentially reinscribes heteronormativity as the preferred meaning of the source text, implying that such sexual practices and identities are always already present in the canon (Jones 81).[6] Because a majority of television and film narratives are based on the adventure genre, Jones argues, happy, successful heterosexual relationships risk stymieing the dramatic narrative by tying down the protagonists to a life of security, stability, and domesticity. The only options that allow the narrative to move forward and continue with their adventure themes either place the protagonist in an unfulfilled heterosexual relationship (think *Moonlighting* from the 1980s) or require the characters to receive all of their emotional support and connection from another same-sex character (Jones 88–89). Foregrounding the same-sex relationship, then, at the expense of the heterosexual one, reinforces the dangers of heterosexuality, while homoerotism allows the narrative and its protagonists to continue to expand the televisual world. Such homoerotism is thus integral to most buddy narratives and not something outside or foreign to traditional media plotlines.

If homoeroticism is already integral to many mainstream fictional storylines, why do mainstream audiences and critics frequently disparage slash and see it as a threat to the media world? Susanne Jung explains this by noting that what is troubling for patriarchal culture is women writing sex for other women: such a sex scene is "doubly transgressive in that it not only violates the notion of female sexual ignorance but also has at its centre that sexuality which since the end of the nineteenth century has been 'constituted as secrecy': (male) homosexuality" (Jung 24). Queer theorists Frederik Dhaenens, Sofie Van Bauwel, and Daniel Baltereyst find it disappointing that so few media scholars have focused on the potential for queer readings of canonical texts and slash's ability to "[embrace] the possibilities of a 'fluidity of erotic identification'"; they conclude that this neglect highlights the ways in which gender, feminism, and fan studies as sociological rather than textual fields continue to dominate research (343). *Sherlock*, to the contrary, has been the site of a plethora of queer interpretations, ranging from homoerotic explorations of the show's queer subtext to complex interrogations of the showrunners' attitudes toward homosexuality and accusations of queerbaiting. The show and subsequent fanfiction provide particularly rich arenas for exploring contemporary attitudes toward the Sherlockian world in combination with characterization and sexuality.

Character and Sexual Identity: Slash in *Sherlock*

Some audiences are surprised when fans interpret John and Sherlock's friendship through a slash lens and argue that fans are "reading too much into the show" and applying contemporary understandings of sexuality to what is, at its source, a Victorian friendship. Fans, however, point to several elements within the show itself that raise questions—either implicitly or explicitly—about the nature of the two men's relationship.[7] As implicit evidence, they cite the deep eye contact in the drugs bust scene at the end of "A Study in Pink" and numerous violations of personal space across all four seasons.

Television's small screen led TV cinematographers early on to use extreme close-ups to bring greater detail to shots and to emphasize character interactions. Placing two characters close together, well within Western society's expectations for personal space, implies a degree of personal and emotional connection between the characters that can seem to exceed traditional friendship. Sometimes termed the "Starsky and Hutch syndrome," this type of shot suggests the characters are inexorably drawn to each other and unable to resist touching one another (Bacon-Smith 33). Another example from *Sherlock* is the escape scene in "The Reichenbach Fall" (S2E1), in which John and Sherlock hold hands as they escape from

John/Sherlock "eye sex" (*Sherlock*, "A Study in Pink")

the police. Because the characters are handcuffed together, running in tandem becomes challenging. Sherlock's suggestion that John "hold [his] hand" as they escape, and John's response, "Now people really will talk," allows fans to interpret the scene as implicit confirmation of the characters' desire for a romantic connection. By making this explicit in the dialogue and cinematography, a queer reading emerges from the show's subtext to its context.

Fans also often mention the dinner "date" scene at Angelo's in "A Study in Pink" (S1E1), during which John inquires about Sherlock's sexuality. (A more recent exploration of Sherlock's sexual history takes place in his mind-palace, as rendered in 2016's *The Abominable Bride*.)

> JOHN: "You don't have a girlfriend, then?"
> SHERLOCK: "Girlfriend? No, not really my area."
> JOHN: "Oh, right. Do you have a boyfriend? Which is fine, by the way."
> SHERLOCK: "I know it's fine."
> JOHN: "So you've got a boyfriend."
> SHERLOCK: "No."
> JOHN: "Right. Ok. So you're unattached, like me. Right. Good."
> SHERLOCK: "John, um, I think you should know, I consider myself married to my work, and while I'm flattered by your interest, I'm not really not looking for any . . ."
> JOHN: "No, no, not asking . . . No. I'm just saying, it's all fine."
> ("A Study in Pink")

Fans also reference several comments and jokes about whether or not Sherlock is John's boyfriend, ranging from Angelo bringing them a candle for the table, since it's "more romantic" ("A Study in Pink") to the inn-keeper apologizing in "The Hounds of Baskerville" for not being able to provide John and Sherlock with a double bed. For fans invested in a queer reading of the show, these examples both provide evidence of a queer sub-text (what some fans label the "Johnlock Conspiracy," which claims Moffat and Gatiss ultimately plan for the two characters to end up in a roman-tic relationship) or, conversely, evidence of queer baiting (playing with audience expectations and hopes that a queer relationship exists between Sherlock and John, only to mock the possibility of such a union).[8] Either way, general audiences cannot deny that the scripts make several refer-ences (at least one in nearly every episode) to John and Sherlock's rela-tionship and how other characters in the show perceive them, including as (potential) romantic partners, so it's no surprise that Johnlock slash is the most popular published *Sherlock* fanfiction on the web.

Plausible and Logical Plot

Kate_Lear's "The Love Song of John H. Watson" provides an ex-cellent entry point into canonical *Sherlock* slash. An established relation-ship fic, the basic storyline revolves around John taking Sherlock on a tour of historic crime scenes on Valentine's Day. Because Sherlock is gener-ally suspicious of any kind of sentiment and corporately sponsored holi-days, John tricks him into the tour by claiming that it's to celebrate Luper-calia, an ancient pre-Roman festival observed between February 13 and 15 to avert evil spirits and purify the city, releasing health and fertility (see the Wikipedia entry "Lupercalia"). Over the course of the evening, John takes Sherlock to several crime-related pubs, one of which used to sell corpses to local medical schools (4); another, The King's Arms, where, in 1811, "an unknown assailant murdered the three people who lived above it" (4) (the man originally accused of the crime, John Williams, died in prison awaiting trial only to be exonerated later); and The Ten Bells, "the pub where the Ripper allegedly first spotted several of his victims" (7). They pass the Metropolitan Police's Black Museum, a repository of major crime and police evidence located in New Scotland Yard and mention stopping by the location of the Crippen murders before finally stopping at home at 221b, which, John claims, was once the site of another crime: "In 1895, Oscar Wilde was given two years' imprisonment for being in love with another man," John explains to Sherlock on the steps of 221b, "and I just thought . . . well, I just thought that . . . we're lucky" (11–12). The entire premise of this slashy Valentine's Day fic—taking Sherlock on a romantic tour of "centuries-old crime scenes" (6)—is both plausible and logically consistent with both the show and the original Doyle canon. In Doyle's "Scandal in Bohemia," for instance, Watson writes that any kind of emotion in Holmes is like grit in an instrument; it obscures his microscopic view of the world. In the show, Sherlock is famously dismissive of sentiment, from the ending of the very first episode ("A Study in Pink"), where he deduces that John carries his sister's old phone, to his triumph over Irene Adler in "A Scandal in Belgravia." Although some viewers and critics may argue that any kind of romance between Sherlock and John—whether in the Doyle canon or on *Sherlock*—is implausible and violates canon, Kate_Lear's premise for "The Love Song of John H. Watson" provides one example of slash that achieves logical consistency with both.

Kate_Lear grounds her fic specifically in Doyle as well as in *Sherlock* by referring to Doyle storylines, settings, and characterization. Early in Kate_Lear's "The Love Song of John H. Watson," for example, she mentions Sherlock's frustration with a case involving a client who found a piece of broken glass in his chicken. Sherlock is disgusted with the client's intention to sue the supermarket for compensation until he discovers that the alleged broken glass is actually "the blue carbuncle of Lady Something-or-Other that had disappeared six months previously" (2), a clear reference to Doyle's famous Christmas story, "The Adventure of the Blue Carbuncle" (1892). The fic also mentions established canon (and fanon) elements from *Sherlock*, mixing it (sometimes incorrectly) with Doyle references. The beginning of her story, for example, establishes "the great love of Sherlock's life . . . London, in all its busy dirty, loud, sparkling glory. Sherlock loves to be at the centre of it," John writes, "like a spider sitting in his web, and he knows it like another person would know the body of their lover, like John is slowly getting to know Sherlock's" (3). This evokes Doyle's *Study in Scarlet*, with Watson's early observations of London as "the great cesspool of the Empire." (This line, this time in Sherlock's voice, is echoed in the middle of "The Empty Hearse" [S3E1] and again by John at the start of *The Abominable Bride*, where it most closely adheres to the original.) It alludes as well to Holmes's detailed knowledge of the city, echoed in Sherlock's familiarity with the city's backstreets, as evidenced by John and Sherlock's taxi chase in "A Study in Pink" (S1E1). In John's description of Sherlock

Lear also embeds a reference to Moriarty: "a spider sitting in its web." "The Love Song" was originally published in 2011, thus before "The Reichenbach Fall" aired in 2012; however, Moriarty is described as a "great spider" in Doyle's "Final Problem," the source story for "The Reichenbach Fall," and Moriarty and Holmes are clearly presented as psychic doubles in the original story as well. Enmeshing these layers of citation into her fanfic provides Kate_Lear with several points of entry into the various Sherlock Holmes worlds and firmly establishes her fic as canon compliant on multiple levels.

"The Love Song" also firmly sets its storyline within *Sherlock*'s world by making specific references to the show's other characters and their personalities. Standing outside the Black Museum at New Scotland Yard, Sherlock is delighted to learn from John that when the new headquarters at New Scotland Yard was being built, the builders one day found an unidentified female torso in the basement. The police, who never discovered the responsible party, was led at the time by a man named Anderson, the name of Sherlock's Scotland Yard nemesis on the show (8). The fic's references to secondary characters further ground it within the broader elements of *Sherlock* and its world.

Consistent Characterization and Canon Compliance

To be believable, fictional characters must be seen as "autonomous beings, not as mere plot functions" (quoted in Pearson, "Kings of Infinite Space" 6). Writers and creators thus need to follow a consistent pattern in forming their characters. David Bordwell's formalist analysis of film (and literary) character provides a particularly helpful framework for analyzing canonical characterization. Bordwell argues that adaptations must consider the following principles when adapting a fictional character for the screen (or another media): embodiment, dialogue, gestures, recurrent motifs (repeated behavior), and traits exhibited in the character's speech and actions (Bordwell 15). Audiences thus come to slash and other forms of fanfics already primed: these readers encounter an original fanfic with prior knowledge of the fictional characters' embodiment, dialogue, gestures, recurrent motifs, and traits. Fans have met them already— not only in the source text but in the actors' themselves. As Francesca Coppa elaborates, "We know who these characters are because we know the actors who play them, and we bring our memories of their physicality to the text, so the reader is precharged, preeroticized" (Coppa, "Writing Bodies" 235–36). The actor's physical embodiment of the character becomes one of the primary ways in which *Sherlock* fan writers (re)invoke the world of the show, particularly in erotic fanfiction like slash and real person fic, as discussed in chapter six.

One of the primary ways "The Love Song of John H. Watson" and other slash fics recreate and reinforce *Sherlock*'s world is through characters' recurrent motifs and personality traits, particularly their portrayals of Sherlock. The very first line of Lear's story represents the commonly held assumption that Sherlock Holmes is some kind of high-functioning sociopath, as he is portrayed in the series. The fic starts: "Almost everyone who encounters him, including the entirety of the Met, thinks that Sherlock Holmes is a heartless bastard. Brilliant, but ultimately heartless" (Lear 1). Such a declaration seems at odds with the impetus of slash and romance fic, but Lear is clearly using this to set up the real Sherlock Holmes only John Watson knows.[9] Lear's Sherlock, much like Moffat and Gatiss's, loves "the puzzle and the chase" (Lear 3), whether in solving a crime or in deducing John's needs and desires. Remaining consistent with both Doyle's and the BBC's characterization, Lear's Sherlock also plays the violin: "Sherlock is a tremendously skilled player, and will often lose himself for hours in the music, but John has also known him to be quite content not to touch it for days when he's happy and absorbed in a case" (Lear 2). Similarly, Lear's John also mentions Sherlock's past cocaine use, noting that he's only interested in the drug "when he's between cases and complaining bitterly that he's about to die of boredom" (Lear 2), both of which themes appear in the early Doyle stories and in the first and second seasons of *Sherlock*. Lear's Sherlock, as well as Doyle's and the BBC's, is a victim of his own over-active brain. He needs constant application or distraction to keep his mind from churning itself into bits. John's job in the show is to "make it all stop" (Lear 19). And in slash, he often does this with his body.

Not only does "The Love Song of John W. Watson" include the show's main characters, it also refers to them in ways consistent with Moffat and Gatiss's syntactic stylistics and speech patterns as expressed in the show's dialogue. For instance, when stating that he doesn't like referring to Sherlock as his boyfriend (it's too juvenile), John mentions that "Sherlock refers to his own brother as his arch-enemy," a clear reference to "A Study in Pink," in which Mycroft is first introduced as a red herring for

Andrew Scott's Moriarty (Lear 3). John also directly quotes from the show, modeling Mycroft's, and later Sherlock's, speech patterns, when he describes how Sherlock "doesn't have friends" (Lear 3). Mimicking characters' speech patterns and identifiable catch phrases serves as an important means for fanfic authors to invoke and recreate the show's world. While other genres of fanfic (most notably, crack!) may be all about violating canon compliance, fans most often accuse fics of being out of character (OOC) when characters speak or act in noncanon-compliant ways. Thus, characterization, particularly within the context of world building, is the most important element of fanfiction writing and consumption.

Embodiment and the Fetishization of Sherlock's Body

Slash differs from other genres of fanfic in its focus on the physical embodiment of the characters and what they do with their bodies. Given this emphasis, perhaps it is not surprising to see how slash fanfic turns the focus on the romantic and physical elements of the characters' sexual relationship into a fetishization of the actors' costumes and bodies. Such physical fetishization occurs frequently across all fandoms, and fans have created various tags and shorthand phrasing for particular obsessions and body parts: eye!porn, bicep!porn, neck!porn, and hand!porn are all frequent tropes in slash fiction and in Sherlock fic, in particular. Once "The Love Song" begins to focus more on the physical aspects of John and Sherlock's relationship, several references are made to Cumberbatch's legendary cheekbones. Other slash fics frequently mention Cumberbatch's cupid's bow mouth, but "The Love Song" calls only general, eroticized attention to Sherlock's lips. Another fetishized element of Cumberbatch's Sherlock is his dark, curly hair. It has become so iconic that the producers even had a custom wig made for the end of 2016's Victorian *Abominable Bride* episode when Sherlock is back in the present day dealing with Moriarty's alleged return from the dead. Cumberbatch's iconic dark curls make an appearance midway through Lear's story when the characters begin to kiss; John describes how he "gently . . . cups Sherlock's head, working his fingers into the warm mess of curls" (Lear 14). The "warm mess" of Sherlock's curls here seems to symbolize his inability to maintain his stoic self-control in the face of John's desire. Even Sherlock's costumes, such as his now famous Belstaff coat, act as instantly recognizable character keys, and Lear's fic makes a few general references to "the loose edges of [Sherlock's] long coat" (Lear 12), its lapels "billowing around him" (Lear 6). In fact, it features significantly in an aborted back-alley sex scene in the story, serving to shield the characters' actions and bodies from random onlookers.

The final fetishized aspect of Cumberbatch's body is more prevalent in fanon than in the canon of the actual show. Sherlock's fingers—their length and delicacy—are frequently mentioned in erotic fanfics and are often the object of John's fantasies about Sherlock's body.[10] Sherlock's fingers receive two mentions in "The Love Song"; they serve as a point of fascination for John and an entry point into Sherlock's seemingly repressed sensuality. Once the two characters return to 221b Baker Street to engage in their Lupercalia sex, John comments that "Sherlock's fingers are sensitive . . . and often cool and tasting of violin rosin, and as John lets them slide between his lips he wants to repeat the action on another part of Sherlock's body entirely" (Lear 15). Here, Lear clearly links fanon's obsession with Sherlock's sensual fingers (hand!porn) with other elements of *Sherlock*'s and Doyle's world through their connection to his canonical violin playing. Thus, the passage serves a double purpose, linking the story's slash elements to both fanon and canon world building. In another passage, Sherlock eroticizes his own hands because of how they highlight his difference from, and complementarity with, John and his body: "Sherlock likes the sight of his own long, narrow fingers twined with John's shorter, blunter ones; he said once that it was 'aesthetically pleasing' and the words had stuck in John's head, since it had been the closest Sherlock had ever come to anything even remotely complimentary or romantic, at least before this evening" (Lear 18).

Such fetishization of the characters', and thus the actors', bodies serves to break the characters into individualized components. Perils arise from such fetishization, however. First, it risks objectifying the characters (and actors), with the added danger, particularly among straight writers and readers, of fetishizing gay sex and homosexual or bisexual characters and people.[11] As Kristina Busse explains, many gay, lesbian, and bisexual writers often are subjected to homophobia, even within seemingly welcoming slash and fanfic communities, and these writers and audiences object to how slash and nonheterosexual relationships are presented without any "sociocultural and historicopolitical context" (Busse, "My Life" 211). By breaking down the characters into eroticized parts, slash risks dehumanizing the characters and the actors playing the roles on the show, even while it highlights the specific elements that go into a characterization. Focusing on Sherlock's mouth, cheekbones, curls, and fingers, for example, underscores some of the consistent character elements that help shape *Sherlock*'s world—both in the television show and in contemporary fanfic.

Traits and Verisimilitude

Ultimately, the verisimilitude of *Sherlock*'s world in "The Love Song of John H. Watson" lies in its application of Sherlock's deductive methods to the newly developing erotic relationship between the two characters. At the heart of the romance is John's understanding of Sherlock's nature. He knows Sherlock is both suspicious and disdainful of traditional Valentine's Day activities, so he tailors his wooing to Sherlock's interest in crime scenes and murder. Similarly, once the two end up in bed back at Baker Street, Lear describes Sherlock using the same deductive skills he applies in crime solving to deduce John's desires. John's entire seduction plan when they return to the flat is to get Sherlock to deduce what turns him on: "'Tonight I'm not going to speak to tell you what I'm imagining doing with you,'" John explains to Sherlock. "He leans forward so that their lips are barely touching as he murmurs, 'You're going to have to deduce it'" (Lear 13). Sherlock immediately joins in on the game: "Sherlock knows John's body, as he studies it with the same sort of attention he gives to crime scenes," the text states. "He knows that he likes having his neck kissed, and that the gentle scratch of fingernails over the sensitive skin of his inner thighs makes him gasp, and also that he has a weakness for Sherlock's voice [another fanon fetish], especially when it's rough and breathless with sex" (Lear 17). Sherlock's knowledge of John's body and what turns him on reinforces their connection as "soul mates" and their top billing as the world's one true pairing (OTP). Lear uses Sherlock's canonical characterization as an intellectual and a detective with unparalleled observation skills, as well as his innate curiosity, to motivate and intrinsically link his sexual behaviors in the scene to the nonsexual characteristics he exhibits in the TV show and in the Doyle canon. By making Sherlock's sexuality consistent with his other major traits, Lear maintains the canonical elements of the world, even when describing scenes and relationships that do not exist in the official canon. While some hard-core

Doyle fans maintain that Sherlock Holmes would never feel or experience sexual desire, let alone for another man, for fan audiences, Lear's portrayal of a sexualized Sherlock appears to be "in character" because she bridges several canonical elements from the plots, settings, and characterization with established fanonical interpretations of the show and its characters. A slashed Johnlock relationship becomes fanonical because of its consistency with, and recreation and reinforcement of, the show's world.

Gender, Sex, and Sexuality in Slash Fiction

Emphases on sexual identity and sex acts highlight fan studies' theoretical shift from gender analyses to the role of sexuality, thus that Rhiannon Bury's 2005 proclamation that "the axis of slash needs to be shifted to sexuality" (Bury 80) has occurred. Although Bury prefaced her statement by saying "I am not suggesting that gender is irrelevant," for other critics such as Lamb and Veith, slash is, in fact, "gender neutral." Slash fics like those in the *Star Trek* fandom, they argue, "remove gender as a governing and determining force in the love relationship" (254); they instead present the two male characters they discuss as "whole people who are psychologically neither 'masculine' nor 'feminine'" (254). They continue their argument with the conclusion that women are drawn to slash because they find masculine sexuality appealing and because they are sexually attracted to men's physiques, noting, rather problematically, that "most women are heterosexual" (254). While space does not allow me to challenge or complicate Lamb and Veith's broad generalizations about slash readers' gender and sexual identities, I do want to comment on the assumption that male slash characters are somehow genderless simply because both are men. The implication is that if slash characters are male, their gender doesn't matter, that gender only matters in contrast (that is, when one of a pair is masculine and the other feminine or, perhaps, when the pair are both female, because femininity is always marked in contrast to masculinity as the norm). This assumption, however, merely highlights the hegemonic power of patriarchy to convince us that masculinity is somehow an unmarked gender. Masculinity itself is not gender neutral. For many readers and critics, that the protagonists are male characters involved in a homoerotic relationship is precisely the point. Patriarchy still includes the power, privileges, and autonomy that go with masculine identities and sexualities in today's culture.

My work intersects with debates over slash as pornography or romance, and particularly with Bury's desire to shift the axis of slash to sexuality, where slash fics investigate, extend, and challenge canonical world building through their explorations of queer sexual identities. I want to invert Constance Penley's claim that "slash does not stop at retooling the male psyche; it goes after the body as well" (Penley, "Brownian Motion" 158) and look instead at how changing the way those sexualized bodies interact affects (or doesn't) character identity, canon, and world building.

"A Cure for Boredom"—A Pornographic Romance

"A Cure for Boredom" is a canonical slash fic involving voyeurism, sex with strangers, and public sex acts, to name a few of its themes and motifs. The premise is that Sherlock doesn't understand human sexuality, so John allows Sherlock to test what turns him on by observing John in various sexual situations. This includes "borrowing" Mycroft's membership to an exclusive sex club where Sherlock arranges John's sex partners and the sex acts they will perform. John does not get to choose his partners, has no prior knowledge of which sex acts he will participate in, and is not allowed to touch his partners during the act unless Sherlock expressly permits it. During many of the encounters, Sherlock directs John's partner to do specific things to John, which helps John come to the realization that he is, in fact, sexually attracted to Sherlock. In his exploration of his own burgeoning sexual desire, John expresses anxieties over whether Sherlock is attracted to him or even able to engage in a sexual relationship with another individual. Spoiler alert: the two finally admit their feelings to each other, although Sherlock expresses anxiety over his control issues and the story ends with them in a monogamous relationship outside of their continuing sexual encounters in the club, still arranged and controlled by Sherlock.

Like Kate_Lear's "Love Song of John H. Watson," "A Cure for Boredom" spends a lot of time establishing the show's canonical characters, particularly through references to in-world dialogue, gestures, repeated motifs, and traits. For instance, Martin Freeman's John often clenches his left fist in the show, a remnant of his PTSD hand tremor and the nerve damage from his shoulder injury. In "A Cure for Boredom," John is seen "scrubb[ing] at his forehead with one hand" early in part 1, a gesture Martin Freeman frequently adopts in the television show. Interestingly, John's body is often left undescribed or unnoticed by the writer, perhaps because John serves as the reader's "everyman" and entry point into the story; it might be distracting to describe the narrator's physical characteristics, mannerisms, or traits. Fanfic authors pick up on these canonical, in-world gestures and motifs and use them to ground their fictional world in the world of the show.

Since most slash fics are from John's point of view, Sherlock's body, gestures, and traits are frequently described in detail, making him both the other and the object of John's (and the reader's) desire. One of Sherlock's most portrayed physical gestures, for example, comes from the original Arthur Conan Doyle canon: Sherlock steeples his fingers beneath his chin while ruminating on a case, a gesture commonly known in fandom as Sherlock's thinking pose. In "A Cure for Boredom," emmagranto1 early on reinforces readers' impressions that her Sherlock character is canonical by referring to him smiling and sitting in a chair, "steepling his fingers" (part 1). The gesture appears again in part 3 when the author writes that John "glanced over to see Sherlock staring up at the ceiling, his fingertips pressed together in what John called his 'thinking pose,'" and again near the end where Sherlock spends much of the day "reclining on the sofa in hard-core thinking mode" (part 7). The references seem to have been deliberately spaced throughout to periodically reinforce Sherlock's canonical character at the beginning, midway, and ending of the story.

"A Cure for Boredom" similarly reinforces John and Sherlock's characterization through its emphasis on the repeated actions or motifs associated with each character. Once again, as in "The Love Song of John H. Watson," Sherlock is described as playing his violin (part 4). Also, in a reference to the ending of "A Study in Pink" (S1E1), John mentions Sherlock's aversion to eating and his tendency to see his own body as mere "transport": "He knew that attempting to feed him was pointless, but the cup of coffee he placed on the floor next to the sofa was empty an hour later, so he felt a small bit of accomplishment there" (part 7). Later, the fic once again mentions Sherlock's eating habits, this time even more closely mirroring the dialogue in "A Study in Pink." Sherlock and John's interrupted plan to get Chinese food resumes after they have eliminated taxi driver Jefferson

Hope: "'Hungry?' John asked Sherlock once the police had released them for the night. 'Starving. Thai?' 'At this hour?' Sherlock smiled. 'I know a place.' John grinned and followed him down the pavement. Sherlock eating was always a good sign" (part 7). Such references simultaneously situate the fic's characters in the world of the show and enlarge the canon by further grounding these citations in the world of Arthur Conan Doyle's Victorian London. For fans immersed in both worlds, such references increase the sense of immersion, play, and pleasure they experience through the fan adaptation.

Dialogue and Canonicity

In "A Cure for Boredom," emmagrant01 frequently uses dialogue and characters' speech patterns to reaffirm the story's connection to the BBC world. For instance, upon their first meeting in "A Study in Pink" (S1E1), Sherlock tells John all of his own "faults," including playing the violin and that he "frequently [doesn't] talk for days on end." These traits establish Sherlock's character early on in the show, particularly in his relationship with John as his flatmate. It's no surprise, then, to see this line almost verbatim late in "A Cure," when John worries about how Sherlock is processing their sexual relationship:

> [John had] spent the day in anxious thought. Even worse, he and
> Sherlock had barely spoken all day. That wasn't particularly unusual,
> of course—Sherlock sometimes went days without saying a word.
> It hadn't bothered John before, but something had shifted between
> them in the last twenty-four hours, something important. (Part 6)

Something integral to Sherlock's character, almost to the point of being unmarked, becomes noticeable and important once the characters' sexual dynamics begin to change. Thus, what seems on the surface to be simple use of canonical dialogue accrues new meaning within the newly sexualized context.

"A Cure for Boredom" relies more heavily than "The Love Song of John H. Watson" on dialogue references to reinforce the fic's connection to the BBC world. For instance, John's quip, "I may be a sub, but I'm not some fucking wilting flower. If I don't want to do something, you'll know. I invaded Afghanistan, remember?" (part 8) immediately places the new sexual relationship between John and Sherlock within the context of the season one opener, "A Study in Pink," where Sherlock teases John for being "ridiculous" because he invaded Afghanistan. The fic also includes other playful references to season two, including numerous references to Sherlock not knowing when John is away from the flat in "A Scandal in Belgravia" (S2E1). Early in that episode, John is out in the field investigating a case while Sherlock directs him via Skype, dressed only in a sheet (perhaps this scene was even an inspiration for the dom/sub dynamics of emmagranto1's story?). When Sherlock reminds John that he will no longer leave the flat for cases scoring less than a "seven," John tells him he was away in Dublin when Sherlock allegedly told him this. John's comment, "Do you just carry on talking when I'm away?" ("A Scandal in Belgravia"), gets picked up in "A Cure" after Sherlock has asked John to pick up a guide to the London gay scene: "'Did you bring it?' 'Bring what?' 'I asked you to look for a copy of *QX* while you were out.' 'You do realize that when I'm not here, I can't actually hear you,'" John responds (emmagranto1 part 3). One additional humorous reference includes Sherlock drugging John's coffee in "The Hounds of Baskerville" (S2E2). John uses this experience in "A Cure" to hint that he still doesn't trust Sherlock's attempts to be conscientious: "John yawned and raised an eyebrow at the cup of coffee Sherlock held out to him. Sherlock rolled his eyes. 'You can't think—.' 'I don't,' John said, taking the cup. 'But I haven't forgiven you either.' Sherlock smiled tightly and to his credit, said nothing. John took a sip of the coffee" (emmegranto1 part 3). All of these canonical references seem to reassure readers that they are still in *Sherlock*'s world, even though the personal dynamics between the two characters differ from their portrayal in the show, including their questioning of their own sexual identities.

Embodiment and Fetishization

Interestingly, although "A Cure" is much more sexually explicit than "Love Song," the fic spends much less time discussing the characters' bodies and their connections to the actors playing them. Like Lear's fic, John is once again drawn to Sherlock's fingers. After one particularly arousing scene at the club when John has his first experience with rimming, the two characters return to 221b to discuss what had been so arousing for John about the experience. Both men become turned on during the discussion, and John invites Sherlock to join him in a masturbation session: "Sherlock exhaled shakily. He picked up the packet of lube and turned it over in his long fingers. God, those fingers. John wondered what they'd feel like inside him" (emmagranto1 part 4). As in "The Love Song of John H. Watson," Sherlock's fingers become metonyms for Sherlock's penis and a site of fetishized desire.

Another major component of John's attraction to Sherlock is his voice. Many fans and media critics have commented on Cumberbatch's deep baritone with approval, perhaps most famously expressed by journalist Caitlin Moran, who wrote that it evoked "a jaguar hiding in a cello." The phrase became such a popular internet meme that Cumberbatch was asked to represent Jaguar cars in 2001. Sherlock tells John's partners how he wants them to pleasure John, and John quickly realizes that Sherlock's voice hits several buttons for him. After John has realized how much he gets off on Sherlock choosing his partners, ordering him about, and telling the partners what to do, John does some internet research of his own to figure out what turns him on and to give Sherlock more ideas to experiment with in the club. As John tries to figure out what sex acts he wants to try next, he comes to the realization that perhaps the acts themselves do not matter as much as Sherlock telling him to do them. That is, John realizes he has developed a kink for Sherlock's voice: "John closed his eyes and shivered. The sound of Sherlock's voice alone was starting to be enough to get him going. He didn't know what to make of that, nor of the way he felt when Sherlock took charge like he'd done tonight" (emmagranto1 part 4). Thus, emmagranto1 appropriates a canonical element of Benedict Cumberbatch's portrayal of Sherlock, his voice, and turns that into a key factor in John's (and the reader's) attraction to Sherlock as a character. By appropriating Cumberbatch's physical embodiment of Sherlock's character, emmagranto1 multiplies the layers of association, canonicity, and fanon within the story.

Traits and Verisimilitude

As does Kate_Lear in "The Love Song of John H. Watson," emmagranto1 in "A Cure for Boredom" uses the confluence of John and Sherlock's sexual relationship and its adherence to canonical characterization to reinforce the latent homoerotic elements in *Sherlock*'s world. The premise for the entire sexual experiment in the story is based on Sherlock's canonical/alleged ignorance, inexperience, or dissatisfaction with sexual intercourse. The story starts with Sherlock complaining that John's suggestion that he masturbate to deal with boredom didn't work. Sherlock admits, after John's doctorly prodding, that he was able to achieve orgasm, but that he found it unsatisfactory. This kicks off a discussion about masturbation, arousal, and sexuality that brings the two men into much more intimate connection than had any of their previous life-and-death cases.[12] To try to get at the root of Sherlock's dissatisfaction, John asks him what he thinks about when he masturbates, and he responds: "'What I normally think about. Everything. . . . Experiments, books I'm reading, celebrity gossip, redox reactions in—' John laughed before he could stop himself, and Sherlock's face clouded. 'What else would I think about?' 'Most people think about sex'" (emmagranto1 part 1). From this initial introduction of emmagranto1's Sherlock as a sexual character, he approaches sex the same way he approaches the rest of the world: as an object of science. He states this explicitly in the following section, telling John: "'It may be just sex for you, but it's science for me. This kind of data collection requires careful controls or the information is essentially worthless'" (emmagranto1 part 2). Sherlock's comment about data collection refers to the experiment that dominates the major part of the story. It begins with Sherlock creating an Excel spreadsheet categorizing all of the sexual acts that arouse him and to what level. After observing John masturbate next to him on the sofa one evening after catching Sherlock "gathering data" by viewing internet porn, he realizes that John's arousal is key to his own, and he devises an experiment that would place John in varied explicit sexual situations, with Sherlock recording the data on his own arousal. This connection between Sherlock Holmes's canonical fascination with scientific method, observation, and deduction (found both in the Doyle canon and in other Sherlockian adaptations, including the BBC's) reinforces the reader's impression and desire that the homoerotic John/Sherlock slash is inherent in the Sherlockian canon. Rather than seeing Sherlock and homosexuality as diametrically opposed and therefore canonically noncompliant readings, "The Love Song of John H. Watson" and "A Cure for Boredom" both situate Sherlock's sexual identity within the already established parameters of the Sherlockian world, thus implying that Sherlock's homosexuality and attraction to John are canonical.

Sherlock's Excel spreadsheet on sex provides the best illustration of the connection between his canonical traits (logic, reasoning, objectivity) and his interest in sexuality. When John first discovers the file, Sherlock informs him that he is "'keeping track of twenty different variables that stimulate a sexual response.' He paused and glanced briefly at John. 'Twenty-one, actually'" (emmagranto1 part 1). When Sherlock Holmes faces a human behavior that he doesn't comprehend, it of course logically follows that he would resort to a scientific experiment to explore it. Once John knows of the file's existence—and that it's being used to track his sexual proclivities, in particular—he can't resist breaking into Sherlock's laptop to check it out. What he finds is incredibly Sherlocky:

> It wasn't the sort of thing that would normally have interested him, but the columns were intriguingly headed with words like "oral sex" and "ball gag," and filled with numbers below. The row headings were more difficult to decipher, but there were ten variants being considered for each column. Sherlock had put some serious thought into evaluating his own reactions to porn. John scrolled though, noting that there wasn't much pattern to the numbers, though when various sexual acts were categorized by gender there was definitely a trend towards the male. Interesting, if not surprising. He scrolled to the right, and there were even more columns. The last one was titled simply John. "Oh my god," he whispered, feeling his cheeks flush. (emmagranto1 part 1)

The concept of the spreadsheet was so popular with emmagranto1's fans that she created an example screenshot of what it might look like.

Even emmagranto1, who dreamed up the idea of the spreadsheet, found it difficult to get inside Sherlock's mind to model the different variables and measurements he would use to track sexual arousal. Once John found out that Sherlock was cataloguing their reactions to different sexual experiences, he doesn't see this as abnormal or as any kind of violation of privacy. To the contrary, not only does he find it arousing but he also sees it as "a typically Sherlock response to a problem John had posed" (emmagranto1 part 1). John's acceptance of Sherlock's method of addressing questions about sexuality and identity reinforces the reader's desire for a Johnlock union and acceptance of this emotional connection as always already canonical.

"A Cure for Boredom" continues to reinforce the BBC world once the fic gets into the various sex acts Sherlock arranges for John in the sex club. For instance, John has no idea why he and Sherlock are in a sex club on

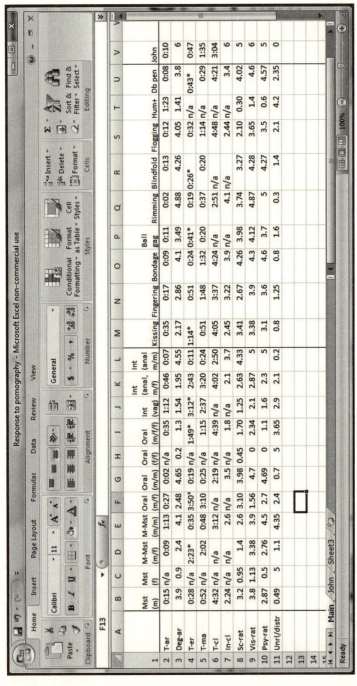

Sherlock's Excel spreadsheet (emmagranton, "Alternate," Archive of Our Own)

their first visit. He goes along with Sherlock's directions, even to the point of engaging in oral sex with two women, Clara and Abby. After he orgasms and the men leave the club, John asks Sherlock what case they were working on there:

"So, the case?"
"What case?"
John frowned. "This case, the one you're working on. When are you going to tell me about it? What are we looking for?"
"I've no idea what you're talking about, John."
"But . . . Then what was this all about?" The moment the words left his lips, it all worked itself out in his mind. The anger that filled him was shockingly intense. "Oh my God. This was part of your experiment? Are you fucking serious?"
Sherlock stared at him, apparently surprised by his reaction. "You looked at my data this afternoon. I assumed you'd worked it out."
(emmagranto1 part 1)

John's assumption that they must be on a case reflects the show's (and the original stories') police procedural format. Like the audience, John assumes Sherlock's action are always motivated by a case. "A Cure for Boredom" can, technically, be classified as case fic as well, since the protagonists investigate and solve a sex trafficking ring later in the story. But by having John assume that their actions in the sex club are part of a case reestablishes the canonical framework of the show within the slash fic: we, like John, automatically approach the plot and characters' actions through the lens of the television show's police procedural framework. By entering through that world, Sherlock and John's growing romantic and sexual feelings for one another are further endorsed.

Throughout all of their sexual encounters at the club, Sherlock seemingly remains the same detached, clinical observer we see in the crime scenes and kitchen lab scenes in the show. In their first sex scene with Clara and Abby, John notes how Sherlock didn't just watch the two women giving him oral sex; "he was observing . . . the entire point of this outing was to collect information" (emmagranto1 part 1). In part 3, Sherlock directs another woman giving John oral sex, and John reads him as "completely clinical, utterly unaffected." John believes Sherlock remains unaroused by the highly erotic scenarios he orchestrates for him, which

Slash, Fanfiction, and (Non)Compliance in World Building   **113** reveals how John sees Sherlock, not necessarily the reality of what is happening with Sherlock himself.[13] Clinical Sherlock is the image John—and the audience—are supposed to have of his character; his detachment is a canonical element of his portrayal in Doyle's stories and in other Sherlock Holmes adaptations over the past century. While John's reading of Sherlock's alleged detachment is canonical, however, it also helps frame the realities of his sexual responses to John's arousal and his own fears about what these feelings mean for his sense of self.

Once John confronts Sherlock with his feelings for him, Sherlock admits he is likewise attracted to John, but he also admits those fears. He tells John:

> "You think we can just have sex and be boyfriends and go on with our lives and be happy, but it's not that simple. . . . I can't just love you, John. I would *consume* you. You know what I'm like. You know what would happen. . . . I want to fucking own you. I want to see you do things you cannot possibly imagine. . . . I want to do things to you, things that frighten me. I want to watch other people do things to you. I want to hurt you and . . ." His eyes locked on John's and he stopped. His face paled, as if he'd just realized he'd said those words out loud. (emmagranto1 part 8)

Sherlock pales when faced with the realities of his desire for John. He believes that he and John cannot have the kind of relationship that other men have in contemporary society, and that somehow his possessive desire for John and his need to control him and his sexuality are so far outside acceptable behavior that he should be denied the kind of companionship and sexual love other people experience. When John tries to reassure him that his feelings are normal, Sherlock still denies that their relationship is okay. John proclaims to Sherlock, "'I am so fucking in love with you that I will take anything you'll give me,'" but Sherlock becomes "even more distraught. 'That's precisely the problem. It's happened already. You couldn't say no on Sunday, and if Annie hadn't put a stop to it, I effectively would have had you raped, and I would have enjoyed it, and I would not have given a shit about what you wanted until it was too late. That is why this can't happen, John'" (emmagranto1 part 8). Sherlock is referring to a previous encounter he had arranged with a man, Ryan, to be John's first anal sex partner; however, Ryan and his wife, Annie, change the dynamics of the scene to John penetrating Ryan, because they realize that John really wants Sherlock to be his first anal sex partner.[14] Sherlock believes that his desire for John is literally dangerous, not only to his own self-preservation but also to John's well-being. His desire to see John penetrated (and to fulfill John's desire) put John at risk of being raped because Sherlock was too controlling and wouldn't share his plans. Although on the surface, Sherlock's initial rejection of John's feelings could look like the fic rejects the premise of a Johnlock relationship as canon—Sherlock's possessiveness, controlling nature, and clinical attitude toward human behavior and sexuality preclude him from engaging in normal relationships—I argue his hesitancy and fear are actually more canonical exactly because they reflect his initial characterization as being logical, antisocial, and disinterested in sex.

In some ways, "A Cure for Boredom" does some of the feminist work described by critics like Penley, Jenkins, and others in showing male characters' understanding of male sexuality from a feminist point of view. For instance, as John takes different sexual positions in his various encounters (giving and receiving oral sex, penetrating and being penetrated by women and men, and so on) he begins to look back on his previous sexual behavior and practices in different ways. When charged by Sherlock to give blow jobs to three different men in the public sex room, for example, John expresses discomfort with his first encounter because of the man's inconsiderate force: "It seemed what Green Shirt really wanted was to fuck his mouth, and John soon gave up trying to use his tongue. He focused instead on hanging on and breathing at regular intervals, all the while cursing himself for any time he'd been this inconsiderate during a blow job" (emmagranto1 part 5). Later on, when John gives Sherlock oral sex without a condom near the end of the story, he thinks about how he wasn't expecting or used to male ejaculation:

> It wasn't until John had a mouthful of semen that he realized he'd forgotten about that part entirely. It wasn't bad—it wasn't like he hadn't tasted it before—but it felt like quite a lot more in his mouth than he would have expected based on personal experience. . . . It was a weird sensation—he was definitely never going to take that for granted again. (emmagranto1 part 8)

Giving a blow job for the first time forces John to change his subject position and to sympathize with other individuals (primarily women, in his experience) who had been in a similar position. John's homosexual experience here thus translates into making John a better lover—for both men and women.

By the end of "A Cure for Boredom," even the canonical setting has been changed and infused with John and Sherlock's new sexual relationship. John comments in the final chapter, "It was astonishing to stand in this spot where they'd had so many arguments and conversations, where Sherlock had paced and ranted about cases and lack thereof, where they'd built this friendship over the last year—and share a kiss" (emmagrant01 part 8). The conclusion resituates 221b Baker Street as a site of desire, restructuring the canonical space into an erotic/romantic space. Rather than seeing the slash story as separate from or in opposition to the canon, the Sherlockian world itself becomes the site where this pairing becomes or always already is possible. Both 221b and Sherlock's world become places of possibility: "It was incredibly freeing to think that this didn't have to be anything, didn't have to follow any prescribed pattern," John observes at the end of the tale. "They could make it whatever they wanted. God, the possibilities" (part 8). Sherlock and John's relationship explores typical patterns of heteronormativity for the characters and allows them—the characters and the fans—the space to believe "anything was possible" (part 8).

Although mainstream audiences may think slash violates *Sherlock*'s world, this is not necessarily the case. To the contrary, many fans and critics argue that slash is inherent in the show itself and that slash fanfic merely fleshes out a queer subtext already present from the first episode. The significant number of subtextual references in the show to how other characters see John and Sherlock's relationship—Irene Adler calling them a couple ("A Scandal in Belgravia"), Mrs. Hudson surprised when John announces he's going to marry Mary Morstan ("The Empty Hearse"), to name two—suggest that a Johnlock relationship actually exists within the show's textual context and is therefore canonical for fanfiction adaptation. Although the genre seems to alter the characters' established identities by changing their sexual orientations, the primary characterization remains consistent with the original world. Sherlock still looks like Sherlock and acts like Sherlock; John's characterization, appearance, and mannerisms remain the same in slash, despite the sexual relationship with Sherlock. *Sherlock*'s canon is complex, as attested by the producers' frequent comments regarding the myriad influences and references in their version. Although they explicitly deny that John and Sherlock are in a romantic relationship, however, a slash pairing is clearly not necessarily noncompliant.

CHAPTER FOUR

GENDERING *SHERLOCK*'S WORLD
Biology, Gender, and Characterization

Building on the focus of sexuality, characterization, and identity, let's look at *Sherlock* fanfictions that explore the relationship among gender, characterization, and world building. The "genderswap" label, used by fans and scholars to describe stories where characters have become differently sexed, contributes to how we theorize sex and gender and simultaneously risks reinforcing and potentially limiting common cultural understandings of the differences between the two concepts. Very little research has been published on genderswap fanfiction, however, either as a genre or through case studies, perhaps because of confusion over sex versus gender and what genderswap actually signifies.[1] As such, let us analyze the ways fans test the limits of the fic world through their explorations of gender and characterization. Since world building is ultimately a question of characterization, fans can make dramatic changes to characters' bodies, identities, and sexuality while remaining consistent with the world—as long as the characterization remains canonically compliant.

Over the past thirty years, transgender studies has shifted away from feminism and queer theory, from which it emerged, to explore the various ways individuals experience gender in a contemporary, embodied world (Stryker, "(De)Subjugated Knowledges" 2–3). Originally concerned with breaking down the cultural links between sex and gender, transgender theorists challenged the structuralist notion that gender was merely the mimetic sign of an ontological sexual identity. Rather, building on the work of Judith Butler, they argued that sex was not, in fact, a stable or unified referent but rather performative, "a variety of viable bodily aggregations that number far more than two. The 'wholeness' of the body and 'sameness' of its sex are themselves revealed to be socially constructed," just like gender identity (Stryker, "(De)Subjugated Knowledges" 9). While this earlier iteration of transgender theory can be defined in terms of Butlerian performance studies, more recent articulations have reinforced the importance of the "lived complexity" of gendered bodies in a post-9/11 world where nations define and police the borders of bodies and identities just as they do states and nations. Genderswap fanfiction provides another way to understand the physical embodiment of canonical and noncanonical characters, specifically "how bodies mean, how representation works, and what counts as legitimate knowledge," both inside and outside the academy, especially in relation to characterization and world building (Stryker, "(De)Subjugated Knowledges" 8–9). By foregrounding gender expectations and how they are both attached to and separate from biological sex, genderswap fanfiction complicates assumptions about character identity and encourages readers to see sex and gender as co-dependent rather than as separate aspects of a character's identity. Even though changing the gender and sexual identity of a canonical character may seem, on the surface, to violate the source text's world, changing a character's sexual identity or practice does not necessarily mean the character is acting out of character or violating the world. In the case of Sherlock and John, both characters' canonical gender identities include stereotypically masculine and feminine elements; therefore, changing the character's biological sex does not change the canonical characterization; whether the characters' bodies are male or female, their behaviors remain compliant with the world of the show.

Sherlock fanfiction is perhaps uniquely suited to serve as a genderswap case study. The popular modernized update of Arthur Conan Doyle's classic detective presents two diversely gendered characters. On the one hand, Benedict Cumberbatch's Sherlock is as cold and intellectually dynamic as his Arthur Conan Doyle Victorian counterpart, and Martin Freeman's John Watson fully embodies the military ethos and medical acumen of the original. On the other hand, Cumberbatch's Sherlock's asexuality, his unruly enthusiasm, and his mercurial mood swings could easily be gendered as feminine, just as Freeman's Watson's nurturing caretaker persona could be.[2] Each character's ability to embody both stereotypical masculine and feminine gender behaviors simultaneously within his male sexed body—

and the other characters' reactions to those behaviors—makes them intriguing sites for exploring the relationship between gender identity and canonicity.

Sherlock is also a great fit for analysis because of the popularity of its eponymous protagonist. Genderswap fanfiction purposefully uses familiar characters to reify the cultural significance of that character and to simultaneously distance the audience from previous portrayals; such characters carry all of the cultural capital of the original canonical figures as well as the defamiliarization needed to challenge traditional gender and sexual stereotypes. Even if an audience member has never seen *Sherlock*, they *know* who Sherlock Holmes is and what his character is like because the role has had pervasive cultural appeal over the past century. Studying *Sherlock* genderswap fanfiction allows us to see not only how predominantly female audiences co-opt this century-old character but also how they explore and theorize relationships between the body and gender identity within an already established fictional world.

(Re)Defining Sex and Gender: What Is Genderswap?

Readers familiar with gender theory find the genderswap label problematic because it can seem to confuse sex and gender.[3] By definition, genderswap depends on gender as its primary category as it describes stories about characters swapping *sexed* bodies.[4] Actress Lucy Liu's portrayal of a female-bodied Joan Watson on CBS's *Elementary*, for example, provides an example of a genderswapped John Watson. While such body swapping often combines with implicit and explicit analyses of gendered behavior(s), cultural expectations, surveillance, sexuality, and so on, using gender as the root of the term privileges socially constructed behaviors over the material reality of the physical body.[5] Most often the gender-swapped character's gender behavior does not actually change, however; rather, the character's gender behavior remains consistent with the sex of the original character (or at least with its original canonical depiction). The focus then becomes not what happens when a male-gendered character becomes female-gendered, but how the character's surrounding world—other characters, institutions, and so on—changes in response to the same behaviors differently *sexed*. Since the character's gender behavior does not substantially change in genderswap fanfic, the character remains canonically compliant with the original fictional world, even though the gendered identity may have changed.

To simplify, sex is generally considered to be biologically determined while gender is culturally constructed, although even these basic definitions are currently under debate.[6] Male and female are terms used to denote a body's sex, referring to its (potential) reproductive capacity, chromosomes, and genitalia.[7] In contrast, gender refers to the social construction and cultural expectation of gendered behaviors or, in the words of transgender theorist Susan Stryker: "Gender is the social organization of bodies into different categories of people" (Stryker, *Transgender History* 11). The emphasis here, of course, is on both "social organization" and "bodies." Gender is a cultural category used to privilege certain behaviors over others by assigning those behaviors to specific sex characteristics.

At heart, genderswap fanfiction explores the cultural constructedness of gender, interrogating what theorist Judith Butler describes as gender performativity and the role that physical embodiment plays in gender identity.[8] Individuals perform gender identity through various behaviors ranging from clothing choices (women's skirts, high heels, and tight-fitting clothing; men's loose clothing, low-heeled shoes, and hats) to how they move their bodies and use their voices to the activities in which they participate. Culturally, we expect male-bodied persons to behave (perform) in masculine-gendered ways (ambitious, protective, aggressive, assertive), and we expect female-bodied individuals to behave in feminine-gendered ways (nurturing, weak, passive, submissive). Such alignment is often referred to as cisgender: literally, gendered behavior aligned with its assigned biological sex.[9] Gender theorists emphasize that such behaviors are learned at an early age by watching and mirroring people we admire, and while it may be easy to criticize such descriptions as stereotypes, they describe how most people define and police gender in their everyday lives. Children, parents, teachers, and friends all conspire to correct any behaviors that do not seem to match a person's perceived sex.

Debates about the relationship between biology and gender continue to dominate much of contemporary feminist and gender theory, especially in transgender studies.[10] Many poststructural transgender theorists in the late twentieth century, including Leslie Feinberg, Sandy Stone, Cressida Heyes, and Susan Stryker, focus primarily on performativity and identity politics, arguing that gender is a culturally constructed performance per-petuated by its own continuous reenactment and that the body itself is as much a re-presentation of identity as the behaviors and actions one attributes to it. More recently, contemporary transgender theorists have criticized such poststructuralist gender approaches, claiming they ignore "the embodied experience of the speaking subject" and how culture acts upon that body (Stryker, "(De)Subjugated Knowledges" 12, Nagoshi and Brzuzy 435, Lane 149).[11] Embodiment refers both to the corporeal body and to the ways an individual materially manifests and lives the life of a specifically sexed and gendered person. As many biologists and trans* theorists have noted, the physical manifestations of biological sex—which include genetic composition (XX or XY), reproductive organs, genitalia, and secondary sex characteristics—all affect how a person identifies as a sexed individual and how society sees, interprets, and acts upon that individual; this is where genderswap fiction concentrates most of its in-terrogations. Genderswapped Sherlock and John often *act* the same way they do in the TV show; however, because they are now in female bodies, other characters *react* to them in different ways. How people interpret bio-logical identifiers—that is, how they choose to express their biological sex through their gender identities and how others react to them—is similarly a form of embodiment. As a concept, embodiment attempts to capture how individuals manifest gender through their physical selves—and, con-versely, their physical selves through their gender—in ways that are inclu-sive of both biological and cultural factors.[12]

Rather than separate the two, genderswap ultimately highlights and complicates the interconnectedness between the physical embodiment of sex and gender behaviors; it concretely grounds characterization, canon, and world building in the physical bodies of the characters.

While earlier critics possibly overlooked the ways characters physically embody gender identity, focusing solely on the biological sex of gender-swap characters simultaneously risks an essentializing discourse that posits masculine and feminine behaviors as being naturally tied to male and female bodies, respectively. If genderswap stories "use changes of sex to explore how [characters] experience the embodiment of gender" (Lothian), then studies of genderswap fanfiction must include both gen-dered behaviors and sexed bodies to explore how the two together con-tribute to individual identity and to how society perceives, constructs, and categorizes them—and how they help define the world. The central tenet of world building requires fans and readers to always create and read the fictional characters within the terms and limits set out by the initial casting in the show. For *Sherlock*, this means writing and reading Sherlock and John through the lens of Benedict Cumberbatch's and Martin Freeman's physical appearances, mannerisms, and gendered and sexualized behaviors. The very concept of genderswap fanfiction itself forces us to reimagine characterization as it has been established in the show and to recognize sex and gender as mutually codependent, rather than separate, influences on identity formation and world building.

"I Want a Female Sherlock Holmes": Fan Responses to *Sherlock*

Analyzing an individual fandom through a particular theoretical lens can reveal important trends, patterns, and attitudes, and the central corpus of *Sherlock* genderswap fanfiction grapples with the relationships among gender behavior, identity, embodiment, and/in the fictional world. *Sherlock* has a large and active fandom ranging across multiple online platforms (LiveJournal, Archive of Our Own, Fanfiction.net, Tumblr, Twitter, Facebook, and others), and while Sherlock Holmes fandoms historically have been dominated by men, *Sherlock* is the first adaptation with a predominantly female audience. Several critical debates over the show's portrayal and overall lack of female characters and perceived misogyny have dominated both Web forums and the media, illustrating that representations of women, gender, and sexuality are critical to the audience's interaction with and reception of the show and its world.[13]

While there isn't space in this chapter to discuss the politics surrounding *Sherlock*'s female characters and viewers' specific responses to the show, some fans cite such arguments as motivation for writing and reading genderswap fanfiction. Writer Parachute_Silks, in her author's note to the story "Astronomy," in which she loosely adapts the Arthur Conan Doyle story "A Scandal in Bohemia" to include a romantic holiday to Prague taken by Sherlock, John/Joan, Mycroft, and Lestrade, explained that she turned all of the male characters into women "as a slightly desperate reaction to this show's female character problem" (Parachute_Silks 2010a). Parachute_Silks seems to be referring to what is commonly known in fan lore as "Rule 63," a feminist response to the underrepresentation of women in television and film: "For every given male character, there is a female version of that character, and vice versa" ("Rule 63"). Representation isn't about simple numbers, however (that is, requiring the same number of male and female characters, regardless of characterization); rather, significance, characterization, and value are all of importance. Rule 63 requires a matching and equal female version of every male character, with the same values, work, and characteristics. Parachute_Silks's fem!John becomes a female-embodied version of Freeman's male!John from the show; even though his body and gender identity have shifted from male to female in "Astronomy," he remains canonically consistent with the *Sherlock* world in his behavior and characterization. For writers like Parachute_Silks, shifting canonically gendered behavior from the show into female-embodied fanfiction characters allows her both to address a perceived lack of female representation on the show and to implicitly explore the relationship between gender behavior and biological sex.

Representations of women characters are similarly important for bloggers and viewers. Blogger Shadowfireflame argued that women fans want the equivalent of the heroic male protagonist famous throughout canonical Sherlock Holmes lore:

> Okay, so I'm coming to realize that it's not just that I want a female genius (though I'll take those!). I actually want an *arrogant* female genius. Someone irritating, confident, abrasive, demanding. I don't want a cute little girl who demurely and quietly provides her brain powers to the betterment of humanity; I want a woman with charisma who explodes onto the scene, verbally eviscerates everyone, and then sweeps away with her massive intellect. Yeah . . . in short, I want a female Sherlock Holmes. (Shadowfireflame 2011)

The characteristics typically associated with the canonical Holmes figure (both in *Sherlock* and other adaptations)—irritating, confident, abrasive, demanding, capable of eviscerating everyone with his massive intellect—are all behaviors typically gendered masculine in Western society. Women, Shadowfireflame rightly articulates, are expected to be cute, little, demure, and quiet; they are supposed to dedicate their intellect to helping others and improving the overall quality of life. Shadowfireflame doesn't want a female character *like* Sherlock Holmes; she wants a female Sherlock Holmes.[14] Genderswap transfers or applies a beloved canonical male's gendered behaviors to an equally engaging female, allowing readers to challenge culturally accepted norms for gendered behavior and to identify with clever, charismatic protagonists while keeping the fictional world intact. The central tension of many such stories becomes the social reaction of others to the different gender embodiment of characteristics, thus bringing sex back to the forefront of analysis.

BAMF!John and Fem!John—One and the Same?

Based on the preponderance of fem!Sherlock fanfiction stories on Archive of Our Own and other such sites, Shadowfireflame isn't the only person interested in a female Sherlock Holmes.[15] The majority of gender-swap Sherlock stories on the web take place within *Sherlock*'s world and focus on fem!Sherlock, often but not always paired with a fem!John. While both characters exhibit both cis- and transgendered traits in the original show, John's feminine behaviors seem more easily accepted and translatable between male and female bodies; that is, fem!John characters are not often seen to be conflicted over their gender identities in the same way that fem!Sherlocks often are.[16] Sexed male, the show's Martin Freeman as John Watson assumes feminized roles in his relationship with Sherlock, depending on Sherlock's needs at the time. He purchases groceries, manages their finances, and maintains their flat, and his training as a doctor means he also takes responsibility for Sherlock's health. Many of guy!John's behaviors tie in with what Marxist feminists identify as women's unpaid productive labor: unpaid domestic/house work that supports the continuity and reproduction of the family unit. Historically, women's activities within the home—cleaning, preparing food, bearing and raising children—have not been considered work in capitalist society. Work in the capitalist definition relates to productive wage-earning employment outside the home. Reproductive labor was aligned with women's political and economic position in the home and within the structure of marriage. In Holmes and Watson stories and pastiches following the classic Victorian-era Arthur Conan Doyle pattern, housework was taken up by Mrs. Hudson, as their housekeeper. As single men in the twenty-first century, however, *Sherlock*'s John and Sherlock take on the reproductive labor role in their household (although Una Stubbs's Mrs. Hudson continues to do some household work for them, such as dusting, cleaning floors, and bringing tea); living together as roommates also facilitates the approximation of a heteronormative relationship whereby one person—John Watson—becomes culturally feminized by assuming these household responsibilities. The TV show, like much of the genderswap fanfic, then, often reifies traditional gender norms rather than challenging them. These feminized behaviors carry over into genderswap stories like Parachute_Silks's "Categories."

Alternating between fem!Sherlock's and fem!John's (Joan) point of view, "Categories" begins by describing both characters as young girls. Fem!Sherlock has a failed sexual relationship with Sebastian from "The Blind Banker" (S1E2) while at university before becoming a consulting detective as an adult. Even though both Sherlock and John are now sexed female, the story follows the canonical Arthur Conan Doyle and BBC canonical meeting between Sherlock and John at St. Bart's, after which they move in together and begin to develop sexual feelings for one another. The story concludes with fem!Sherlock and Joan working a case for Sebastian in France and confronting him about his treatment of fem!Sherlock at university. Fem!Sherlock retains her masculine aloofness and independence within the story, but Joan is shown as caring and emotionally sensitive, much like Freeman's guy!John is portrayed in the TV show. While fem!Sherlock "is not one to appreciate people trying to look after her," Joan likes caring about people: "Love and responsibility come natural to her" (Parachute_Silks, "Categories").[17] Including the word "natural" here to describe fem!John's behavior may strike a dissonant chord for readers. Joan's characterization may look, on the surface, as if it reinforces traditional gender dynamics of woman-as-caretaker. It is natural, that is, instinctual, for Joan to nurture fem!Sherlock, something that is directly tied to her womanly biology; Joan's characterization is cisgendered and therefore does not challenge cultural expectations for women's behavior. Such a characterization is also consistent with BBC!John's portrayal on the show, however, which makes the term *natural* a bit more slippery. Joan's natural preference for taking care of fem!Sherlock could come either from her female biology or from her tie to the show's original portrayal of John's character. Fem!Sherlock is still brilliant, arrogant, and rude, while fem!John remains supportive, loyal, and caring. In a sense, then, the exact same behaviors from the show remain consistent with the world; only the bodies and gender identities are inverted in the genderswap story. Fem!Sherlock's arrogance is now portrayed as masculine, while fem!John is now cisgendered. By giving readers two female genderswapped characters exhibiting differently gendered behaviors (the former stereotypically masculine, the latter stereotypically feminine), but both of which remain consistent with their male personifications in the original show, gender-swap fanfiction stories like "Categories" reinforce the canonical world of the show even while inherently challenging audience notions of natural gender roles in relation to sex and disrupting the traditional binaries of sex/gender and masculine/feminine.

Along with BBC!John's feminization in both the show and in fanfiction, several other stories keep John's canonical military career at the forefront. In Mad_Maudlin's "In Arduis Fidelis," for example, Jane Watson emphasizes male BBC!John's cis/masculine characteristics, including his history in the military and his physical prowess. The story loosely follows the plot of "A Study in Pink" (S1E1) and portrays a nonlinear retelling, from Jane's point of view, of her first meeting with Sherlock, her frustrating therapy sessions, and her sense of purposelessness and resentment after being injured and discharged from the army. The focus on her father–son-like relationship with her dad, her childhood experiences learning to shoot and hunt, and her skills with weapons all highlight the cisgendered elements of BBC!John's military career, behaviors typically associated with men's experiences. Shifting those masculine characteristics into a female body highlights the cultural assumptions we make when encountering a sexed individual. Unlike fanfiction's seeming easy acceptance and transference of male!John's more feminine transgendered behaviors, however, such masculine behavior when embodied in a woman can cause concern and conflict.[18] Even though Jane's character still behaves in canonically consistent ways, the text constantly reiterates cultural rules for women's behavior: "Women didn't serve in frontline positions. Women weren't marksmen. Women didn't get shot" (Mad_Maudlin). Clearly, the assumption here is that women, as a group, do not participate in war or violence; such activities are not cisgender for women. And yet, by placing John's canonical (male) characteristics in a woman's body, "In Arduis Fidelis" simultaneously reinforces and challenges those generalizations. The phrase, "Women didn't get shot," denies Jane's experience and makes it an impossibility; as a woman, she couldn't possibly have gone to war or have been injured, since, according to contemporary attitudes, women didn't do that. At the same time, however, Jane does get shot in the story, meaning she has the same masculinely constructed experiences as BBC!John.

By shifting the same behaviors from a male sexed body to a female one, Mad_Maudlin both challenges gender expectations and highlights how embodiment influences our reactions to those behaviors. Therefore, even though Mad_Maudlin technically changes BBC!John's biological sex, which would seem to violate *Sherlock*'s canon, by keeping Jane's gendered behaviors consistent with BBC!John, the story both challenges preconceived gender norms within the show (and fic) and reinforces the show's world.

Freaks and Geeks: Fem!Sherlock's (Disruptive) Femininity

While audiences find most aspects of male BBC!John's femininity socially acceptable, male BBC!Sherlock's disruptive femininity seems more troublesome.[19] At first glance, Benedict Cumberbatch's Sherlock appears to reinforce the original canon's traditional cismale characteristics familiar to all Sherlock Holmes aficionados: high-level reasoning, emotionlessness, arrogance, audacity, and initiative. Yet one could argue that he also exhibits feminized behavior, for example, his unruly enthusiasm (such as jumping and clapping his hands in excitement over hearing of a new suicide in "A Study in Pink"), his mercurial mood swings and sulking on the couch, his vanity over his appearance, and his snarky eye-rolling, exaggerated shrugs, and heavy sighs.[20] Characters on the show, ranging from Sally Donovan's repeated "freak" to John's begrudgingly affectionate "bit not good," constantly admonish Sherlock toward more socially acceptable (that is, masculine or cisgendered) behaviors. Enthusiasm itself is not consistently feminized, however, either within the show or in Western culture. Men are allowed—and even encouraged—to be unruly and enthusiastic in the context of sporting activities and events, for example; only when Sherlock shows enthusiasm for morbid topics like death and crime does John step in: because Sherlock is being enthusiastic in the wrong way. Similarly, John chastises Sherlock in "The Great Game" episode for not being feminine enough—that is, Sherlock does not show proper emotion or compassion when the hostages are in danger or when the old woman hostage dies in the bomb explosion. Rather than being criticized for unruly feminine behavior while embodied as a male, Sherlock seems to be constantly violating the limits and expectations for both masculinity and femininity.

Unlike fem!John, fem!Sherlock seems in constant conflict with gender expectations when female-bodied in genderswapped texts. Male!Sherlock's freakishness in the canon gets recontextualized as a specifically gendered critique in the fanfiction where male characters, in particular, play an important role in policing women's gender behavior. At the beginning of Parachute_Silks's fem!Sherlock/fem!John story, "Categories," for example, a young female Sherlock tries to keep her university boyfriend, Sebastian, interested in her, first by pretending to fulfill traditional cisfeminine stereotypes: she hides her deductions and intelligence and tries to "make conversation—and the phrase is perfect, really, because that is very much what it feels like, that she is creating something artificial" (Parachute_Silks, "Categories"). She cannot keep up the charade, however; she "tries less and less to pretend not to know things," and when she is herself in front of Sebastian's friends "he snaps at her, tells her not to be such a freak, and his friends snigger and make jokes [fem!]Sherlock doesn't understand or particularly want to" (Parachute_Silks, "Categories"). The central tension of such scenes is the social perception of the female embodiment of masculine gender traits that make this fem!Sherlock a freak in the eyes of patriarchal society. Sebastian ends up dumping fem!Sherlock for another woman who looks just like her: "pale and dark-haired and clever"; but this woman "isn't cleverer than [Sebastian] and thinks he's brilliant and goes to the Conservative Society meetings with him" (Parachute_Silks, "Categories"). Because she does not fulfill Sebastian's (and society's) expectations of her as a woman, fem!Sherlock is belittled, emotionally damaged, and ultimately ostracized from her university social group. Male!Sherlock, however, is similarly ridiculed by police officers Sally Donovan and Anderson, who doubt his ability to read the details of a crime at one glance. Cumberbatch's Sherlock is othered by his co-workers and even by his closest friend. In "The Reichenbach Fall," (S2E3), for example, John, in a fit of pique, accuses Sherlock of being a machine; likewise, in "The Hounds of Baskerville" (S2E3) he chastises Sherlock for not having any friends. Sherlock's intellectual acumen and his freakishness in "Categories" are therefore not necessarily the result of his newly regendered body; rather, they are canonically consistent elements of his character from the original storyworld. The *contrast* between canonical Sherlock's masculine intellectualism and its embodiment in a female body, however, highlights audience gender expectations for male and female behavior and the particularly high cost of going against cultural expectations of femininity.

SomeoneElsesDream's fem!Sherlock story, "And Then You Wake," explores the ways in which men and women define and police their peers' appropriate gender behavior and sexualized bodies. The majority of the text closely follows the show's "A Study in Pink" and "The Great Game" episodes, beginning with John's Afghan injury and fem!Sherlock being violently assaulted and raped as a student at Cambridge University. At the beginning of the story, fem!Sherlock is surprised in a deserted alcove by three male university students who immediately begin criticizing her masculine behavior. They accuse her of "running around like a boy" on campus and of thinking she is smarter than everyone else (SomeoneElsesDream). The first assailant then proceeds to restrain fem!Sherlock, pressing her into the wall, querying, "Do you even have a cunt? Or are you some kind of freak?" A second man raucously suggests she has a "dick," and the third proceeds to grope her chest and force her down on the floor before proclaiming "she's hardly a girl at all" because of the small size of her breasts. One of the attackers brutally rapes fem!Sherlock before Mycroft appears and prevents the rest of the men from assaulting her. "And Then You Wake" problematizes the mistake of equating gender identity with the physical embodiment of the canonical character. While the men in the text seem, on the surface, to reinscribe the idea that "cunt" or "breasts" equals "woman" (and "dick" equals "man"), the tone of the story and fem!Sherlock's reactions clearly show the reader that this concept is to be questioned. Rather than her body, Sherlock's behavior and personality dictate her consistent characterization within the world of the show. Similarly, one could argue that simply highlighting the assumed connection between a woman's genitals and her gender identity simultaneously reveals cultural stereotypes about womanhood and critiques them. Such analysis of the relationship or relationships between biological sex and gender identity is key to recent North American transgender theory, the focus of this chapter's final topic.

Transgender Theory and Trans/Genderswap Fanfiction

Transgender fanfiction—that is, fanfiction with characters who transition from one sex or gender to another—is even more underresearched and undertheorized than current genderswap scholarship, most likely because it is quite rare.[21] Trans/genderswap fanfiction takes the basic premises of genderswap to an entirely new level by adding a trans* component to an already genderswapped character. To clarify, gender-swap narratives in themselves do not qualify as transgender fanfiction; rather, trans* stories feature a character whose gender identity is dissociated from his or her assigned sex identity and who may or may not seek to transition to the other sex. Adding the genderswap component to such narratives, however, significantly complicates them. Before the story begins, the author recasts a canonically male character, such as Sherlock Holmes, as female and then places the character in a narrative world in which that fem!Sherlock is transgender. Thus, male Sherlock becomes fem!Sherlock becomes female-to-male (FTM) Sherlock.[22] Such doubling and redoubling highlights a primary concern of transgender theory today: the intricate relationship between gender identity and embodiment. Likewise, embodiment is also a key element in fictional world building and characterization.

By changing a canonically male character into a female character, genderswap authors often seek to restore (or challenge) the relationship between the character's sexed body and his gender comportment by re-aligning gender and biological identification in the fictional world; behavior that may have seemed cis in the original becomes misaligned in the swapped character, forcing readers to rethink their assumptions about the (implied) relationship between sex and gender. The decision to re-embody that character in the canonically sexed body, however, again raises several important questions. Why not just write a male Sherlock Holmes who seeks to transition to female? Why add the complexity of transitioning back to the original sex? What does drawing attention to biological sex, in addition to gender, add to such stories? Such moves seem to simultaneously question the origin of sex identity and to reaffirm the important role the body plays in gender identity and characterization.[23] As transgender theorists Elliot and Roen explain, "The body is not equivalent to the organism but only comes to take on form and meaning through representation" (247). Such representation does not only occur through the individual and his/her presentation to the world of a body and personal gender identity (through clothing, naming, behaviors and so on); it also occurs through powerful visual and textual representations across cultures—including fan productions. While traditional genderswap fanfiction seems to dissociate gender behavior from the body, trans/gender-swap narratives—following the trajectory of contemporary transgender theory—remind readers that the body plays an important role in determining identity and shouldn't be subsumed under gender labels.

Much of recent transgender theory focuses on the relationships among embodiment, gender, and identity, particularly around the issue of sex reassignment surgery (SRS). Some trans* theorists criticize what, to them, seems to be an overemphasis on the importance of genital surgery, arguing that medical practitioners often take advantage of transgender patients by raising idealistic expectations and promising often unrealistic results from reconstruction surgeries (Elliot and Roen 250). Others, such as Rubin (1998), Ramachandran (2008), and Lane (2009), emphasize how important the physical body is to gender and sexual identity. For these theorists, "body image is the psychic representation of the body for the subject. There can be a difference between the body image and the corporeal body—but it is the body image that we act on in the world" (Lane 149). Many transgender individuals report dissociation between their bodies and identities. For instance, transgender theorist Cressida Heyes, describing her own transition, felt "a deep sense of unease with [her] body" and "often wished (including for periods of years at a time) to be in a different body" (Heyes 1097). Another research subject, FTM "Babe," similarly described feeling "trapped in the wrong body," and he anxiously sought genital surgery to "correct" this "aberration" (Elliot and Roen 250). Making sure that the body matches the individual's psychic self-image is crucial for many transgender people. While poststructuralist arguments about the social constructedness of gender are immensely important to our understanding of how gender is learned, acquired, and performed, ignoring embodiment and relying solely on the "artificiality" of gender—which genderswap, in isolation from sex, runs the risk of doing—may diminish the need many transsexuals feel for sex reassignment surgery and, more broadly, negate the gender/sex dissociation many transgender people describe (Nagoshi and Brzuzy 432).[24] By exploring the connections between gender, identity, and physicality, trans* fanfiction highlights the importance of the characters' actual bodies in determining canonical characterization and world building, which will become even more significant in the following chapters on alternate universe fanfic and real person fic.

FTM!Sherlock and the Importance of Embodiment

Many characters in FTM Sherlock genderswap fanfiction claim their identities do not match the physical manifestation of their selves; that is, they feel as if they inhabit the wrong physiques.[25] In a sense, the characters (and writers) are questioning the relationship between readers' canonical understanding of the characters' behaviors and self-identities and their physical descriptions and representation in the world, ultimately asking: What makes a character canon compliant? Many of the attitudes expressed toward female bodies in FTM fanfic resemble Western attitudes toward women. Most female readers are familiar with how the Western media acculturates women to hate their bodies—to see physical developments like growing breasts and menstruating as embarrassing or even disgusting and to seek constantly to reshape, reform, and redesign their bodies (whether through clothing, diet, or plastic surgery). Perhaps not surprisingly, several FTM!Sherlock stories spend a considerable amount of time on how the onset of puberty was particularly problematic for a character's sense of identity. For example, Ishmael's "Body of Evidence" (from the longer *Bodies* series on AO3) describes a young FTM!Sherlock disgusted with her body. Born female, Sheridan Olivia Holmes enjoyed typical "boy" activities as a child, like exploring the outdoors and getting dirty. Her family was constantly disappointed that she wasn't more interested in traditionally feminine things like wearing frilly dresses and playing with dolls. Young Sheridan, however, resented her body and the changes it went through at puberty, viewing it as a kind of betrayal. When early in the story she sees her pregnant Aunt Matilda, she describes Matilda's stomach as a "grotesque flesh balloon" and the fetus as a "parasite." When her female family members tell her she, too, will want to have a child of her own one day, Sheridan is terrified. She wants to keep her boyish prepubescent body and all of the freedoms that presumably go with it:

> None of them understood. You didn't want to do anything but grow taller. You liked your skinny hips and flat chest. You hated the idea of carrying a *thing* inside you, of bleeding every month without any say in it. You didn't know why having those parts meant you wanted the things people expected you to.
>
> You knew biology, knew your body's betrayal was inevitable. (Ishmael)

She hates the idea of menstruation and childbearing, two obvious biological functions of the female body. Clearly, Sheridan recognizes how society equates the shape of her body and its functions with who she is supposed to be as an individual, yet she rejects this role and points out such problematic assumptions. Even though Benedict Cumberbatch's Sherlock, being a man, doesn't go through any of these biological changes, fanon has adopted Sherlock's professed disinterest in food as an indicator of his own discomfort in his male body. This uneasiness is often portrayed as anorexia, body dysmorphia, or another body image disorder in traditional *Sherlock* fanfic, so FTM!Sherlock's desire to resist the limits of biology is consistent with canonical portrayals of Sherlock in the show and in fandom.

Other trans* fanfics base their regendered characterizations on other already existing canonical elements, such as Sherlock's drug use. Red's "A Room Untended" tells a similar story of a FTM!Sherlock who struggles through puberty, rejecting her female body and its attributes. FTM!Sherlock tries to stave off puberty through starvation, ultimately turning to cocaine and drug addiction when this tactic fails. By the young age of 16, Red's FTM!Sherlock is "disgusted" by her developing body, "the onset of menses, the steady development of breasts, the nearly undisguisable distribution of what fat remained on [her] body" ("A Room Untended"). Even though Red's FTM!Sherlock comes from a strongly matriarchal family and is raised to believe that her sex has nothing to do with her abilities or intellect, she rejects her female identity and, after sex reassignment surgery, transitions to being male. The story ends on a rather wistful note, with FTM!Sherlock hoping he can one day share his history with John and reveal the fact that he "did not emerge fully formed into this world, complete as [he was]" (Red, "A Room Untended"). Red's FTM!Sherlock seems to view his transitioned self as complete rather than fragmented, faulty, or perhaps more simply, in transition. For transgender FTM characters like Ishmael's Sheridan and Red's FTM!Sherlock, the disconnection between the physical and mental manifestations of the self cause them to reject their bodies as faulty, and these faulty bodies become damaging to the characters' sense of self.

On the one hand, Etothepii's "Seems So Easy for Everybody Else" appears to reinforce these cultural hostilities toward female bodies. From a young age, FTM!Sherlock, Sophie Charlotte Holmes, is told that being a girl isn't good enough. When she brushes some maggots off a rotting rat skull in the playground, the boys grudgingly tell Charlotte she is *"almost as good as a boy"* (Etothepii; emphasis added). She learns early that boys like Mycroft are "smart and strong and fierce," and they "go off and have adventures." Girls are instead told to be pretty and "empty-headed" (Etothepii). As a result, she sees her female body as her enemy; menstruation is "just another way her body fights her, changing against her wishes, unstoppable and uncontrollable" (Etothepii). As she matures into a young woman, her unhappiness grows.

> She doesn't know why she's unhappy. She just . . . she doesn't like herself, her body, the way it looks. It's pretty enough, in a feminine sort of way. It's fit, and her muscle memory—for combat, for the violin, for archery, is superb.
> But.
> But she looks in the mirror and she thinks, *This isn't who I want to be*.
> She doesn't know why and this bothers her the most. (Etothepii)

Later in the story, Charlotte catches a glimpse of herself in a mirror and "she hates her reflection with a vehemence that surprises her. She looks wrong—awkward and uncomfortable and unhappy. *I don't want to be that woman*, she thinks" (Etothepii). The transgender element adds another level of complexity to the story, however. Clearly, Charlotte is experiencing a strong dissociation between her biological body and her gender identity. Psychologically, she identifies as masculine, and she even begins using a male pen name when corresponding with the Metropolitan police; the constant reminder of her female body confounds her and causes an intellectual and emotional dissonance that leads her to drug addiction and overdose. But this masculine identification is exactly what makes Charlotte canon compliant with the original world. Even though the writers have changed the dynamics of the character's gendered bodies, whether by genderswapping or through the complexities of gender reidentification in trans* fanfiction, Charlotte's desire for alignment between her body and her self highlights the elements that make Sherlock *Sherlock*. Fanfic writers ground these FTM!Sherlock characters in the original world—

through Sherlock's intellect, rejection of physical limitations, drug use, and outsider status—thus keeping the characters canon compliant even as they change them radically in fundamental ways.

Transgender theorists Elliot and Roen maintain that the body is not just a physical reality; it is, rather, an "unconscious manifestation" of the self, which "might or might not 'correspond' with anatomical sex" (247). The body Charlotte sees in the mirror does not necessarily reflect the one she sees in her mind (the canonical Sherlock), the one she may think is a more accurate representation of her self. Charlotte's comment that "she doesn't like herself, her body, the way it looks," syntactically connects her sense of self directly with her body, its physical manifestation (Etothepii). The three—self, body, appearance—all become one. Even though she is fit and athletic, Charlotte "hates her reflection with a vehemence that surprises her" (Etothepii). With no distinction between the body and identity, then in hating her body Charlotte must hate herself. One way to escape from this self-loathing is to change the physical manifestation of that self.

FTM!Sherlock characters ultimately emphasize the importance of analyzing sex as well as gender through the genderswap genre; but at the same time, they reflect a conflicted stance on embodiment, gender identity, and characterization. As we've already seen, many stories emphasize the dissociation many transgender people experience toward their corporeal bodies, with several characters expressing outright resentment and hatred of their sexed selves. Very few stories choose to have the FTM!Sherlock character pursue sex reassignment surgery, however. Red's "A Room Untended" starts with FTM!Sherlock's claim, "It had occurred long enough ago that you had considered the surgery a complete success," which one can assume refers to SRS. Most trans/genderswap writers in the *Sherlock* fandom choose to focus on embodiment and transgender—not transsexual—issues, implying that genital reassignment surgery only addresses cosmetic elements of sexual identity. For a character like Ishmael's Sheridan in "Body of Evidence," masculinity and masculine identity are not necessarily centered on male biology at all; while she binds her breasts and moves about in the world as an adult man, she/he "had no particular desire for a penis" (Ishmael).[26] Sheridan can be a man without having a male body. Similarly, Charlotte in Etothepii's "Seems So Easy for Everybody Else" is suspicious of SRS: "And even if she *does* want to be male, what does it matter? She can't actually change her chromosomes, just force her body into a facsimile of masculinity" (Etothepii). While Charlotte believes that maleness is embodied, one must go deeper than the external copy of masculinity she argues SRS provides. For her, sex is immutable, genetic, inside the body, not outside, and unchangeable by modern surgery. We can also read this as an insight into canon and characterization. Character, like sex or gender identity in Charlotte's case, is immutable in world building. As long as the character remains consistent with the original world, even if her gender identity and biological sex are changed, then the world remains intact.

Problems with terminology, confusion between sex and gender, and debates over gender performance versus embodiment all point to the importance of language and representation when discussing gender identity, characterization, and world building. Language, in particular, is frequently used as a way to structure the self. For instance, individuals are often forced to choose between the binary of male or female when filling out forms, which frustrates Sheridan in Ishmael's "Body of Evidence." Although Charlotte in "Seems So Easy for Everybody Else" distrusts SRS and its ability to make her a man, the story ultimately argues that representation—specifically that found within language—is where true ontological power resides.[27] Three-quarters of the way through the story, Charlotte admits defeatedly that she "can't see [transitioning to a male] happening, no matter how hard *she* tries" (emphasis added); then, there is a break before the narrative returns: "*He* gives up arguing with himself about it, eventually" (Etothepii; emphasis added). Through this subtle shift from the feminine to masculine pronoun, the reader experiences both a linguistic and ontological shift. As Judith Butler explains, "Within speech act theory, a performative is that discursive practice that enacts or produces that which it names" (Butler, *Bodies* 13). The linguistic move from feminine to masculine pronoun in Etothepii's story highlights the cultural (historic, linguistic) construction of gender identity; by calling herself "he," Charlotte transitions to Sherlock in a Butlerian and Lacanian sense. She/he is performing masculinity through language, labels, and identity. This is simultaneously an ontological shift as well. Immediately after the pronoun shift, Mycroft arrives in Sherlock's apartment and confronts him: "'You've been pretending you're a man.'" Sherlock's response—"'I'm not pretending'"—firmly establishes his ontological shift in identity (Etothepii). In the Cartesian sense, by calling himself "he," Sherlock now literally defines himself as male. By the end of the story, Sherlock is able to recognize himself in the mirror "without hating how he looks" in a way that previously, as a female, he could not or did not. This is a double recognition for the reader in that Charlotte's transition to Sherlock reconfirms what she knew all along: that *Charlotte is Sherlock*, even in a transgendered body. The characterization throughout remains compliant with Sherlock's portrayal on the show and within fandom norms and expectations.

Analyzing specific fanfiction genres and individual fandoms gives theorists insight not only into fan practices and reimaginings of canonical work but also into the ways in which we, as a society, define ourselves. Looking at genderswap fanfiction, specifically, not only helps us to understand a specific genre within fan writing but also how fans understand and articulate complex ideas like sex, gender, and identity and how those categories are constructed both in the *Sherlock* world and in various fan practices. As fans become more and more creative with the *Sherlock* world, they begin to experiment with the very foundations that make that world unique. Questions of sexual orientation, gender, and sexual identity are integral to how writers formulate and understand character, so analyzing how *Sherlock* writers craft their own versions of Arthur Conan Doyle's characters, and then seeing how fans challenge, expand, and sometimes re-inscribe those characteristics, provides fascinating insights into how writers construct characters within the *Sherlock* world, what limits those characters' identities, and how fans work within the show's world to actively invoke and rewrite it.

Throughout the various genderswap and trans* fanfic examples in this chapter, the protagonists' characters remain consistent with the world of the show, even when their physical bodies—and the characters' own relationship to those bodies—change. As film theorist David Bordwell reminds us, character is defined and established by physical behavior, major traits, observable projections of personality such as gestures, facial expressions, particular speech patterns/syntax, and recurrent motifs that serve to make a specific character unique from others within the storyworld (15). Fem!Sherlock and Fem!Jane *look* like feminized versions of Cumberbatch and Freeman in their bodies, but their behaviors, while sometimes challenged by themselves and by other characters, remain canonically consistent with their portrayals in the original show. Fem!Sherlock and FTM!Sherlock are intelligent, logical, arrogant, domineering, and dismissive of emotion and physical needs. Similarly, fem!John is the same caretaker *cum* military badass she was in the original world. In a sense, genderswap and transgender fanfic are ultimately about the embodiment of character. Genderswap authors change characters' biological sex, which sometimes results in discord between their gender identity and their physical bodies and often creates conflict with how other characters perceive and respond to them. These conflicts reveal important sociopolitical issues surrounding femininity and masculinity in Western culture while also providing insight into how character is formed, represented, and recreated in storyworlds and in transmedia extensions like fanfiction.[28] We will return to the importance of embodiment in the chapter on real person fiction, but first we will explore how character acts as the linchpin in the radical re-envisioning found in alternate universe fanfiction.

CHAPTER FIVE
OUT OF THIS WORLD
Sherlock's Alternate Universe Fanfiction

Sherlock's material world is uniquely situated compared with other large fictional worlds (*Lord of the Rings, Game of Thrones, Harry Potter*) due to the hundreds of film adaptations, thousands of textual appropriations, and perhaps innumerable cultural appropriations (ranging from ads for Beecham's pills in the 1890s to Sherlock Homes Construction in Aspen, Colorado, to quick cash at surelockloans.com) over the past century. Millions of tourists travel each year to Holmes's digs at 221b Baker Street—ironically located at 239 Baker Street—to immerse themselves in the furniture, trappings, and case evidence of the world's only consulting detective. More recently, *Sherlock* fans, in particular, have explored cinematic locations used in the show's filming; fans leave notes, love letters, and clever canonical references in red phone boxes and in dusty windows at St. Bartholomew's Hospital, the location of Sherlock's death at the end of season two's final episode, "The Reichenbach Fall." Fans post selfies on social media from Speedy's Café on North Gower Street (lovingly called "Faker Street" by *Sherlock* fans worldwide), the actual location of the show's 221b Baker Street apartment. (The showrunners wrote the preexisting Speedy's into the show.) More so perhaps than other popular transmedia worlds today, *Sherlock*'s world is real. Fans can visit, see where Sherlock Holmes (and BBC's *Sherlock*) lived, and imagine key moments from the canon. With such a strong footing in material reality, it is perhaps surprising that so many *Sherlock* fanfics place the characters and actions in alternate universes (AUs), that is, time frames, countries, situations, or fictional worlds completely disparate from the show's established canon. AUs highlight, perhaps more than any other fanfic genre, the extent to which a fictional world is defined by character, *not* by the actual world or setting itself. Fans can change every material element (physical location, nation, profession, sexual identity, gender identity) *except* the foundational character elements, and the fictional world will still remain intact.

What Is Alternate Universe Fanfiction?

As we've discussed earlier, genre plays an important role in fanfic and is often used as a key framework through which fans can approach the canonical world.[1] Slash, genderswap, omegaverse (a fanfiction world where the characters mirror the biological characteristics of wolf packs, with individuals presenting as alpha, beta, or omega sexual orientations and identities), hurt/comfort, angst, and so on, all provide their authors with particular tropes, themes, and parameters through which to approach the source text. While genres often overlap (for example, one could write a slashed genderswapped story, as did Parachute_Silks in "Categories," discussed in chapter 4), most of these genres when applied to *Sherlock* use the basic premise and setting as a given: Sherlock is a detective; John is a doctor just returned from Afghanistan; the stories take place in modern-day London; and so on.[2] Alternate universe fanfiction, in contrast, changes most of the major canonical elements that typically define the show's world.

Often confused with crossover fanfiction, which places one world's canonical characters into another already established fictional world (think Sherlock and John at Hogwarts), alternate universe fanfic imagines an alternate reality, with the characters living in new, unfamiliar settings, having new careers, and/or existing in a different time and place.[3] This new world can follow the basic rules and parameters of the real world (adhering to our basic understandings of physics and natural laws, acknowledging concurrent religions and belief structures, and possessing similar social, cultural, and political formations), or it could depart radically from current understandings, introducing elements such as new species, magic, or temporal-spatial changes. Rather than filling in the interquel and intraquel narrative gaps, as discussed in earlier chapters, AU fanfic is more typically interested in "tone, mood, character, [and] style" than in continuing, extending, or filling in canonical plot points (Mittell, "Strategies" 273).

Many readers often confuse *alternate* and *alternative* when discussing this genre; however, *alternative* means "different" and *alternate* means "taking turns" (Booth, *Digital Fandom* 5). In contrast to possible worlds theory, which posits that multiple worlds exist simultaneously, alternate reality or alternate universe fiction presents a new world as the real and only world in existence. The actual world, known as the "base," is thus set up in opposition to and surrounded by a constellation of satellite alternate worlds, often called a universe (Pavel 51, 64). While any canon-compliant fanfic technically could be categorized as a satellite possible world, AU fanfics tend to dramatically change one or more defining canonical element from the world to imagine the characters in new situations, new premises, and new timelines. Popular *Sherlock* AUs, for example, have Sherlock and John as professional tennis players competing at Wimbledon (and falling in love); they can be college students; they can be fathers of a clone child; they can own a coffee shop or a tattoo parlor; they can be WWII spies. Even though writers may change virtually every aspect of the setting, time period, details, whatever, the one thing that most critics and fans agree must stay consistent is characterization. More fans get upset when Sherlock and John act out of character—OOC—than for any other possible alteration. Tentacle porn? Fine. Sherlock falling for a woman? No way.

Sheenagh Pugh, who has provided some of the most in-depth scholarship on AU fanfic to date, argues that AU stories are "deliberate departures from canon" (61) that allow fans to "think again" about primary aspects of the world (62). Some critics see AU fanfic as a particularly effective genre for commenting on contemporary social issues such as LGBTQ+, military conflicts, and identity politics (Coker 3.7), while others see the genre as a way of liberating characters from their authors' control (Pugh 56). Slash, genderswap, and other fanfic, as we explored in chapters 3 and 4, provide many fans with opportunities to take control of the major narratives influencing contemporary culture. But while slash and genderswap fanfics allow fans to challenge cultural norms regarding sexuality and sexual identity, particularly by reframing them through iconic characters such as Sherlock Holmes and John Watson, AU fanfic allows authors to challenge the fundamental concepts of authorship and world building.

When critics argue, however, that AU stories "diverge" (Pugh 36) and even "stray significantly" from the source text (Stein and Busse, "Limit Play" 196), moving away from and to an extent challenging the source text's established world, they are simultaneously reaffirming the centrality of the canonical world as the base from which AUs diverge. As Marie-Laure Ryan explains, possible worlds are organized hierarchically around a centralized base; their identities as possible worlds are always already defined in opposition to the actual world (Ryan, *Narrative* 99–100). Similarly, AU fictions constantly reinscribe the source world as its base or "discursive referent" (Stein and Busse, "Limit Play" 196). All fanfictions, but particularly AUs, operate through their connection with the source text, whether in terms of origin or in terms of point of view (Ryan, *Narrative* 101). Thus, rather than canon divergent, AU fic retains canon as its central reference point, as something to stray from—as long as the characters remain compliant with the original world.

Setting and Environment

While AU fanfics may remain canon compliant, however, what constitutes canon seems to change when analyzing this genre. While setting/environment was a key element in the *Sherlock* television show itself, in the creators' transmedia franchises such as Sherlock: The Network video game, and in previously discussed genres such as slash and genderswap fanfic, many critics agree that, in AU, canon primarily depends upon character, including physical appearance, mannerisms, behaviors, and syntax (Pugh 65–67, Ryan, "Story/Worlds/Media" 32). Jason Mittell describes slash, genderswap, and other similar genres as "centripetal, or character-driven" franchises; AU stories are less interested in expanding the storyworld than in providing added depth and further opportunities to explore the world's already developed characters (Ryan and Thon 15). Such characters can "transcend their original context and their creator[s]" (Pugh 222) and thus prove that "storyworlds hold a greater fascination for the imagination than the plots that take place in them" (Ryan and Thon 19).

This is not to say that canonical setting never plays a role in AU fanfiction. When it does, however, it is often transmuted into another kind of alternate universe version of itself. Many AU stories make specific use of locations from *Sherlock*—among them Angelo's restaurant, Speedy's Café, St. Bart's Hospital, and New Scotland Yard—but, of course, the foundational setting for *Sherlock* remains the iconic 221b Baker Street flat. Both earlgreytea68's baseball AU, *The Bang and the Clatter* (*B&C*), and reckonedrightly's World War II femslash, *No Bangs Without Foreign Office Approval* (*NBWFOA*), include a version of Sherlock's 221b Baker Street flat. *B&C* ends with Sherlock taking John to his UK apartment, even though the majority of the story takes place in the United States: "John stood in the middle of 221b Baker Street. . . . It looked exactly the way he had pictured their flat to look, the way Sherlock had described it, with the busy wallpaper and the cozy fireplace and the bedroom big enough for a nice-sized bed" (chapter 36). Although description of the flat is limited, the references to the wallpaper and fireplace are sufficient to invoke the show's readily identifiable set for any knowledgeable fan. And even though reckonedrightly situates historic AU *NBWFOA* in war-torn 1942 London, she begins her story of Special Ops training and espionage in the flat on Baker Street: "A flat had been provided for her on Baker Street, so close to the headquarters it might as well have been attached to it. Number 221b comprised a creaking couple of Victorian rooms which were, with a particular cruelty, furnished for two" (prologue).

Unlike many other *Sherlock* AUs, which frequently take place outside of the UK, Jupiter_Ash's beloved tennis AU, "A Study in Winning," mostly takes place in London, so including 221b Baker Street is not as difficult as in other stories. "A Study in Winning" imagines John and Sherlock as finalists in Britain's famed Wimbledon tennis championship. John, aging out of his tennis career and suffering from a past shoulder injury, decides to announce his retirement from the sport, but not before attempting one last hurrah in the nation's Grand Slam tournament. There, he meets and falls in love with the notorious British-born French player, Sherlock Holmes. Beset by paparazzi and tormented by Sherlock's arch-rival, Jim Moriarty, the two make it all the way to the final championship, where John defeats Moriarty to take home the coveted trophy.

John is first taken to Sherlock's flat after an early altercation with Moriarty and notices the "quiet London road" "very close to Regent's Park" and the "small café" next to Sherlock's door, both clear references to *Sherlock*'s filming location on North Gower Street (chapter 3, chapter 4) as well as 221b Baker Street's real proximity to Regent's Park; thus, Jupiter_Ash is able to conflate the actual world of modern London with the fictional television show's real filming locations. As John enters the apartment for the first time, he points out several items that fans easily identify as references and appropriations from the show's original set:

> Up involved seventeen stairs and a door that led into a cosy but cluttered main room. It was undeniably Sherlock's. Tennis equipment and paraphernalia littered the room. Tennis balls lay abandoned against walls and under chairs, rackets were discarded on the table or sofa, some of them with broken strings. A skeleton stood in one corner, a paper racket clasped by its bony fingers. Boxes sat everywhere, some opened, some not. Clothes, shoes, racket covers, books, trophies. "Is that a skull?" he asked pointing to the mantelpiece. "Training partner," Sherlock said. "Well, when I say partner . . ." (Jupiter_Ash Ch. 3)

Jupiter_Ash situates her text both in the Arthur Conan Doyle world, with its reference to 221b's seventeen steps, and in the BBC *Sherlock*'s flat, with its moving boxes, cluttered paperwork, books, and skull ("A Study in Pink"). Instead of having a bull skull with headphones over the desk, Jupiter_Ash incorporates a full human skeleton with tennis racket. Rather than merely reproduce the BBC set, Jupiter_Ash overlays the setting with the accoutrements of her AU: tennis balls, tennis rackets, and other tennis paraphernalia consistent with the alternate world she has created. And yet by incorporating Doyle's seventeen steps and *Sherlock*'s skull, she also clearly overlaps her AU with these Sherlock Holmes universes.

Performance in a Leading Role

World compliance becomes even more difficult in AU fanfiction when the storyworld is located outside of the UK, as we see in Mad_Lori's Hollywood!AU, *Performance in a Leading Role* (*PIALR*). One of the most popular *Sherlock* fanfics of all time (AU or otherwise), *PIALR* provides the material for an in-depth case study of the ways in which AU fanfics remain canon compliant through characterization while expanding and contradicting the material world itself. In *PIALR*, Sherlock is an Oscar-winning actor known for his demanding and irascible temper, while John Watson is a famous rom-com boy-next-door actor whose career is failing as he begins to age out of prime romantic movie roles. The two are cast in a high-end independent drama directed by Ang Lee (of *Brokeback Mountain* fame) in which they have roles as distraught lovers; in a case of life imitating art, the two fall in love but must hide their burgeoning relationship from the Hollywood press for fear it will damage their professional relationships.

Because most of the action in *PIALR* takes place in Hollywood, little mention is made of the iconic London sites so familiar in other *Sherlock* fanfics. Mad_Lori does incorporate two iconic England locations, however: the canonical Sussex cottage where Doyle's Sherlock Holmes retires to keep bees, and the BBC's legendary 221b Baker Street flat. As an Academy Award–winning actor, Sherlock's flat in *PIALR* is much more luxurious than the version from *Sherlock*: "Sherlock's building was a tall column of flats, Victorian and posh, right round the corner from Regent's Park. . . . There were five flats, apparently, A through E. He pushed the button for B" (chapter 8). Mad_Lori makes sure to remain consistent, however, and does so using a few key Sherlock world elements: the address—specifically, the apartment designation "b"—and Sherlock's haphazard style. Much as in the show, *PIALR* Sherlock's flat is "cozily Bohemian, full of squashy furniture and oddball prints on the exposed brick walls and tattered Persian rugs. . . . Books were everywhere, and a large flat-screen telly was shoved into the corner like an afterthought" (chapter 8).

Mad_Lori makes sure to include iconic set design elements in her story, such as the canonical jackknife on the mantelpiece and Sherlock's skull (both highlighted in the first episode of season one) to firmly situate her story within the world of the BBC show: "There was a pocketknife stuck through a stack of letters on the mantel next to a skull. John picked it up. 'Poor Yorick,' he muttered, laughing at himself for pulling out the very hoariest of hoary old jokes" (chapter 8). Of course, John's "Poor Yorick" quote is even more ironic after Benedict Cumberbatch's record-breaking run as Hamlet in London's West End in 2015. Even though Sherlock and John aren't often at the Baker Street flat in *PIALR*, this world consistency satisfies fans' desire for more *Sherlock*: more character development, more setting, more of the objects and syntax—more *Sherlockian* world. Such attention to the vast and detailed narrative space of the established world reassures readers that they are still in the storyworld they know and love—even if most of it takes place in Hollywood.

Mad_Lori also adds her own world-building elements by including photo images of setting locations at the end of key chapters. Some of them, like Sherlock's Sussex cottage, link directly back to the original Sherlock

Holmes world created by Arthur Conan Doyle. The original stories' only genealogical and personal information provided on Holmes indicates that his "ancestors were country squires," his grandmother was the sister of the French artist, Vernet, and he retires to Sussex to care for bees (Doyle, "The Greek Interpreter" 683; Doyle, "His Last Bow" 325). Mad_Lori also includes an image of John's L.A. house, referred to in the story. By linking to real-world locations not originating in either Doyle's stories or *Sherlock*'s world, Mad_Lori affirms the verisimilitude of her own alternate universe. Such locations are known as "immigrant objects." While "native objects" are items originally invented by the source text's author and included in the BBC franchise, immigrant objects have been imported into the *Sherlock* world, either from the actual world or from other fictional texts (Pavel 29). Importing immigrant objects or locations into *PIALR* brings the reality of the alternate universe that much closer to our actual world and increases the reader's immersion in the AU. Even though so much of *PIALR* is foreign to *Sherlock* audiences, who are often heavily invested in the Britishness of Sherlock Holmes as a character and London as the primary setting for his adventures, grounding the AU in concrete architectural images helps the reader accept this Hollywood AU as not only possible but believable as well.

AUs and Realism

Not only is Mad_Lori's *Performance in a Leading Role* consistent with *Sherlock*'s world, it is also consistent with our contemporary media landscape, further emphasizing the story's verisimilitude. Mad_Lori blurs the line between real life and the fictional world by incorporating real media personalities in her story, including Ang Lee, Ellen Degeneres, and A-List actors Rachel Wiesz and her husband, Daniel Craig. The online fic also incorporates several pieces of fan art that support the realism of the story, including art by Marielikestodraw of John and Sherlock's fictional *Entertainment Weekly* cover promoting *To a Stranger*, based on Mad_Lori's textual description:

> The photographer had put them both in black shirts and shot against a black background, so they appeared to float. They were back to back, turned so that John was three-quarters to the camera and Sherlock was three-quarters away. Sherlock was looking back over

his near shoulder, John down and toward Sherlock. They both had thoughtful, serious expressions on and the black-and-white image made them both look like – well, like movie stars. Whoever had done the image processing had restored the color in just their eyes. Sherlock's alien verdigris and John's deep blue peered out from under their lids. . . . The cover had been kept mostly free of text except above the masthead and the title of their article in the lower right. "Men on a Mission: Sherlock Holmes and John Watson shoot for career rejuvenation and a leap forward for gay cinema in 'To a Stranger.'" (Mad_Lori chapter 12)

Other fans created art based on the story's mention of *Time* magazine's coverage of John and Sherlock's coming out story. A few *PIALR* chapters consist of transcripts from publicity appearances on the *David Letterman Show*, *Ellen*, and *60 Minutes*. References are made to blog posts by Perez Hilton, the *Huffington Post*, fan forums for Sherlock and John—all reinforce the realism of Mad_Lori's alternate universe story. She makes it seem more than a possible world in which Sherlock and John *could* be movie stars; in this world, Sherlock and John *are* movie stars.

Syntax

Not only do AU authors try to place their canonical characters in new yet familiar locations, they also make sure to follow the characters' specific syntax or way of speaking as established in the canon. Characters seen as acting or speaking inconsistently with canon expectations (excluding some aspects, however, such as emotions and relationships) may generate fan accusations that the writer is portraying Sherlock and John out of character. Use of syntax, speech patterns, and specific quotations and catchphrases all highlight the fanfic's reliance on, and connection with, the original world. Some AU fics incorporate iconic dialogues from the show with minimal adaptation, like earlgreytea68's baseball coach Lestrade telling John in *The Bang and the Clatter*, "Sherlock Holmes is a great baseball player. And someday, if we're very, very lucky, he might even be a good man" (earlgreytea68, *B&C* chapter 1), which closely reproduces Lestrade's comment made first at the end of "A Study in Pink" (S1E1) and again at the end of "The Final Problem" (S4E3): "Because Sherlock Holmes is a great man. And one day, if we're very, very lucky, he might even be a good one." Lestrade's speech pattern in *B&C*, along with Sherlock's "Well, when I say partner . . ." from "A Study in Winning" (Jupiter_Ash chapter 3), recreate both *what* the characters say in the canonical source text and *how* they say it. Both earlgreytea68 and Jupiter_Ash recreate the speech patterns found in the original show to provide their fanfic characterization with deepened verisimilitude. How Rupert Graves's Lestrade and Benedict Cumberbatch's Sherlock speak in *Sherlock* is important to the audience's perceptions of their characters; recognizable speech patterns help cement a character's identity to that of the actor playing him, and this cohesion carries over and strengthens the characterization in fanfic as well.

Quotation is another form of canon reference and world building, and several AU fanfics use specific cues, such as an eight-year-old girl named Rachel asking for John's autograph in "A Study in Winning" (a reference to the pink lady's dying clue in *Sherlock*'s "A Study in Pink"). Some AUs reference important character backstories as a means of explaining or acknowledging their texts' deviations from established canon. For instance, in earlgraytea68's *Bang and the Clatter*, Sherlock observes that John regrets not becoming a doctor, a part of the foundational John Watson identity going back to the Arthur Conan Doyle stories. Instead, earlygraytea68 references this canonical element and uses it to fill in the character's thwarted backstory to help explain his current professional trajectory: even though John never finished his pre-med university training, his baseball nickname "The Doctor" preserves that legacy in his work training pitchers and catchers.

In addition, *The Bang and the Clatter* recreates several popular scenes from the BBC show, almost word for word, including Sherlock's request early in "A Study in Pink" to borrow Mike Stamford's cell phone (here requested of John), and the opening scene of "The Great Game" (S1E3), in which John walks into 221b to discover Sherlock shooting bullet holes into the wall in boredom (changed here from a smiley face to the pentagon of baseball's home plate). Likewise, Jupiter_Ash's "A Study in Winning" also reproduces iconic canonical moments like John's frustration at Sherlock breaking into his password-protected laptop in "The Blind Banker" (S1E2) and the taxi ride deduction in "A Study in Pink" (S1E1) where John asks Sherlock how he knows so much about him. Even though some of these AUs seem far removed from the reality of the TV show's actual world, by constantly referencing the characters' speeches in the original show and transferring original scenes into new AU contexts, the authors clearly indicate to their readers where their stories fit into the larger *Sherlock* world. Baseball!AU Sherlock telling Baseball!AU John that he "prefers to text" (earlygraytea68, *B&C* chapter 1) tells the reader that *this* Sherlock is also *their* Sherlock; the same Sherlock who solves crimes and banters with John Watson in modern London is also the one who wins the world series in *The Bang and the Clatter* or Wimbledon in "A Study in Winning" or who fights German spies in 1940s France in *No Bangs Without Foreign Office Approval*. By focusing on how the characters speak and (re)producing what they say, AUs reaffirm the show's world as the center and establish their own relationship to it.

Again, looking at *PIALR* as an extended case study, we see that Mad_ Lori picks up several of *Sherlock*'s most identifiable syntax styles and uses them throughout her story. Syntax and vocabulary mean more than just world choice and ways of speaking, although those are important elements. They also refer to the speech patterns used, in this case those of the original show, which are then reproduced in fanfic and other transmedia outlets. Sherlock, for example, in "A Study in Pink" states that "All that matters to me is the work" and that his body is just "transport"; both phrases are used in *PIALR* to establish the consistency of Sherlock's characterization between the story and the *Sherlock* world. In the story's first chapter, Sherlock considers whether to accept the offer to appear in Ang Lee's new film, *To a Stranger*, and he tells his agent: " 'I don't care about the money. All that matters to me is the work. I just want something interesting, something challenging' " (chapter 1). Later, Harry, John's sister and personal assistant, similarly reinforces Sherlock's canonical characterization, telling John: " 'Sally [Sherlock's PA] says all he cares about is the work. How did she put it? The rest is transport' " (chapter 3). By repeating these elements of Sherlock's characterization, *PIALR* reinforces the idea that, even though this is a Hollywood!AU with Sherlock and John as A-list actors, they remain the Sherlock and John we know and love from the television show.

PIALR also references canonical plot elements, including for example Sherlock and John going out for Chinese food at the end of "A Study in Pink." Such references become part of the framework or pattern of the fanfic storyworld. Take-out Chinese is a popular trope in *Sherlock* fanfic, precisely because it frames the ending of the first show in which the two protagonists meet and are introduced to viewers. Such behaviors thus become part of the syntax of the world itself and are reproduced over and over again in various participatory outlets, making it unsurprising to *PIALR* readers that John enters Sherlock's studio hired flat with a bag of Chinese food after they get together to work on the script (chapter 4). Such habitual behaviors signify character behaviors that, upon being repeated, establish a particular character as canonical.

"A Connected Set of Objects and Individuals": Character Overview

Another way Mad_Lori builds world consistency in her Holly-wood!AU is by incorporating most of *Sherlock*'s characters in new Hollywood roles. For instance: Lestrade becomes Sherlock's agent, Sally Donovan his personal assistant, and Mrs. Hudson another actress in the cast of *To a Stranger* and one of Sherlock's favorite people. Mike Stamford works as John's agent, John's sister, Harry, is his personal assistant, and both John and Sherlock later hire Irene Adler as their publicist. Jim Moriarty, of course, is a foul human being, although a successful actor and Sherlock's competition during awards season. In *The Bang and the Clatter*, earlgreytea68 makes Mike Stamford into John's sports agent, Lestrade becomes Sherlock and John's baseball coach, and Mrs. Hudson is the team's owner. In "A Study in Winning," Lestrade is Sherlock's tennis coach, while Mike Stamford acts as John's physical therapist. In each of these stories, the writers ground their alternate universe version using the character parameters found in the show; even though an individual character's job may have changed technically, their relationships to the protagonists remain compliant with the world. Thus even though the setting, context, and character interactions may have changed significantly, the authors reinforce the world of the show by foregrounding subsidiary characters. These adapted characters become part of the setting, much like 221b Baker Street does, even when they appear in different incarnations.

Undoubtedly, the main protagonists from the original world constitute the most important element in AU fanfiction. Even though they are often cast in different roles in AU worlds, they retain the major characteristics that make them recognizable to any reader familiar with the original production. The more a fanfic veers away from the source text and the world of the show, the more important consistency in the main characters becomes in keeping the fic aligned with fan expectations. As Sheenagh Pugh articulates,

> Even readers who don't claim themselves as "character junkies" . . . won't stand for interpretations that strike them as wildly off-beam. . . . You can set the story in a different timeline, cross it with other fictions, write before it began or after it ended, or even make it go in a different direction. But in the end you must work with a particular set of people and whatever situation you put them in they must behave and speak like themselves. (65–67)

Pearson's analysis and Bordwell's six key elements for establishing character in film and television provide helpful structures for understanding how fanfic emphasizes character in world building: environment; speech patterns; psychological traits or habitual behaviors; physical characteristics or appearance; interactions with other characters; and biography (Pearson, "Anatomising Gilbert Grissom" 41–42, 43). We've already briefly discussed environment and speech patterns; the following section will focus on the significance of habitual behaviors and physical characteristics.

Character: Habitual Behaviors and Mannerisms

Perhaps because so many *Sherlock* fanfics are written from John's point of view, little time is spent on his canonical appearance and mannerisms. John begins the BBC series limping from a psychosomatic leg injury, and he is frequently seen clenching his left fist in response to a tremor related to his PTSD. In reckonedrightly's historic femslash *No Bangs Without Foreign Office Approval*, the fem!John/Joan's character has a limp early in the story, the result of a recent accident rather than a war injury. When Joan first arrives at Wanborough Manor for her special ops training, she is seen stopping just inside the doorway, "leaning on her cane" (chapter 1). The text includes eighteen additional references to Joan's injury, reinforcing her connection to BBC!John and his psychosomatic limp noted in "A Study in Pink" (S1E1). Similarly, in earlgreytea68's *Nature and Nurture* (*N&N*)—one of the more canonically consistent AUs discussed here, since it so closely follows the show's basic premise that Sherlock and John are London-based detectives, but with a clone baby—makes several mentions of John having a limp when he first meets Sherlock. In chapter 2, Sherlock observes that John's limp no longer hinders his progress around the city:

"Your limp, John," Sherlock reminded him, looking almost amused that he'd forgot it.

But he *had* forgotten it, in the midst of everything else that was happening to him. "Oh, God," he said, "that *was* forever ago, wasn't it? Do you think I'd still be limping along with a cane, if I hadn't met you?"

"Yes," answered Sherlock, readily.

"Thanks for the vote of confidence," John replied, drily. (*N&N* chapter 2)

Even though John never limps in the two-hundred-thousand-plus-word fic, earlygraytea68 uses it to ground her character in the original world of the TV show. *Sherlock*'s fans know that John returns to London from Afghanistan with a distinct (psychosomatic) limp that requires him to use a cane and initially prohibits him mentally from participating in Sherlock's madcap life.

Another frequent identifier for John is his hand tremor, the result of nerve damage from his shoulder wound. Although the reference never appears in Jupiter_Ash's "A Study in Winning," John's hand tremor is mentioned at least three times by earlgreytea68 in *The Bang and the Clatter*. Like the use in *No Bangs* of Joan's limp and cane in its first chapter, "A Study in Winning" introduces John's hand tremor in the opening paragraphs as explanation for why he is considering a move to a new expansion team and possibly retiring from baseball. These thoughts arise following a physical therapy session with Mike Stamford:

John bristled but told himself it wasn't Mike's fault. Mike was doing the best he could with a client who was washed up, had decidedly seen better days. John looked down at his trembling hand, flexed it, and tried to will it still. It was odd, most days his shoulder barely bothered him, and that was where the injury had been. It was the rest of it that he couldn't shake, the tremor in his hand, the abrupt stiffness that could come over his leg sometimes when he rose from a crouch to try to gun down a runner at second. (chapter 1)

While Baseball!AU John's injuries have nothing to do with military service, earlgreytea68 still uses them to situate the character in the show's underlying canon even as she transmutes that storyline and world into an American baseball narrative. Similarly, earlgreytea68 doubly embeds John's tremor late in her story in a scene between John and Mycroft that verbatim recaps the characters' first encounter in "A Study in Pink." When Mycroft first kidnaps John in that episode, he observes: "'You have an intermittent tremor in your left hand. You're under stress right now, and your hand is perfectly steady.' The man dropped his hand and sent him a smile John didn't like. 'Welcome back,' he said, and then he walked away, swinging his umbrella jauntily" (chapter 7). By layering the syntax of the show over John's physical mannerisms, earlgreytea68 doubly reinforces her AU's dependence on, and intertwining with, *Sherlock*'s world.

While John is often seen blogging or writing in alternate universe fics, as he does in the show, one major behavioral element for Sherlock's character—which, again, comes from the original Arthur Conan Doyle canon—is his violin playing. In Watson's original list of Holmes's "limits," he lists his violin playing at number 10 and immediately follows with:

> I see that I have alluded to his powers upon the violin. These were very remarkable, but as eccentric as all his other accomplishments. That he could play pieces, and difficult pieces, I knew well, because at my request he has played me some of Mendelssohn's Lieder, and other favourites. When left to himself, however, he would seldom produce any music or attempt any recognized air. (Doyle, *A Study in Scarlet*, chapter 2)

Holmes's canonical violin playing becomes a foundational character element in "A Study in Pink" (S1E1) when John and Sherlock are first introduced in St. Bart's lab, and it is referenced in all of the AUs analyzed here, ranging from brief character-establishing scenes as in *No Bangs Without Foreign Office Approval* (chapter 14) and in *The Bang and the Clatter* (chapter 4), when John first visits Sherlock's flat. In other instances, for example, in earlgreytea68's canonically compliant *Nature and Nurture*, Sherlock's violin playing serves as a key element of the setting and overall quality of life at 221b Baker Street:

> John woke to the sound of Sherlock's violin, which was such a common occurrence that he rolled over and pulled the duvet tighter around him and prepared to doze for a luxurious few additional

minutes, secure in the knowledge that Sherlock was absolutely fine because he was playing his violin. (chapter 2)

John's comment that Sherlock's nocturnal playing is a "common occurrence" highlights the fanonical importance this character element has achieved in *Sherlock* fanfics overall.

Sherlock also incorporates several behaviors that clearly demarcate earlgreytea68's Holmes as channeling the Benedict Cumberbatch incarnation. For instance, Sherlock ruffles his hands through his hair in several *Sherlock* episodes ("The Blind Banker," "The Sign of Three");[4] he sulks and throws himself on the sofa in 221b; and he narrows his eyes when he makes deductions. Sherlock's most identifiable and often cited mannerism, however, is his uber-canonical thinking pose. The gesture, first described in Doyle's story "The Red-Headed League," appears frequently in *Sherlock*, with Cumberbatch steepling his fingers in a prayer position either in front of his mouth or directly under his chin, from "A Study in Pink" (S1E1).[5]

Sherlock's thinking pose is such an iconic mannerism that it is referenced in every fic discussed in this chapter. Some writers, such as reckonedrightly, closely align their character descriptions with Doyle's in the original stories: "With that Sherlock took refuge on the sofa, stretching out, fingers pressed together as in prayer. There he stayed, silent and still for the best part of an hour" (reckonedrightly chapter 4). Even though *No Bangs Without Foreign Office Approval* is both a historic AU and femslash, fem!Sherlock is described sensuously as "touching her lower lip with the tips of her fingers and frowning, her eyes fixed with uncanny steadiness on Joan" (reckonedrightly chapter 1), thus keeping her character aligned with the original Sherlock's description. Other writers, such as Mad_Lori, make much briefer mention of this mannerism; for instance, actor!Sherlock merely sits on the couch, "his hands steepled under his nose" (chapter 4). Other fanfic authors simply invoke the fanon name for Sherlock's gesture, inserting the label "thinking pose" directly into their descriptions. In *Nature and Nurture*, John observes Sherlock watching the ballet, noting he was "leaning forward in his seat, his fingers steepled into thinking pose [*sic*] while his eyes avidly tracked the dancers' movements on stage" (earlgreytea68, *N&N* chapter 47). In earlgreytea68's baseball AU, Sherlock is seen in a restaurant with his "fingers steepled against his mouth in what John was recognizing was his thinking pose" (*B&C* chapter 8). Both descriptions recall to the reader's mind the several scenes from the TV show in which Sherlock is filmed in this position at key points in the narrative and evoke the nineteenth-century Arthur Conan Doyle world as well.

Perhaps because of its significant length (156,000 words), Mad_Lori's *Performance in a Leading Role* is able to incorporate several additional behavioral and psychological elements foundational to Cumberbatch's Sherlock. In addition to Sherlock's violin playing and thinking pose, Mad_Lori's Sherlock struggles with reading other people's emotions and social cues. In the show, Sherlock often has to look to John to see if his comments and behavior are "not good" ("A Study in Pink," "The Great Game"), reflecting *Sherlock*'s particular take on Sherlock as possibly being on the autism spectrum.[6] Mad_Lori writes in *Performance in a Leading Role*, "Sherlock . . . often found the behavior of other people and the ways of society incomprehensible" (chapter 5). He is likewise depicted as being perceived as "cranky and superior and critical and judgmental and totally intolerant of anyone's shortcomings" as well as "cold and emotionless. Detached. Frigid. Unsympathetic" (chapter 12, chapter 9), all of which makes him an unpopular actor to work with, even though he's won an Oscar. He "constantly battled boredom and was always hoping for work that would excite him" (chapter 16), a trait highlighted in "The Great Game" (S1E3) when John finds Sherlock shooting a smiley face into their flat wall. All of these psychological traits and behaviors work to align the AU's characterization with that of the show's world, even when several major elements of that world have been changed. By reproducing John and Sherlock's specific mannerisms and behaviors, fanfic authors invoke the visual elements of the original world and concretize their characters' images in readers' minds.

Physical Attributes

The most emphasized element in AU characterization, however, is the characters' physical attributes. As previously discussed in chapter 3, many fanfic writers fetishize the characters' physical appearance, focusing on and often sexualizing their various body parts. With *Sherlock* as the fanfics' source, this means aligning the main characters' bodies with those of the actors who play them on-screen. Over and over again in fanfic the fetishization of the actors' bodies becomes central to understanding and portraying the fictional character. Because the fictional character is inseparably embodied by the actor playing the role on-screen, the actor's body becomes fetishized *as the character*. This connection between the actors' bodies and the specificity of fanfic character descriptions may be somewhat unique to fics based on television shows (and other serialized media franchises, I would argue). In contrast to TV characters, David A. Black argues, famous theater characters such as Hamlet, Romeo, and others, do not become physically tied to the specific actor(s) who play them. Garrick, Olivier, and even Cumberbatch may all be famous for their Hamlets, but this does not cement in audiences' minds that Hamlet should always look like any of these actors. Television actors, on the other hand, seem particularly tied to their roles, and the characters become "resistant to abstraction" in ways that other literary and theatrical characters do not (Black 105–6). This "character/actor join," as Black describes it, creates a "uniquely powerful identification of actor with role" (105), perhaps because of the scope of the TV audience and television's ability to broadcast repeat performances throughout and beyond a show's run. While this character/actor join will be studied in further detail in the final chapter on real person fic, personal appearance is a significant method by which AU fanfic authors connect their stories to the world of the source text. Even though the majority of the canonical elements have changed—everything ranging from setting, time period, context, profession, conflict, and even gender—the consistency of characters' looks, along with their behaviors, work to create the impression that an AU is still "in world," even when its entire premise is to be out of that world.

John

Many *Sherlock* fanfics are told from John's point of view, logically resulting in fewer descriptions of John's character overall. When he is described, however, the depictions follow particular patterns that clearly align his character with Martin Freeman's portrayal in the BBC show. He is often described as having boy-next-door good looks and deep blue eyes and as being stubborn, independent, well-liked, loyal, sometimes jealous and possessive, and not afraid of a fight. In *The Bang and Clatter*, earlgreytea68's John is described as having "dark blue eyes. . . . His mouth might be set in a firm line. John had a stubborn mouth. Even when he was not being stubborn, even when he was smiling, the stubbornness lurked there, in the creases of the lines around it" (chapter 5). These physical attributes are often isolated from the rest of John's physical body, a hallmark of festishization, particularly in film studies. Cinematographers and photographers often frame a scene or image by highlighting or excluding particular facial features, thus fragmenting the actor's body into small, identifiable pieces. These individual pieces (an eye, mouth, nose, or other body part) then come to stand in for the whole, becoming imbued with symbolic meaning and weight.

In contrast, abundantlyqueer's *Two Two One Bravo Baker*, a slash military AU in which Sherlock meets John while on a mission in Afghanistan, provides one of the few occasions when we see John through Sherlock's eyes. First, the narrator describes John's face and military cropped hair as "suntanned and sun-bleached to almost the same shade of dark gold, and his eyes look startlingly blue by contrast" (chapter 1). When the two men engage in their first sexual encounter, the POV switches to Sherlock:

> He brushes his fingers of both hands into John's hair, his eyes fixed on the short gold and silver strands as they bristle past his fingertips. He draws the edge of his thumbnail down the creases between John's brows, along the half-moon creases at the corner of his mouth, and

then down the cleft in his chin. John's smile is just a gleam in his eyes as he studies Sherlock studying him. Sherlock moves his fingertips over the curves of John's face, over the wind- and sun-roughened skin, and the pale gold creases etched in the deeper tan around his eyes. He touches John's mouth, tracing the thin bow. (abundantlyqueer chapter 3)

Sherlock's fingers tracing John's features act as a metaphor for the ways the fic repeats and recalls Martin Freeman's physical attributes in the actual world of the show. As the reader follows the path of Sherlock's fingers, she is both reminded of and (re)familiarized with the character's looks and thus reimmersed into the original storyworld.

Strikingly, Mad_Lori's famous AU fic *Performance in a Leading Role* seems to rely so much on fans' prior knowledge of John's looks that she includes practically no outright physical description of John's character in the entire 156,000-word story. All readers see is "a generic boy-next-door, the die-cast Unthreatening Male," and that his hair "gleam[ed] like gold" and his eyes "glow[ed] deep blue like an aquarium" (chapter 10). In many ways, this assemblage of body parts—blue eyes, blond hair, stubborn mouth—are generic; yet, the AU remains in world since the reader comes to the text having already gained knowledge and expectations of the character. Fanfics, as adaptations, depend on intertextuality. Reading becomes a Bakhtinian dialogical process in which readers continually oscillate between the source text and the fanfic, filtering the fanfic elements (genre, setting, character) through what they already know about the world. Fanfics thus become palimpsests, at once obscuring and preserving the memory of the source text as it "resonates through repetition with variation," giving readers the pleasure of familiarity and repetition (Hutcheon 8, 21). The reader's previously established expectations of the world frame the AU and help to fill in any missing gaps in description or behavior.

Sherlock

In contrast, because so many AU fics are from John's point of view—and John is frequently seen falling in love with Sherlock—most AU fanfics spend considerable time on Sherlock's mannerisms and looks, all of which again serve to place Sherlock firmly within the world of the show rather than solely in the new alternate reality. The sheer number of examples highlight how much time fanfic authors invest in establishing Sherlock's character, emphasizing how important character consistency is to world building in fanfiction overall. What really stands out when considering Sherlock's characterization in AU fanfic, in particular, is the intensity with which fans fetishize Benedict Cumberbatch's appearance. Perhaps the most exaggerated example is in earlgreytea68's *Nature and Nurture*, an AU focusing on Sherlock and John's adoption of a cloned child version of Sherlock. Even as an infant, baby Oliver has the same physical attributes as his fictional father as portrayed on-screen by Benedict Cumberbatch:

> The ridiculous thing was that the child looked like Sherlock. He was so tiny that he was still flailing around, not in control of any of his limbs, barely able to hold up his head on his own, and yet he looked like Sherlock, his hair in dark swirls on his skull and his eyes the pale blue-green-gray that John had almost grown immune to. And, when he screwed up his face and wailed his displeasure with the universe, John had to admit the resemblance was complete. (*N&N* chapter 1)

Baby Oliver has Sherlock's dark hair, "pale blue-green-gray" eyes, and personality, even though he is only an infant. Even though earlgreytea68's John recognizes the ridiculousness of a clone baby looking exactly like Benedict Cumberbatch's Sherlock, the AU can't help but doubly emphasize the canonical character elements linking the fic's Sherlock with the BBC's canonical version.

Fans seem to break Cumberbatch's Sherlock down into four fetishized features: voice, eyes, hair, and mouth, and in most cases, each feature is sexualized through John's attraction to Sherlock. For instance, in *The Bang and the Clatter*, earlgreytea68 has John describe how, "as much as [he] tried to pay attention to the lecture, Sherlock's voice was incredibly distracting, and he found that vast periods of time passed where he wasn't bothering to translate the words, just letting the timbre of his cadence wash over him" (chapter 5). Cumberbatch's famous baritone, likened to a "jaguar hiding in a cello" (Moran) and employed in various audiobooks, film narrations, and advertisements (including for Jaguar automobiles), is frequently the subject of voice kink *Sherlock* fanfic. In some fics, Sherlock's voice is enough to send John tumbling into orgasm, even without any additional physical contact.

Sherlock's eyes (*Sherlock*, "The Reichenbach Fall")

More frequently cited features include Cumberbatch's distinctive eyes, notable for their heterochromia iridis, a condition in which pigmentation effects make his eye color seem to change depending on his clothing, the lighting, or the background. Fanfic descriptions of the results of this condition vary widely. At one end of the spectrum, Sherlock's eyes are described as "practically colorless" (abundantlyqueer chapter 1), "unusual" (earlgreytea68, *B&C* chapter 10), and even "unearthly" (Mad_Lori chapter 9). For John in *The Bang and the Clatter*, Sherlock's eyes remain a point of fascination, much like his voice: "Sherlock turned onto his side suddenly, his unusual eyes fastened on to John, all blue and green and gray, and God, what color was that supposed to be? People shouldn't have eyes like that" (chapter 10). Part of the fascination with Sherlock's eyes is in the indeterminacy of the color, but another is their focus. Sherlock's eyes "fasten" on John in the passage just quoted; likewise, in Mad_Lori's *Performance in a Leading Role*, Sherlock "pins" John with his eyes: "Sherlock kept him pinned in place with his eyes, those unearthly verdigris eyes that every cinematographer he'd ever worked with had worshipped in close-ups and side-lighting" (chapter 9). Mad_Lori's elision between her Hollywood!Sherlock and the actual world's Cumberbatch!Sherlock erodes the boundaries between the fictional and the real world. Sherlock's eyes are not only distinctive but they are also a key character element through which he deduces others' characters and the clues he searches out. Thus, fetishizing this particular physical element cements his intellectual acumen, his canonical profession as a detective, and his physical attractiveness as centered in Benedict Cumberbatch's body, all combining to reinforce Sherlock's canonical characterization even in the most outlandish of AUs.

Several AU fics reinforce their compliance with the storyworld through canonical references to Sherlock's dark, curly hair. Sometimes it's the only recognizable character element offered to identify Sherlock, as in this text from *Performance in a Leading Role*: "Missing: one Oscar winning actor. Thirty-four years old, six feet, dark brown hair. Dead sexy. If found please return ASAP to bed of John Watson. Generous reward is offered" (Mad_ Lori chapter 10). In other fics, Sherlock's hair becomes an eroticized feature of Sherlock's body. In *The Bang and the Clatter*, which heavily fetishizes Sherlock's body as a method of recentering the AU in the canon, John is often distracted by Sherlock's hair:

> He'd at least wet his hair, and John couldn't help but think that was
> his vanity striking again, getting the hat-flatness out of it. Sherlock's
> obvious preoccupation with his hair made John itch to run his
> fingers into it, muss it up, twist curls into his fists, and make Sherlock
> as thoroughly debauched as his hairstyle seemed to promise he
> would be. Sherlock's ridiculous attractiveness was kind of annoying.
> (earlgreytea68 chapter 5)

John observes that even for Sherlock's fictional character, his hair plays a key role in establishing his identity and sense of self. John postulates that Sherlock's obsession with his hair is both a sign of his vanity as well as a preoccupation, and John seeks to debauch his hairstyle until it matches John's own perception of Sherlock's character and sensuality. The TV show frequently shows Sherlock fluffing his hair ("The Blind Banker," "The Sign of Three"), particularly when looking at his own reflection, and Cumberbatch's vocal, public dislike of his *"Sherlock* hair" keep this aspect of his appearance in the public's eye. As a result, Cumberbatch's locks frequently become a focal point for news stories, interviews, celebrity photos, and fan discourse, so it's no surprise that AU fanfics call on such a frequently commented-upon physical characteristic to reinforce a connection to the show's canonical world.

The other physical attribute most commonly used to establish Sherlock's character in AU fanfic is his Clara Bow mouth. Cumberbatch's lips are a scintillating topic for both celebrity media and fan art in the real world. In various media interviews and images on the web, he is seen biting his lower lip, touching his mouth, and brushing his fingertips across his lips, perhaps as a result of his smoking habit. Regardless, Cumberbatch's mouth, along with his voice and eyes, remain objects of fascination for his fans and the general public alike. Used for speaking, eating, kissing, and other things, perhaps it is no surprise that his mouth is the most sexualized feature of Cumberbatch's character (a close second to his fingers, as discussed in chapter 3). John in *Performance in a Leading Role* proclaims "epic poems [should be] written about it" (Mad_Lori chapter 16), while a baseball fan in *The Bang and the Clatter* tells a reporter, "His mouth is pure sex" (earlgreytea68 chapter 1). John tests out this observation early in the fic as he watches Sherlock face down a batter:

> His lower lip was caught between his teeth as he frowned in concentration and the camera panned slowly out, capturing all of him as he coiled into leashed energy and then flung the ball toward home . . . . The camera zoomed in again to Sherlock's face, his mouth this time curved into a self-satisfied smile, and John decided that the woman's comment was not a non sequitur at all. Sherlock Holmes's mouth was *pure sex*. (earlgreytea68 chapter 1)

We see the same elements in Sherlock's AU character—the lip biting, the half-smile—that fans see both in the actual TV show and in the real-world media. John goes on to describe Sherlock's mouth as "pornographic," especially as he watches Sherlock eat:

> Sherlock's pornographic mouth fastened around a spoonful of tiramisu. The effect of it made John so light-headed that he momentarily reconsidered every decision he'd made in his life that had brought him to this point, sitting opposite a pitcher he was supposed to catch, simmering slowly with lust. Then Sherlock's tongue darted out to lick up a bit of whipped cream at the corner of his mouth and John thought, sod it, he was clearly the most brilliant decision-maker of all time to be enjoying this moment. (earlgreytea68 chapter 2)

These extended scenes combine several canonical elements into one fetishized physical attribute. In the aforementioned example, John's fascination with Sherlock's mouth is connected to the characters' canonical dinner at Angelo's restaurant, seen in "A Study in Pink" (S1E1). Similarly, by fetishizing the act of eating, *The Bang and the Clatter* also highlights another key characteristic found in the *Sherlock* fanon: John's role as Sherlock's caretaker and his fanonical efforts to get Sherlock to eat and feed his transport. Compounding these elements with Sherlock's canonical appearance solidifies the AU's connection to *Sherlock*'s world, even when the main characters are romantically involved American baseball players.

Physical characteristics are so important that even the most extreme alternate universes remain faithful to Cumberbatch's and Freeman's looks. For instance, in reckonedrightly's genderswapped slash World War II AU, *No Bangs Without Foreign Office Approval*, Joan and fem!Sherlock are described consistently with the show's canon, even though they are both characterized as female. Like Freeman's Watson, reckonedrightly's historicized fem!Watson has "dirty blonde hair" but cut into a "rumpled, unfashionable bob" (chapter 2) and "a tiny dip in the middle of her chin, another at the tip of her nose" (chapter 5). As we saw with many genderswap fanfics discussed in chapter 4, Joan is uncomfortable in her feminine body and worries that she hates herself: "But there she was; hating not her starchy collar or her baggy uniform skirt or her scratchy khaki stockings, not even her meaty thighs or her frizzy hair or her leg, but something about herself" (reckonedrightly chapter 2). Situating Joan and Sherlock's love story within a more conservative, war-torn World War II culture provides reckonedrightly the space to challenge contemporary cultural discomfort with homosexuality in ways that make the reader believe that this is an issue from the distant past and not for our (more idealized) present. Even with so many aspects of the canon changed in *NBWFOA*, Joan's physical description still turns her into a feminized Martin Freeman and allows readers to see the connections between this universe and the world of the show.

Again, because most of *NBWFOA* is from Joan's perspective, it includes significantly more description of Sherlock's characteristics and physical appearance. Joan's first impressions of Sherlock are of her "spidery fingers passing over thin eyebrows, pointy cheekbones, full lips, a strange, clammy sort of paleness. She was pretty. No, she was far from pretty. She was probably closer to beautiful, in an unfamiliar and bad-tempered way" (reckonedrightly chapter 1). Touching on many of the physical elements we've already discussed, Joan fetishizes Sherlock's eyes, "so pale Joan couldn't quite work out their colour" (chapter 1) as well as her clothing. Within *Sherlock* fandom, Cumberbatch and Freeman's costuming is a frequent point of interest, so much so that the popular fan site, *Sherlock-*

ology, devotes a section to the actors' costumes, including information on where fans can get their own versions. Particular items from Sherlock's wardrobe—his Belstaff coat, his suits, and a particular purple Dolce and Gabbana dress shirt featured in "The Blind Banker" (S1E2) and "The Great Game" (S1E3)—make frequent appearances in *Sherlock* fanfic as identifiable canon markers.

Even though *No Bangs Without Foreign Office Approval* takes place in 1942, reckonedrightly was still able to dress Sherlock in clothing similar to the canonical versions. One of the first times Joan sees Sherlock, for example, she notes her "civilian clothing—a dark purple blouse which was really too small on her and a black skirt which, as Joan watched, fanned out and fluttered as she set herself down onto her bed" (chapter 1). While reckonedrightly has to find some historical equivalents, replacing Sherlock's Spencer Hart suits with fem!Sherlock's black dress skirts, for example, other elements like BBC *Sherlock*'s Dolce and Gabbana purple shirt are easier to incorporate while remaining consistent with the story's genderswap premise. Interestingly, however, the author kept some male!Sherlock clothing, like Sherlock's Belstaff coat. Joan describes seeing Sherlock wearing "what looked like a man's greatcoat . . . draped around her shoulders; it rippled and flapped in the wind, slicing up the quiet rustle of the grass behind her with swathes of navy-black" (reckonedrightly chapter 2). While men's and women's fashion certainly would have been different in WWII-era Britain, reckonedrightly seems to be cautious as to what could constitute canonical equivalents, perhaps out of concern that too much canon deviation (time period, setting, profession, gender, sexuality) risks violating the world of the show and, consequently, believability and audience immersion. Perhaps by keeping Sherlock's Belstaff as a "man's greatcoat," reckonedrightly more easily treads the difficult line between alternate universe and the *Sherlock* world, in which Sherlock's masculinity derives from the nineteenth-century Arthur Conan Doyle universe.

Alternate Universe Fanfic and Possible World Theory

Alternate universe fanfics explicitly frame the fanfic's connection to the established *Sherlock* world by foregrounding how the AU relates to the already established world. The original storyworld defines the foundational parameters to which all fanfics adhere. Beyond transporting and adopting the primary characterization elements established in the original world, several AU fanfics use the trope of alternate realities to highlight the ways *all* fanfic reimagines other possible directions the original storyworld could have taken. Uniting the different versions, however, is consistency of characterization as defined in the original world. At a simple level, for example, although the majority of *The Bang and the Clatter* is about an American baseball AU, author earlgreytea68 can't resist the chance to explicitly explore the concept of possible worlds inherent in fanfiction. When talking to Sherlock about whether he regretted not going to medical school, baseball!John states: "I don't regret it, not really, I just . . . I wish we got more than one life, you know? I wish I could know what would have happened if I'd gone that route" (chapter 2). AU fics explore exactly that opportunity: What if canonical figures got more than one life, and what would have happened if they'd followed some other specific route?

A popular *Sherlock* fan author writing as bendingsignpost regularly explores possible worlds in his AU fics. Known for his work *Bel Canto*, a *Sherlock/Phantom of the Opera* crossover, as well as the vampire AU, *Stranger at the Gate*, his most interesting series dealing with this question is the Watches Universe. A two-part story comprising *The World on His Wrist* (*TWOHW*) and "Elsewhere Come Morning" ("ECM"), the story has John time-jumping across four different parallel universes every time he falls asleep. John is conscious of the world changing, but he doesn't know what causes it or how to fix it. As the summary for *The World on His Wrist* explains: "The AU of AUs: First, he is shot in Afghanistan (again). Second, he wakes on a boat. Third is pain, fourth is normalcy, fifth is agony, and sixth is confusion. By the tenth, he's lost hope" (bendingsignpost, *TWOHW* Summary).[7] John uses different watches (analogue or digital, brown leather band or black) to help him keep track of each universe as he travels. In one world, John is still a surgeon at a Chelmsford hospital; he never went into the military, his life never intersects Sherlock's, and he follows Sherlock's career and life through the internet and news. In another modern-day London world in which John doesn't meet Sherlock he gets another roommate, the divorced Derek, and lives his post-war life *sans* "skulls or experiments or taxidermied animals with headphones on" where John can "safely open the fridge and Derek loves a good movie reference" (bendingsignpost, *TWOHW* chapter 3). Because John is conscious of the world swapping, he begins to recognize the infinite number of alternatives he may be experiencing across multiple possible worlds. When he thinks about the basic plot the reader knows from *Sherlock* (which John thinks of as his primary life, that is, *the canon*), he recognizes that every possible outcome has already happened in an alternate universe:

> Everything happens somewhere. Somewhere, outside of John's life, Mrs. Hudson did die [referencing the end of "The Reichenbach Fall" (S2E3)]. Or maybe she didn't, Sherlock already dead and Moriarty without a need of a hostage. He doesn't know, not really, but it's all possible. It's all so very possible. (bendingsignpost, "ECM" chapter 4)

Postulating alternate storylines highlights the "fictionality of all narrative" (Mittell "Strategies" 273–74). As Aristotle maintains, "it is not the poet's business to tell what happens but the kind of things that would happen— what is possible according to possibility and necessity" (quoted in Pavel 46). While all fiction provides writers with the space in which to imagine the kind of things that happen in their fictional worlds, AU fanfics apply Aristotle's ideas explicitly to an already established canonical world and, in so doing, provide invaluable insight into canon, characterization, and world building.

John experiences a great deal of confusion moving among his different universes. In one, he goes back to the surgery in London, assures his girlfriend, Sarah, from "The Blind Banker" (S1E2) that "he's all right, and neglects to mention that he may have drunkenly cheated on her with a bloke in a parallel universe" (bendingsignpost, *TWOHW* chapter 5). In the sequel, "Elsewhere Come Morning," John initially tries to get Sherlock to figure out what's happening to him and to help him solve it by using his prior-day knowledge to predict the day's sports scores, news headlines, and other major events. When he finally tells Sherlock what's happening, Sherlock mistakenly thinks of John's experience as time travelling. "'You looked up the scores online in an alternate reality, then travelled back in time by going to sleep,'" Sherlock tries to explain. "'I don't time travel, I reality swap. There's a difference,'" John retorts (bendingsignpost, "ECM" chapter 5). It's important for John that Sherlock understand his experience as an alternate reality, not as the same reality in different time periods, to realize that he is living multiple possibilities for their lives together, not just a nonlinear experience of the same lives. This seems key to understanding the role alternate universe fanfiction plays in world building and canonicity, since the fic's explicit connection to an already established world defines its fundamental parameters. John is still John in every one of the Watches parallel universes explored in the story, even though the plots, settings, and even character relationships are all different. While each narrative thread explores a different alternate reality (as all fanfics do), the characters remain consistent with themselves and with the world of the show. Thus, no matter how many elements are changed within the fanfiction world, as long as the characters remain consistent with the original world, the fanfic stays canonically compliant as well.

These explicit references to parallel universes and alternate realities make the Watches universe exceedingly interesting as an AU. On one level, the various alternate universes provide ample space for John (and bendingsignpost) to explore what identity means. As an individual, John

> never doubted who he is. John H. Watson is Dr. Watson is Captain Watson. He is a doctor and a soldier, a surgeon and a fighter. He is a straight man who will someday marry, have children, and take his family on holiday to Devon in the summers. He will not be an alcoholic. He will not hit his wife or curse his daughter or alienate his son. This is the life he'd chosen, so very long ago when he'd had but one life to choose. He'd chosen this life, trained for it. It's not everything he's ever wanted, but no life is. No one life can be. (bendingsignpost, *TWOHW* chapter 7)

In a sense, John recognizes that he is all of the John Watsons that he experiences in the various worlds: a doctor, a soldier, a surgeon, and a fighter. But he also recognizes that "no one life" can fulfill every dream and identity that an individual might imagine for herself. We can't have everything we've ever wanted; with all of these opportunities, John emphasizes that he chose and trained for the life he's living now, which provides a sense of agency, both for the reader and for the characters and writer.

"Elsewhere Come Morning" concludes with John trying to remain in the one reality where he's happiest—that is, the one where he is in a romantic relationship with Sherlock. As he explains to Sherlock earlier in *The World on His Wrist*, "'I don't want to go anymore.' He wants this, just this, because this is more than enough and he's tired of waiting for it. This is the best of all worlds. He's seen them, he knows" (chapter 5). Because John (like the average fanfic reader) has been able to experience multiple alternate realities where he either doesn't know Sherlock or isn't in a relationship with Sherlock, he can better decide which reality is the best fit for his desires. Much like a fan chooses a specific fandom to follow, a certain OTP (one true pairing) to support, and/or a specific genre of fic to read, bendingsignpost's John knows some of the possible worlds out there and chooses the one to which he wants to remain faithful.

For some theorists, such as Anne Kustritz and Jack Halberstam, AUs also provide authors and readers with ways to challenge traditional patriarchal heteronormative narratives that prescribe "one single life path that ends in heterosexual marriage and children," implying that any other alternatives are abnormal (Kustritz, "They All Lived" 5). As an alternative, Halberstam postulates a "queer time" model to "describe the many alternate ways a lifetime might be structured when the normative ways of organizing time and narrating it into coherence, are abandoned" (quoted in Kustritz 5). Queer time seems particularly apt when applied to AU fanfic, so much of which explores queer identity and nonheteronormative relationships and characters. In proposing various alternate realities and alternate storylines to the original *Sherlock* canon, AUs "offer a gentle form of critique" (Kustritz, "They All Lived" 8), whether of patriarchal heteronormative narratives or of the canon and characterization itself.

Although AUs seem, on the surface, to displace the world of the show with an alternate reality, when we look more closely at the central components of that new world we can identify all of the world elements that made the show so popular to begin with; the story remains, for the most part, world compliant, even if it isn't *canon* compliant. In terms of the example *Sherlock* AUs analyzed here, the iconic 221b Baker Street flat remains a reassuring staple for our protagonists, in one form or another. But even more importantly, the characters themselves remain consistent with those established in the original world, even when the entire surrounding environment has changed. For instance, several different characters pick up and use readily identifiable catchphrases from the original show, and Sherlock and John's physical appearance, behaviors, and temperaments remain consistent with those originally established in *Sherlock*'s world. The amount of time the AU fanfic writers discussed here spend on the physical characteristics of the actors playing the *Sherlock* characters, in particular, reinforces the importance of character in world building. Because character in the case of *Sherlock*'s world is so enmeshed with the physical descriptions of the actors embodying the roles, the actors' bodies become inseparable from the characters they portray. In fact, character identity at times becomes so dominant that fanfic writers and audiences erase the boundaries between fanfic worlds and the *Sherlock* world altogether.

CHAPTER SIX

INVASION OF THE BODY SNATCHERS
World Building and Real Person Fiction

Thus far we have explored the range of *Sherlock* fanfic from mostly canon-compliant case fic to out-there alternate universe stories. Here we explore real person fiction (RPF) and what happens when the boundaries between the fictional world and the real world disappear altogether. As the previous chapter on alternate universe fanfic concluded, fan writers often fetishize and indelibly link television actors' bodies with the fictional character, making character the defining element of the canonical world. When all other canonical elements change—the character's sexual and gender identities, the setting, and, in the case of RPF, even the fictional apparatus itself—fanfic remains in-world as long as the characterization remains consistent with the canon. Moving beyond traditional alternate universe fanfic, RPF erases the boundaries of the fictional world and focuses instead on the actual lives of the actors portraying the characters in the world.

Like many other fanfiction origin stories, most scholars place the beginnings of RPF in 1960s *Star Trek* fandom; however, instances of RPF appear much earlier in literary history, if you include works such as Shakespeare's *Richard III* or Marlowe's *Tamburlaine the Great*. Any fiction written about real people might be called RPF. Steven Spielberg's 2012 Oscar-winning *Lincoln* and Theodore Melfi's 2016 *Hidden Figures* are more recent examples. As frequent and accepted as historical fiction has been in the wider culture, however, its use and reception in fandom has been much more contentious.

Real person fic has been foundational to the Sherlock Holmes fandom for over a century, but in an almost inverted form: rather than writing fiction about real people, Sherlockians treat fictional characters as if they were real. Nearly from Sherlock Holmes's first appearance, fans have persistently treated Holmes and Watson as if they were real people. As T. S. Eliot remarked in 1929, "Perhaps the greatest of the Sherlock Holmes mysteries is this: that when we talk of him we invariably fall into the fancy of his existence" (quoted in Plakotaris 40). Arthur Conan Doyle was delighted to learn that a group of French schoolboys wanted to visit Holmes's flat at 221b Baker Street (Doyle, *Memories* 108), and hundreds of fans wrote letters to Holmes when the Abbey National Bank opened its doors at that address in the 1930s. Doyle also received mail at his home addressed to Sherlock Holmes and requests for information and memorabilia relating to the great detective: "I get many letters from all over the country about Sherlock Holmes," Doyle told the *Bookman* magazine. "Sometimes from schoolboys, sometimes from commercial travelers who are great readers, sometimes from lawyers pointing out mistakes in my law. One letter actually contained a request for portraits of Sherlock at different periods of his life" (Doyle, quoted in Stashower 132). One of the author's earliest, and oddest requests, came in 1890 from a tobacconist in Philadelphia who asked for a copy of Holmes's monograph on tobacco ash (Montgomery 98). For fun, Doyle sometimes sent postcards in response lamenting that the detective was away and unable to respond personally, and he often cheekily signed such missives "Dr. Watson," perpetuating the illusion that Holmes and Watson were real figures (Stashower 132). When Doyle gave speaking tours in the United States, audiences were often disappointed the man was not, as described, "a cadaverous looking person with marks of cocaine injections all over him" (Jann 13). Some early Sherlock Holmes fans, then, believed Holmes and Watson were real people and often saw Arthur Conan Doyle himself as a stand-in for his fictional creation.

Keep Holmes Alive societies in the 1930s helped perpetuate the illusion that Holmes and Watson were historical figures, and these organizations created and participated in several fan practices to memorialize Holmes and Watson's real lives. The Amateur Mendicant Society of Detroit, for example, presented a plaque to St. Bartholomew's Hospital commemorating the first meeting between Holmes and Watson in the hospital's lab. The plaque, now located in the hospital's on-site museum, reads: "At this place New Year's Day, 1881 were spoken these deathless words: 'You have been in Afghanistan, I perceive' by Mr. Sherlock Holmes in greeting to John H. Watson, M. D. at their first meeting" (Rennison 44). Since then, fan organizations have commemorated other significant sites from the canon, including a plaque at the Reichenbach Falls in Meiringen, Switzerland, memorializing the plunge over the cliff of Holmes and Moriarty in "The Final Problem," and a plaque denoting Watson's lunch meeting with his army buddy, Mike Stamford, at the Criterion restaurant in Piccadilly, which led Stamford to introduce Watson and Holmes at St. Bart's, as recorded in *A Study in Scarlet*. Even the modern-day Sherlock Holmes Museum at 239 Baker Street has a fake blue heritage plaque claiming the location was Holmes's residence and office in the early 1880s. Such memorialization helps past and present fans retain the belief that Holmes and Watson were historical figures in 1880s London.

"Great Game" scholars' mock publications claimed that Arthur Conan Doyle, rather than being the creator and author of the Sherlock Holmes character, was merely Watson's literary "editor," something that has irked the Doyle estate no end for decades. Sherlockians worldwide continue to contribute to a range of Great Game scholarship—detailing Holmes's lineage, critically reviewing Watson's alleged medical journal articles on ocular surgery, and offering alternate theories about Holmes's cases—and receive wide circulation through the *Baker Street Journal*. The authors of these essays write about Holmes and Watson as if they were real, building an entire body of scholarship and speculation around the alleged lives and accomplishments of fictional characters.

Outside scholarship, Sherlock Holmes aficionados frequently blur the line between the stories' fiction and the characters' presumed real lives. Each year on January 6, for example, the Baker Street Irregulars and the Sherlock Holmes Society of London host a weekend of celebrations in honor of Holmes's birthday; of course, Holmes's actual birthdate is unknown, but the global societies have agreed on a common date on which to recognize the great detective's appearance in the world. When new members are invested into the Baker Street Irregulars each year at the annual birthday bash, they are assigned a moniker based on a character from the original stories, assuming the character's identity and name for purposes of all BSI correspondence. In 1968, more than forty Sherlockians (and twice as many reporters!) dressed up as Holmesian characters and made a pilgrimage to the Reichenbach Falls in Switzerland to reenact Holmes's hand-to-hand battle with Professor Moriarty, with Society President Lord Gore-Booth playing Holmes and lead barrister Charles Scholefield as Moriarty. The battle was momentous enough that it was the lead story that evening on the BBC World Service. As of 2012, the London Society had traveled to Switzerland seven times times (Sherlock Holmes Society). Sherlock Holmes fandom is remarkable for this investment in the reality of the characters in the world, not just in their realism within the stories. From the outset, fans engaged with the characters outside the texts as real people and indicated a desire to extend the world of the stories into their own lives.

Unlike the Great Gamers, who seek to become the literary characters themselves, a contemporary fan's first encounter with a text is often through a media franchise already populated with particular actors with unique appearances and mannerisms. These fans' mental images are thus formed from the first by actors rather than from their own imaginative constructs. The actor's body becomes imbued with aspects of the fictional character, sometimes to the point where, for audiences, the actor and the role merge. Real person fic explores the ways fanfiction fetishizes actors' bodies to the point that they see the actors as indistinguishable from the characters. Fans of *Sherlock*, in imagining personal encounters with the performers who play their favorite *Sherlock* characters, ascribe to the actors particular lines and mannerisms established in the TV show, as if they constituted the actor's actual personality, manner of speaking, and behavior. Fans construct RPF stories in several ways, and all of them raise important ethical and ontological questions concerning reality, fiction, embodiment, identity, and performance.

RPF Genres

Like other fanfic genres, RPF contains various subgenres. The most popular, self-insert RPF, recounts a first- or second-person tale in which the author imagines meeting or being in a relationship with a favorite celebrity; while some self-insert fics create an original fictional character who meets the celebrity, often these characters are thinly veiled representations of the author's identity and fantasies. This thin veil is perhaps one reason why so many fans dislike and distrust RPF: self-insert fanfic aligns closely with Mary Sue fanfiction, which inserts an idealized version of the author into the fictional world as simultaneous savior and primary love interest of the canonical character. Some fans, such as Lucy Jones, a One Direction slash writer, distinguish between RPF and self-insert fic altogether: "The whole point of RPF is that it's fiction: your characterization is fictional, the setting is fictional, the plot is fictional. . . . [Self-insert is] no longer completely fiction, because the person writing it isn't fictional, even if they are placed in a fictional environment" (quoted in Arrow 327). We'll go more into the differences between real and fictional persons a bit later, but Jones's claim is fascinating in how it differentiates between fictional characterizations of the author and fictional characterizations of the real people about whom the author is writing. Why is the fictional representation of Benedict Cumberbatch, for example, more imaginary than a fictional representation of the writer? RPF raises these questions, and more, about the (alleged) separation between reality and fiction.

One way to avoid dealing with a fictionalized author is to explore observer RPF. Observer RPFs "voyeuristically fantasize" about the private lives of favorite celebrities, including putting celebrities from the fan's favorite media franchise in slash relationships with other real-life people (Busse, "I'm Jealous" 256); the author or a simulacrum of the author rarely appears in such stories. Some fans (called "Tin Hats" because of their alleged similarities to conspiracy theorists) have been accused of taking these observer fantasies too far by claiming that their imagined celebrity romantic relationships actually exist in the real world and that the celebrities' agents and producers are conspiring in a cover up to conceal them (B. Thomas, "Fans Behaving Badly" 174). Such attitudes and behaviors perhaps explain why even many fanfiction authors view RPF with suspicion, portraying it as a "delusional" attempt, by young female fans in particular, to fulfill their personal fantasies of having a real-world encounter or relationship with the object of their adoration (Arrow 325–26).[1] While self-insert and observer fanfics have been around since the late 1960s, new social media platforms have created opportunities for more developments in RPF. Originating on Tumblr in 2010, "imagines" are a version of self-insert RPF that strive to break down the lines between fictional character and reader. Rather than creating an original fictional character or writing in first or second person, imagines ask the readers to literally insert their names, eye color, hair color, and other physical characteristics at designated places in the fic to personalize it as much as possible. Imagines sometimes involve readers with real-world celebrities; at other times, they engage the reader in a fantasy with a favorite fictional character. In the Imagine "Sherlock Whispers (Sherlock x Reader)," a fluff fic (a story primarily focused on fuzzy, happy feelings), author 1001Fangirls imagines what Sherlock might say in his sleep. Although the fic begins in second person—"'Sherlock!' pulling the cold hand out of the fridge, *you* debated what *you* were going to do with the hand" (emphasis added)—the story quickly turns to the Imagine trademark signal "(y/n)" ("your name") format: "You heard a small whisper coming from the man in front of you. Leaning in closer to him, you hear another whisper. '(Y/n), (y/n), come here.' He started shifting a bit, and you feared he was waking up already, but he was just rolling in his sleep" (1001Fangirls). While some fans might find such interrogatories jarring, others argue that not limiting the reader by name or description allows for greater immersion and verisimilitude (Angelfire "Imagines"); the reader becomes the character by inserting her own name, eye color, and hair color. Much as traditional RPFs and other fanfics focus on the physical attributes and personalities of the actors playing the fictional characters, imagines invite the reader to bring her own body into the fictional world. The reader, by bringing her real body into the fictional construct of the fanfic, helps break down the boundaries between her real identity and the fictionalized encounter with the actor. Regardless of whether fans insert themselves directly into fics with real celebrities or creatively imagine a celebrity's private life without their personal intervention, however, RPF frequently meets with criticism both within the fandom world and outside it for its alleged violation of the boundaries between fictional and real worlds and between characters and real people.

The Ethics of RPF Fanfiction

While most debates about the ethics of RPF take place within specific fandoms and in fandom fora, more recent critics (Thomas, Arrow, McGee, Hagen, Busse, and Piper) have begun to explore the ramifications of the genre for larger fannish practices. Arguments against RPF are numerous. Fanlore has labeled the genre "wrong, creepy, very extremely icky," "a horrific breech of bad taste, common sense, and basic human rights," and "the height of bad manners and bad taste" (Fanlore, "RPF"). Other condemnations include "offensive" (Busse, "My Life" 215–16) and a violation of the celebrity's right to privacy (B. Thomas 175; Fanlore, "RPF";

Busse, "My Life" 215–26). Some fans even argue that RPF turns people into objects, denying them their basic human rights (Fanlore, "RPF) or their personhood (McGee 175–76) and subsequently dehumanizing them (Piper 2.4). Some fans deem the practice so "dangerous" that it borders on illegality and even libelous treatment of celebrities (Fanlore, "RPF"), although other fans counter that since erotic fanfic, particularly RPF, "does not require actors or any other real people to perform" actual sex acts, "readers don't have to worry about the objectification or exploitation of these people," unlike in film or photographic pornography (Coppa, *Fanfiction Reader* 14). RPF advocates maintain that it is acceptable because it merely offers textual *representations* of the actors' bodies; it does not involve the actual bodies themselves.

Fans writing RPF are aware of the positions opposed to their chosen genre, and their stories often reference these fandom attitudes and their own fears of being attacked for writing in this particular genre. For instance, in the AU *Performance in a Leading Role*, author Mad_Lori explicitly states in a note in chapter 3 that the fic is *not* RPF:

> I'd like to just clarify one thing: THIS IS NOT RPF. This story is in no way real-person fic. There are cameos by real people in it, yes, because of the setting of the story and it was easier than making up a whole bunch of fellow actors and directors to populate Hollywood (that's harder than it sounds). But Sherlock and John are characters. Neither of them are meant to be skins over the actors who play them, whom I hope they do not much resemble except in the physical. Their personalities and backgrounds are meant to reflect their characters, not the personalities of the actors. (Mad_Lori chapter 3)

Mad_Lori explains that while her *Sherlock* AU takes place in the real world of Hollywood film and references real actors, the story itself should not be confused with RPF because none of the real characters play a major role or are fully developed. *Performance in a Leading Role* isn't a story about Benedict Cumberbatch and Martin Freeman, the actors who play Sherlock Holmes and John Watson on the BBC's *Sherlock*, Mad_Lori asserts; it's a fictionalized story about fictionalized characters more than one hundred years old. Mad_Lori distinguishes subject matter or focus, main characters, and peripheral characters. Because Sherlock and John are fictional and are portrayed in a fictionalized version of contemporary Hollywood,

they are not "meant to be skins over the actors who play them" (Mad_
Lori), even though it is often the very transparency of that skin between
actor and character that allows fans to explore fictional worlds through
their own creations.

Splix71, author of the RPF *Method Act* expressed similar fears on her
Tumblr that readers would attack her or her fic because of its genre:

> There are several people who have said "I don't like RPS [Real Person
> Slash], but I like this!" which is also fantastic, but I'm petrified that
> I'm going to freak [readers] out at some point and I'm going to get my
> head chomped off. I get that some people abhor RPS/RPF. Different
> strokes. I didn't care for it myself for some time. . . . Later on, I read
> a book by Michael Korda called *The Immortals*, which is, at its core,
> explicit John F. Kennedy / Marilyn Monroe fanfiction and figured fuck
> it, he's getting paid, I'm not going to have any compunctions about
> reading it or writing it for free. . . . Probably the best thing to do is to
> presume that everyone knows what they're getting into and won't wig
> out. (Splix71, "Real Person")

While more fans and critics take time to explain why RPF is unethical,
some also do attempt to defend or justify the genre, whether by comparison with commercially produced historical fiction or in terms of postmodern identity. For instance, emmagrant01, the author of the *Sherlock* slash
fic "A Cure for Boredom" discussed in chapter 3, praised Splix71's *Method
Act* while sharing her own concerns about RPF:

> I remember back a decade ago when I was squeamish about RPF.
> Heh. And then I wrote some . . . and realized that it was really just
> another kind of fic. Celebrity fantasy fic has a tremendous history
> outside of and predating modern fandom, so it's not like this is a new
> thing, you know? Like a lot of what we write, it's intended for our own
> consumption, and that is perfectly fine IMNSHO. (emmagrant01,
> "eep")

For emmagrant01, RPF is a legitimate genre because it has a long history
in the commercial literary tradition.

The popularity in the early 1990s of popslash and boyband RPF helped
dispel many qualms against the genre. Recently, scholars including
Kristina Busse, Francesca Coppa, Jennifer McGee, and Ross Hagen have

observed that changing attitudes toward homosexuality (especially in the lives of public figures), combined with postmodern ideas about representation, identity, and selfhood, have opened up RPF as a serious and accepted form of fan writing. The main underlying question in RPF is whether celebrities are real people or personas (Coppa, *Fanfiction Reader* 102). Many RPF fans and authors argue that "the 'people' being written about are not really people at all. . . . They are fully constructed personas, created for the consumption of the public in the same way entirely fictional characters are" (McGee 174). RPF fans see a celebrity's public persona as different from his or her lived private life (Hagen 48). Once fans understand a celebrity as a constructed persona, that is, as a story composed using public appearances, press releases, and other media paratexts, fanfiction becomes just one more story within that larger body of narratives (Coppa, *Fanfiction Reader* 102). Rather than dehumanizing these public figures by denying them agency and personhood, as some anti-RPF fans argue, RPF actually rehumanizes celebrities by inventing "backstories and inner lives" (Busse, "I'm Jealous" 256).[2]

Celebrity Studies, Selfhood, and Authenticity

Interrogating questions of character, authenticity, and public personas versus internal selves has been a major focus of interest in recent celebrity studies scholarship. Christine Gledhill carefully delineates the difference between fictional characters, real people, and public personas, for example, where film or television characters are "relatively formed and fixed by fictional and stereotypical conventions" (Gledhill 214–15). Previous discussion in this book addressed the significant role of genre in establishing character and inaugurating the parameters outlining how characters can and cannot operate. Authors are somewhat limited by the narrative structures they have chosen in setting out paths for their fictional characters. Characters, therefore are often seen as static entities, rather than accorded the fullness of philosophical concepts composing the notion of persons; characters are, rather, constant public signs signifying meaning within a specific context (Lamb 272, 278). Fictional characters are "nobody in particular," in that literary conventions define them as both unique and a type (Gallagher, quoted in Lamb 272–73). For instance, Arthur Conan Doyle's Sherlock Holmes is both the distinct individual character existing in fin-de-siècle London, solving crimes with his partner, Dr. Watson, and an archetypal fictional detective character-type from the emerging mystery genre who follows genre-specific patterns and conventions. In contrast, persons are private and dynamic, fulfill a narrower idiosyncratic role, and possess "inaccessible particularity" (Lamb 272, 278). For Gledhill, "The real person is the site of amorphous and shifting bodily attributes, instincts, psychic drives and experiences" (214-15). Individual people are much harder to type because they constantly evolve and change. Thus, persons appear to be authentic while fictional characters appear fabricated.

The authentic self, therefore, depends on the opposition of private and public to survive. Utilizing language surprisingly similar to that used to describe media adaptation, individuals are said to possess "an inner, irreducible essence, a 'real self' behind whatever public face, or mask, they might project" (Tolson 445). This real me contains the specific feelings, desires, needs, and abilities that makes each person unique (Guignon 6). As Tolson and others have argued, however, this perception of the real self could be construed as essentialist—that is, as something that is physically and essentially tied to the physical self: the real self is believed to be housed inside the body and is something you are born with rather than something that is culturally constructed and constantly changing. Tolson, in contrast, believes the self is actually the result of an interpretation and performance of these internalized elements (452). Individuals must perform and express these inner constellations to the public world, enabling others in that world to know and engage with the real self hidden behind the public mask. This performance becomes a mediated representation of the authentic self.

Erving Goffman was one of the first to identify the conflation of inner self and performative self in his notable work, *The Presentation of the Self in Everyday Life* (1969). Highlighting the frequent interchangeability of personal and fictional character, Goffman explains: "In our society, the character one performs and one's self are somewhat equated, and this self-as-character is usually seen as something housed within the body of its possessor, especially the upper parts thereof, being a nodule somehow, in the psychobiology of personality" (252). Goffman was the forerunner of a postmodern reconceptualization of the self, led by scholars like Anthony Giddens and Stuart Hall, who argued that the postmodern self was not lodged in some inner recess of the individual's psyche or DNA but should rather be seen as a "process of becoming," a constructed identity always "at play" (Bennett 31). This decentered self took much of its import from the late nineteenth-century philosopher William James, who claimed that

> a man has as many social selves as there are [groups of] individuals who recognize him and carry an image of him in their mind. . . . He generally shows a different side of himself to each of these different groups. . . . From this there results what practically is a division of the man into several selves; and this may be a discordant splitting . . . or it may be a perfectly harmonious division of labor. (Quoted in Guignon 110)

Goffman, Giddens, Stuart, and James are all defining what has come to be known as the persona, the public performance of the internal self, tailored to specific audiences and situations. One doesn't perform the same self for one's supervisor as one does with one's friends or children. The role of the persona is to "form the private life into a public and emblematic shape, drawing on general social types and film roles, while deriving authenticity from the unpredictability of the real person" (Gledhill 214–15). In terms of film and media professionals, an actor's persona is defined and limited by already existing social types, and the public always already sees the celebrity's persona through the previous film roles she/he may have portrayed. The persona becomes an emblem, a sign representing the performer's alleged inner self. Like its derivative, person, persona signals the mask a person wears for the external world (Guignon 35). Admitting that the persona exists seems to imply, by default, an inner self to perform. Thus, the persona's performance appears to fans as an authentic representation of the star's true self: "not as something purposefully put together" but as "an unintentional product of the individual's unself-conscious response to the facts in his situation" (Goffman 70).

Celebrities may have several levels of public persona, as P. David Marshall has argued, especially in the age of social media. A celebrity's public persona is the face used for most public appearances, the industrial model put forward by the celebrity's agent or management team. Several public events demand that celebrities present a distinctly public persona to the audience, including, for example, red carpet events, awards ceremonies, interviews, and press junkets. Fans seem to clearly understand that at these appearances they are seeing the stars' public personas; the celebrity attends the event or speaks with reporters to promote and represent a current professional project. But in other cases, fans may not be able to tell whether they are seeing the public persona or the real celebrity. For instance, Benedict Cumberbatch's viral photograph photobombing U2 at the 2014 Oscars became an internet sensation and inspired dozens of popular memes with Cumberbatch photobombing everything from Leonardo's *Last Supper* to *Doctor Who* (Phillips and Tucker). Similarly, the numerous images on the web of Martin Freeman giving the middle finger to photographers, paparazzi, fans, and other celebrities make fans think they are seeing the real Martin Freeman behind the public persona. One could argue, however, that these public performances of noncompliant selfhood (violating polite protocols at the Oscars, making obscene gestures to photographers) are a form of transgressive intimate selfhood—just another public persona presented to the masses. I use the term transgressive intimate selfhood—originally conceptualized by Marshall as a specifically online persona that seems to reveal a celebrity's real internal, emotional, and psychological states in ways that do not seem to be mediated (Marshall 44–45)—to describe similar public performances in which stars appear to give viewers a glimpse into their authentic, yet transgressive selves.

Social Media, Authenticity, and the Transgressive Self

New social media platforms are changing the face of celebrity/ fan interaction and have provided fans with seemingly limitless access to celebrities' inner lives. Stars can now choose to maintain and curate a particular yet fabricated intimate version of what Marshall calls "public private" identity on platforms such as Twitter and Facebook (Marshall 44–45). While the authenticity of the self represented online can be problematic—famous people can self-edit their profiles, pics, and content, and they can intersperse seemingly private elements with material from their professional, public life (Hills, "From Para-Social" 475)—social media also "promises the revelation of the 'authentic self' via a more immediate, intimate connection with audiences" (Bennett 170). In a public platform where stars seem to reveal their personal thoughts, lives, and relationships, fans can seem to be engaging directly with the star by direct tweeting, commenting, liking, retweeting, and replying. The public, participatory, and open platform on Twitter has potentially changed the typical dynamic between Big Name Star and anonymous fan, replacing an imaginary experience of connection with public, visible conversations that directly involve the celebrity and follower (Hills, "From Para-Social" 473).

Although neither Martin Freeman nor Benedict Cumberbatch is on social media, their authentic selves are often represented through friends' tweets, twitpics, Facebook status updates, and so on. Fans get a glimpse into the stars' real lives through such mediations. For instance, Cumberbatch's best friend and partner, Adam Ackland, published twitpics of Cumberbatch as Ackland's son's godfather. Likewise, longtime school friend and concert pianist James Rhodes frequently tweets about his social interactions with Cumberbatch: "so BendyDick Comeonmybaps comes for dinner and brings cake. Minus a giant slice. Who does that?!" (October 7, 2012). Both of these examples give fans insight, albeit peripherally through his friends, of Cumberbatch's intimate, private self. Likewise, Martin Freeman's former partner, Amanda Abbington, is an active tweeter (@chimpsinsocks) and frequently posts about *Sherlock* filming and life with Freeman. In addition to manufactured home photo shoots with the family and dogs, Abbington also gives audiences glimpses into her private home life with Freeman, commenting on their work, likes, and animals, as seen in a Twitter video of Abbington singing Pharrell's "Happy" to her pet (September 20, 2015). Although *Sherlock* fans never have direct access to Freeman's comments, thoughts, or pictures, they believe these images of his private life are, in fact, private and that they are somehow getting an insider's look into the actor's real life.

The use of Twitter by some of Cumberbatch's co-workers incidentally provides fans with information on the actor's whereabouts and social activities. During the filming of *Star Trek: Into Darkness*, Spock actor Zach Quinto tweeted an image of Cumberbatch with the rest of the cast watching a ball game in a northern California bar (May 5, 2012). After the broadcast of *Sherlock* season three, actress Louise Brealey (*Sherlock*'s Molly Hooper) tweeted about the much-commented-upon scene from season two in which Sherlock, after seeming to jump to his death in "The Reichenbach Fall," bursts through a St. Bart's window and passionately kisses Molly: "Four takes, since you're asking. *professional face* IT WAS TRICKY TO GET RIGHT. #SherlockLives #SherlockSnogs" (January 1, 2014). Brealey's tweet both gives fans a professional's insight into the behind the scenes action and allows *Sherlock*'s primarily female audience to experience the scene vicariously.

Adam Ackland's 2012 twitpic of Cumberbatch riding his bike for the Prince's Trust Foundation illustrates the blurred line between the actor's public private self and the public persona he uses to sell his professional accomplishments, in this case to further a charitable cause. One could argue that posed celebrity photoshoots perform a similar function. Some, like a photo op from a *Dogs Today* article from May 2009, shows what appears to be a casual, informal snap of Freeman, his former partner, Amanda Abbington, and their dog. Others, like a prerecorded image from Reddit.com of Benedict Cumberbatch in a robe drinking tea, gives viewers the impression that they are seeing the real Cumberbatch—sans make-up, sans costume, even sans clothing! The reality, of course, is that all of these images are carefully constructed representations of the public-private persona that the actors' agents want them to project to their fans and are designed to increase viewership, sales, and investment in the actors' characters. Such social media creation leads fans to a sense of intimacy, making them feel they really know the actors, are seeing behind the screen, and are being invited into the lives and homes of the celebrities they cherish.

Given the multiple personas and selves being performed in private, public-private, and publicly professional spheres, fans unsurprisingly sometimes blur the distinctions among actors, personas, and fictional on-screen characters. Many fans seek to know the true private self of the celebrity that is unknown to others (Bennett 30); however, because stars "collapse this distinction between the actor's authenticity and the authentification of the character s/he is playing" (Dyer 21), the distinction is often confusing. Some fans chronicle encounters with the show's actual filming and set locations and activities, a pursuit known as setlock. Setlock photos of Benedict Cumberbatch in his *Sherlock* costumes, for example, complicate the relationship between the fictional character Cumberbatch plays and Cumberbatch as a real person, particularly because he is often seen engaging with fans ostensibly as himself, taking photos of fans with his iPhone while in his *Sherlock* costume, standing in the doorway of 221b, or taking group photos in his *Sherlock* suits. In these scenarios, fans recognize that Cumberbatch is not acting the role of Sherlock Holmes; however, they may not realize that the Benedict Cumberbatch they are seeing smiling and taking pictures with fans is also not the real Benedict Cumberbatch they've come to the set to see and meet. When fans combine these split notions of self and persona with the added element of Cumberbatch actually being in *Sherlock*'s costume, the three identities can become conflated into one.

Television Media, the Character/Actor Join, and Parasocial Relationships

Interestingly, this conflation of fictional character, actor, and persona seems particularly pervasive in the world of television and other serialized media. Karen Lury argues that television performers' defining characteristic lies in the tendency for the distinction between actor and character to become "notoriously blurred" in ways she sees as unique to the genre (118). Such confusion may be fostered by television's seriality and what Fiske describes as newness (150). In television serials such as *Sherlock*, audiences revisit characters, their lives, and their adventures regularly (often weekly) and thus seem to experience time and life events in similar timeframes (Fiske 150). Also, when a show begins to air, the actors usually participate in promotional interviews and appearances across a range of media platforms, from traditional newspaper and magazine articles to digital platforms, television talk shows, and photo shoots. This "contemporaneous cycle of promotion and broadcast" helps effect a slippage between the actor and character, since the audience sees them in both roles simultaneously on different media platforms (Ellis 106). Actor and fictional character thus become entangled in the audience's perception, a confusion that may be intensified by the knowledge that the actors' public appearances are effectively another form of acting, analogous to the celebrities' function within the TV show (Lury 117).

Perhaps one reason the character/actor join (Black 105) from serials is so strong is their power to foster parasocial relationships. Parasocial interactions (Horton and Wohl) describe an audience's identification and connection with media performers. In particular, direct address camera work—that is, shots in which the TV personality looks and speaks directly into the camera, seemingly directly to the audience—led spectators to imagine they had a personal relationship with the celebrity. *Sherlock* has employed such parasocial techniques, even though it is a fictional mystery and not a reality program. In "A Scandal in Belgravia" (S2E1), for example, Sherlock and John confer over an alleged murder case via Skype call. In his arguments with John and the detective inspector on duty, Sherlock speaks directly into the camera, ostensibly to John, but also to viewers.

Skype call (*Sherlock*,
"A Scandal in Belgravia")

According to Horton and Wohl, by directly addressing the camera and, seemingly, the viewer, the audience is "subtly insinuated . . . into the program's action and internal social relationships" where they are then "ambiguously transformed into a group which observes and participates in the show by turns." Many scholars have depicted parasocial interactions as delusional relationships, what Horton and Wohl term "one-sided, nondialectical, controlled by the performer, and not susceptible of mutual development," much like depictions of (female) fans over the last century. As a result, parasocial relationships have suffered significant social stigma in media and sociological research over the past few decades.[3]

The character/actor join is strengthened by television's ability to foster an imaginary social relationship between the actor and the viewer, particularly through the actor's physical appearance. As Tim Edwards explains in his analysis of gendered perceptions of celebrity, audiences primarily look at celebrities (male and female), whether through various performance platforms such as television, film, or theater, or through media outlets such as photographs and other recordings (157). An actor's physical appearance is therefore very important in shaping their persona, identity for, and relationship with their audience, and a star's significance is often measured in physical terms (Gledhill 210–11).[4] Fans often assume celebrities' bodies represent and house their fictional characters. Bodily movement, gesture, and facial expression become spontaneous, authentic language through which audiences can circumvent spoken language in understanding character (Gledhill 210), and the physicality of the actor, in particular, is used to reveal and perform the hidden, authentic self of the character (Piper 6.2). Character behaviors are often categorized into identifiable patterns of gesture, traits, and speech/syntax (Bordwell 13–14; Pearson, "Anatomising" 41–43), but the physical manifestations of character can also be signaled through clothing, insignia, sex, age, racial characteristics, size and looks, posture, facial expressions, and so on (Goffman 24). Television's repetitive serial format allows actors to reify the subtle emotional and psychological elements of their characters within the specific bodily performance.

Celebrity Bodies and/in RPF

Given the focus on performance of inner versus public selves and the importance of the (male) celebrity body in housing and enacting both the fictional and the real self, perhaps it is not surprising that RPF is becoming a more visible and popular fanfiction genre. RPF, in particular, explores these tensions between the real body and the fictional body, between the real world and the fictional universe. Melanie Piper's recent article, "Real Body, Fake Person: Recontextualizing Celebrity Bodies in Fandom and Film," explores the similarities between authorized biopics that focus on the lives of historical figures and the more disreputable world of RPF fanfiction. In both genres, the celebrities' physical bodies (and their star image) are appropriated by the creator to (re)enact a narrative of their personal and professional lives. Piper writes, RPF fanfics, specifically, "appropriate both the signifier of the celebrity's physical, private, off-screen self and the major signifier of the textual star image"—the physical body (2.2). She goes on to note that both biopics and RPFs appropriate the representation of the star's body, not the actual physical body itself, and use the image "as a means of representing character and the 'inner self'" (6.2).

Piper's distinction makes a few important clarifications. First, she attempts to identify and break down the stigma associated with RPF by comparing it to the established and well-received biopic genre. Second, she also sidesteps the most significant critique of RPF: that it invades celebrities' privacy and appropriates their bodies and identities for someone else's personal fantasy. Piper's thesis aligns with the thinking of several other postmodernists, who see both the self and fictional representations of that self as social constructions made up of disparate parts. Our interest here lies in how RPF fans "use the physical body in imagining the private self of a public figure" and the ways that body is mediated through various media (Piper 2.4). My argument builds on Piper's analysis of celebrity bodies in RPF and explores this embodiment in light of world building, canon formation, and (non)compliance in fanfiction.

What Is Canon in RPF?

Because celebrities exist in the real world and RPF fanfiction imagines narratives depicting these real stars' lives, the question of what constitutes canon becomes particularly problematic. Previous chapters focused on the various elements that make up *Sherlock*'s fictional world, primarily, setting, syntax, and the various elements of characterization. On the surface, RPF would seem to have nothing to do with *Sherlock*'s world: fans focus on their objects of interest (actors Benedict Cumberbatch and Martin Freeman) and then imagine them in various real-world scenarios, settings, and relationships. What one finds in Cumberbatch or Freeman RPFs, however, is a fascinating conflation of individual, persona, and fictional character—indeed, of fictional world. The question of world building and canon formation thus comes to a unique head when exploring why and how fans venture into *Sherlock* RPF and the ways in which they comment on and invoke the *Sherlock* world by creating situations that initially seem to lie far outside the show's original framework.

So what constitutes canon in RPF? On the one hand, scholars like V. Arrow and Kristina Busse initially argue that there is no such thing as canon-based RPF, period (Arrow 328; Busse, "My Life" 215). Actors' public personas are created by a vast number of media encounters and displays, ranging from print interviews to photoshoots to public appearances. Unlike a fictional world where the creator(s) or author(s) carefully choose and map out all of the defining elements of the canonical world, real people's lives are full of random moments. Thus, because no "true authority or true owner of the source text" exists, "no single canon source can be claimed" (Busse, "My Life" 215). In addition, the stars constantly add to the warehouse of persona moments, with new movie and TV roles, new interviews, and new public appearances happening all the time. Many fans and scholars likewise recognize that these media moments are manufactured (Arrow 328); they are part of the celebrity machine that works to promote the star's professional, artistic, and economic projects. While critics such as Kayleigh Thomas argue that each piece of celebrity media thus has to be taken as its own individual, unique canon (as noted in Arrow 329), others observe that fans take the disparate pieces of a celebrity's public media persona and use the disparate pieces to construct a "unified fanon, or whole picture of the celebrity" (Arrow 329). The star canon is thus created simultaneously by the celebrity, the media, and the fans (Busse, "My Life" 215).

Fans embarking on establishing a RPF canon based on an actor's real-life experience and media coverage must contend with the constant expansion of the material and even, occasionally, contradictory information and materials. The open-endedness of this material is one reason some scholars maintain that a celebrity canon does not and cannot exist. The mere potential for expansion does not preclude the possibility of a canonical world, however. As Mark Wolf explains, the media landscape includes different kinds of worlds, some of which derive from closed worlds (with established end points) and others of which remain open to new authorized extensions and additions. Both closed and open worlds have established canons, even though the latter may still be in development. Similarly, celebrity lives can also contain a unified canon, even though new experiences are added all the time. The celebrity self is always already mediated through the news, images, sound bites, film images, social media, and so on. If we agree that there is no real inner self, only performance, and that we can only access the celebrity self through mediation, then real authentic selves and mediated personas cannot be differentiated. What we find in RPF is a particular b(l)ending of the real-world celebrity persona and the fictional world, accomplished through an emphasis on the characters' bodies and physical characteristics.

The *Benedict Cumberbatch Sexual Frustration* Blog and RPF

Two sexual frustration RPF Tumblr blogs have been created that center on Benedict Cumberbatch and Martin Freeman. Both blogs are conglomerations of fan fantasies and self-insert fics focused primarily on sexual fantasies involving the authors and the actor in question. Many of the stories on the *Benedict Cumberbatch Sexual Frustration* blog establish a real-world canon through repeated references to Cumberbatch's personal interests and real-life experiences. "A Study in an Education" makes brief mention of Cumberbatch's previous smoking habit and his taste for gin and tonics, while "A Quick Hob-Nob" describes Cumberbatch in his motorcycle gear, a favorite subject in RPF and fan art: "His boots are slumped on the hall floor with his crash helmet, and there are spots of rain on the shoulders of the jacket hung next to your own" ("A Quick Hob-Nob"). Similarly, Splix71's RPF *Method Act* includes a reference to the often-mentioned carjacking incident when Cumberbatch was in South Africa filming *To the Ends of the Earth*: "Benedict's throat felt as if it were packed full of sand. A flurry of terrifying images whirled through his head: South Africa, that dark road, the chaos of that night he thought would be his last" (Splix71 chapter 11). In each of these examples, the fan makes deliberate use of real-world events to help define Cumberbatch's public persona and personal life and establish a consistent fanon of his life.

As we saw with other sexualized fic centered on the main male characters, the blogs focus primarily on fetishizing the dominant physical characteristics of the two actors, many of which have become objects of fascination within fanon. For instance, "A Study in an Education" from the *Benedict Cumberbatch Sexual Frustration* blog highlights Cumberbatch's "blue eyes," "ginger hair," and "the sharpest pair of cheekbones I'd ever seen." Reference to Cumberbatch's distinctive "blue-green eyes" appears again in "A Day at the Beach" as well as in numerous RPFs and other fanfictions. Another Cumberbatch body part frequently fetishized is his fingers. "A Quick Hob-Nob" mentions Cumberbatch's "long fingers curling round the mug" of tea, while "A Summer's Day" describes how "his eyes flit over the pages and when he reaches the last page slender fingers turn the page." References to Cumberbatch's lean hands and long fingers provide one of the most interesting examples of how his body becomes fragmented and hypersexualized within fandom. On the surface, fingers may not be erotic on their own, but in the *Sherlock* world Cumberbatch's hands play a unique role in establishing his character. Not only is Sherlock frequently seen with his fingers steepled under his chin in thought (a reference to the Doyle canon as well), they are also frequently seen in close-up as Sherlock plucks the strings of his violin or plays a tune. Thus, the identification of Benedict Cumberbatch's hands with Sherlock's character is clearly established within the world of the show, and eroticized reference to them in RPF similarly blurs the boundaries between Cumberbatch's real body and his fictional character's body.

Interestingly, Cumberbatch himself has noted the eroticization of Sherlock's hands and acknowledges similar confusion in distinguishing his own bodily features from those of Sherlock. In a March 2015 interview with Rebecca Merriman for Entertainmentwise.com, the actor rejected attempts by fans and reporters to pigeonhole Sherlock's sexuality. When pressed for what Sherlock would be like in bed, however, Cumberbatch replied, "It would be devastating. *I'd know* exactly where to put *my* fingers, where to put *my* tongue, where to put *my—his* I should say—*his fingers, his tongue*. Think about violinists, think about what they can do with their fingers" (Merriman; emphasis added). Not only does Cumberbatch fetishize his own body, through a *Sherlock* lens, but he also forgets, for a moment, that he is not, in fact, Sherlock Holmes. The real person and fictional character blended into one, reinforcing the character/actor join prevalent in television media. In this scenario, even the actor himself forgot the division between his fictional and real bodies.

In other RPFs, fans seem particularly interested in the perceived differences between real-world Cumberbatch and fictional *Sherlock* Cumberbatch. In "A Summer's Day," for example, the author notes Cumberbatch's signature curly hair but "[misses] his natural hair colour"; the current color is recognizably "Sherlock brown" rather than auburn. Thus, the actor's hair only signifies in relation to how it confirms or contrasts with the show's established canon. In another fantasy encounter, "A Day at the Beach," clearly set around the time Cumberbatch was in Los Angeles filming *Star Trek: Into Darkness* (2013), the author initially notes many of Cumberbatch's physical features, including his "trademark crooked smile" and "fantastic ass," before going into detail about the changes his body underwent to prepare for the physical demands of playing *Star Trek*'s Khan: "The change in his physique was simply stunning—I was used to seeing him as skinny Sherlock, but I'd managed to catch a glimpse of his much larger biceps and abdominal muscles" ("A Day at the Beach"). Once again, the fan defines Cumberbatch's real-world physique in terms of how it compares to his canonical *Sherlock* fictional representation, this reinforcing the world of *Sherlock* and eliding the separation between the real and fictional world.

The *Martin Freeman Sexual Frustration* Blog and RPF

In the stories on the *Martin Freeman Sexual Frustration* blog, Freeman is likewise fragmented and fetishized. Physically, he is described in terms including "polite, chivalrous, sarcastic, and smart" ("Over Pancakes and Django"), and his "his long eyelashes, and his button nose"

John at Angelo's
(*Sherlock*, "A Study
in Pink")

("Over Pancakes and Django") and eyes "the blue of deep ocean water, out in the middle of the Pacific" ("A Comic Con Fantasy") are similarly fetishized. His smile is described as "boyish, wide" and his hair as "blonder and his eyes are brighter, bluer, so intense" ("Sunscreen"). As we saw with the Cumberbatch RPFs, fans similarly highlight and repeat specific physical characteristics constituting the actor Martin Freeman in the public eye and the physical world. They also tend to focus on characteristics commonly noted in more traditional fanfic genres. Freeman's deep blue eyes often play a significant role in John Watson's physical descriptions, as does Freeman's dirty blonde or greying hair. Fans also often focus on Freeman's mouth and the frequency with which he purses and licks his lips. One favorite fan scene involving Freeman's frequent (subtextual?) lip-licking is in the dinner scene at Angelo's in season one, episode one when John asks about Sherlock's emotional attachments. John gazes into Sherlock's eyes as he waits for his response to "You've got a girlfriend, then?"

John's subsequent licking of his lips is seen by fans as a subliminal sexual response to Sherlock's availability, and the motif often appears in RPF stories. In the RPF "Sunscreen," for example, Freeman tilts his head "pointedly towards the sun, and then licks his lips (pink tongue wet mouth, the flash of rounded, white teeth)." Beyond describing the simple process of licking dry lips, the author's use of detail further fragments Freeman's already fetishized mouth.

While many more celebrity images and interviews of Benedict Cumberbatch appear on online, the *Martin Freeman Sexual Frustration* blog seems more complex in its treatment of Freeman's persona. In addition to itemizing his physical appearance, several stories also incorporate Freeman's personal interests (music, fashion), blur his fictional character and real-person persona, directly reference and quote from *Sherlock* in the realistic fiction, and consistently make appeals to realism and verisimilitude. A few stories make specific mention of Freeman's notorious mod style; "Over Pancakes and Django" and "Drive" both mention Freeman's fashionable sunglass collection as well as his well-known obsession with music, particularly Motown. In contrast, few of Cumberbatch's personal interests are mentioned online.

"Over Pancakes and Django" also seems to blur the distinction between Martin Freeman, the actor, and Martin Freeman as John Watson (that is, between persona and fictional character) by attributing some of John's canonical—and fanonical—behavior to his real-life person. As James Bennett explains, "Television actors are often subsumed within the character that they play, an illusion reinforced by their intertextual appearances in other media that emphasize a compare/contrast approach to the performer and their character" (14). Although Martin Freeman may not come across as nurturing or particularly domestic in most media outlets, this is part of his Watson portrayal in *Sherlock* and hence is frequently reinforced in traditional fanfiction. Like John in fanon, RPF Freeman is sometimes described as nurturing and as feeling contented when watching his partner eat ("Over Pancakes and Django"), two frequent tropes in contemporary fanfic portrayals of John Watson, as discussed in chapter 4. Another more explicitly *Sherlockian* RPF, from 2011, titled "The One Where Martin Role-Plays as Doctor Watson," specifically sets up a fantasy in which the speaker imagines asking the actor, Martin Freeman, to role play as Dr. John Watson in their private sexual fantasy. In the description leading up to the story, the author clarifies that Freeman would be "acting as John Watson" while she is "just another patient at the practice." The author inverts some of the Imagine genre tropes, such as the use of y/n (your name) by referring to Martin as both Martin/John, clearly indicating the elision between the actor's personal and fictional identities. The speaker has trouble keeping track of Martin/John's identity as the action starts to heat up, calling him Martin the closer she gets to orgasm. Staying true to the role play, however, Freeman corrects her, telling the speaker he is "Not Martin. . . . It's Doctor Watson." This most likely unconscious correction—calling Freeman "Not Martin" rather than "Doctor Watson"—highlights the ways in which postmodern selfhood is identified as a lack, an absence, a form of "play." Freeman here is an absence, "Not Martin," a denial of his inner self and public persona, leaving only the possibilities raised by his fictional character and the fictional world.

This blurring of fictional and real worlds becomes so pervasive that some writers begin repeating *Sherlock* quotes back to the actors in the fantasies. For instance, in "Over Pancakes and Django," the protagonist repeats to John lines Moriarty directs to Sherlock in "The Reichenbach Fall" episode: "'Oh that's clever, awfully clever. . . .' I said sort of drifting off into my pillow." The narrator even comments on her own slippage, "My inner fangirl was seeping out. The whole night, I refrained from quoting *Sherlock*." However, that doesn't stop her from bringing the source of her fascination with Freeman—the *Sherlock* show and Freeman's character in it—into her real-world fantasy.

Several RPF authors on the *Martin Freeman Sexual Frustration* blog specifically call attention to the artificial or arbitrary boundaries between *Sherlock*'s fictional world and the real world by repeatedly asking whether their experiences were real. For instance, the young woman in "A Comic Con Fantasy" asks herself, *"Oooh. Oh my God. This is real, right?"* Even more insightful, the speaker in "Over Pancakes and Django" asserts upon meeting Martin Freeman in real life, "This is not real! I must be dreaming. This only happened in movies. Or in fan fictions." Identifying her experience as a literary trope allows the author to give a knowing wink to her audience, indicating her desire to elide the typical distinctions between fiction and reality.

This blurring between real world and fictional world identities, characteristics, and behaviors, while liberating for some fans and troubling for others, seems to be particularly troubling to the *Sherlock* cast. Even though Cumberbatch himself has at times accidentally forgotten the difference between his personal identity and his fictional character, in other interviews he's expressed discomfort over fans appropriating his body in explicit fictions and fan art. In an open session at Australia's Oz Comic Con in April 2014, Cumberbatch told the audience of his frustrations with the media fabricating a public persona for him that was inaccurate and misleading. He also made strong statements about the separation between his private life and his professional identity: "My work is for the public and my life is for myself . . . and for no one else. That's it. And I understand people are interested. And as you know, my problem is that I probably overshare a bit too much. So, the media loves playing with that" (quoted in Cumbertrekky). Here, Cumberbatch reinforces the idea that the fans at Oz Comic Con are seeing a version of his authentic self that the media often misappropriates, but he also wants to maintain a strong separation between his personal life and his public persona. More specifically in relation to RPF, Martin Freeman's former partner, Amanda Abbington, caused an internet firestorm in an early 2014 interview with online magazine *Zap 2 It* in which she expressed her discomfort with and disapproval of slash fan art. When talking about her fears that her children will Google their father and find fan art, Abbington commented: "I've seen some particularly explicit paintings of Martin and Ben. Let's not say it's John and Sherlock; it's Martin and Ben, because you don't see Basil Rathbone and his Watson. I don't think it's about the characters; it becomes about the actors" (quoted in O'Hare). Abbington's concern is that this fan art is not, in fact, about the fictional characters of Sherlock Holmes and John Watson but rather about Benedict Cumberbatch and her former partner. Her argument is based on the observation that these pictures do not try to artistically represent completely imaginary characters coming from the artist's own imagination, or even other actors who have played these roles; in effect, she's making a distinction between fan art and fic based wholly on fictional literary depictions of characters versus fan products based on other media that include real actors. Since these fan images and RPFs clearly reference her partner's looks, his mannerisms, his modes of speech, and so on, they become pieces of art about *him*, not the fictional character he plays. Hundreds of fans attacked Abbington on Twitter for her criticisms of fandom and the situation became quite thorny.[5] This ethical argument seems to be at the heart of RPF, and perhaps of all fanfic and art, and highlights the blurry boundaries between fan investment and fictional world building.

Method Act, RPF, and the Multiverse

Splix71's RPF/body swap AU, *Method Act*, provides an insightful and creative exploration into the foundational questions underlying persona, selfhood, and fictional world building. Splix71's one-hundred-thirty-thousand-plus-word multichapter RPF explores the consequences if the real-life actor Cumberbatch swapped worlds with the fictional Sherlock Holmes. The story begins in the fictional world of BBC *Sherlock*, with Sherlock working on an experiment in the kitchen of 221b. When he accidentally plugs a hotplate into a faulty electrical socket, he suffers a shock and becomes unconscious. In the real world, Benedict Cumberbatch has just finished a day's shooting on *Sherlock* when he slips on set and accidentally grabs an exposed electrical lead, which shocks him unconscious (Splix71 chapter 1). When both characters regain consciousness, they find themselves in a nondescript white box with "White floor, white walls. . . . Pure white, no doors, no windows, no single seam to offset the whiteness" (Splix71 chapter 1). The two men are able to converse for a brief time before they are each somehow transported into the other's world. In the real world, Sherlock learns that Benedict is in a secret romantic relationship with British actor Tom Hiddleston (adding a further layer of RPF to the tale). While Sherlock and Benedict try to navigate their new worlds without letting on that they aren't who they are supposed to be (and risk being carted off to a mental hospital), they are recalled each evening to the mysterious white box where they try to troubleshoot how to rectify the situation. Ultimately, 221b-world Mycroft locates a physicist who researches multiverses and comes up with a device that allows the men to return to their own worlds.

The multiverse RPF fanfic seems a logical progression from alternate universe fictions. But while stories such as *Method Act* include elements of the alternate universe—the fictional characters are situated in a world and circumstances different from their own, even though the characters maintain their identifiable physical, syntactic, and behavioral characteristics from the original canon—the focus on the actors *behind* the fictional characters raises important questions about the boundaries between public and private, personal and persona identities, and real and fictional worlds. By centering on multiverses, specifically, *Method Act* brings to the forefront the major questions investigated in this book: What makes a fictional world? What are the boundaries between canon and fanon? How do fans explore, expand, and challenge the fictional world through the structural limitations of fanfic genre? Ultimately, how do fans' understanding of character and characterization, in particular, influence their understanding of persona and fictional character?

Method Act raises the possibility of the multiverse during the first encounter between the character and actor in the mysterious white box in chapter 1. Briefly defined by Cumberbatch as "layered, or alternate worlds" (Splix71 chapter 1) and incomprehensibly by Sherlock as "all measured mass energy occurs on the boundary of the multiverse. All non-measured mass energy occurs in the interior of the multiverse. For measured mass energy, inertial mass energy equals gravitational mass energy . . ." (Splix71 chapter 8), the multiverse recalls the possible worlds theory, discussed here in chapters one and five, which differentiates between real worlds and fictional worlds, in the first instance, and between canonical worlds and alternate imaginings, in the second. In traditional RPF, fans imagine an alternate world in which they have access to their favorite star's personal life and inner feelings. They may also construct an experience, a different universe, in which they meet and engage in a personal relationship with that celebrity. *Method Act* combines these various possibilities into an exploration of the "multitude of universes in the Universe" in the real world and fictional world simultaneously (Splix71 chapter 8). Here, real actors and fictional characters swap bodies, experiences, and realities to highlight the ways in which fans often elide real and fictional worlds, particularly through actors' physical bodies and distinctive mannerisms.

Method Act begins with an explicit exploration of identity, selfhood, and persona. The epigraph to the fic is a scholarly excerpt referencing Frick and Frack, a famous Swiss comedy ice-skating duo and film stars who were virtually indistinguishable from one another. The passage from Anthony Everett's "Against Fictional Realism" reads:

> No one was absolutely sure whether Frick and Frack were really the same person or not. Some said that they were definitely two different people. True, they looked very much alike, but they had been seen in different places at the same time. Others claimed that such cases were merely an elaborate hoax and that Frick had been seen changing his clothes and wig to, as it were, become Frack. All that I can say for certain is that there were some very odd similarities between Frick and Frack but also some striking differences. (Everett, quoted in Splix71 Ch. 1).

The Frick and Frack example raises important questions about selfhood and persona, and what makes an individual, while Everett's essay, as a whole, interrogates and responds to various theories about fictional realism, in particular in relation to character and identity. Among other texts under analysis, Everett briefly explores Arthur Conan Doyle's world of Sherlock Holmes and the way readers and critics "simultaneously [talk] about Holmes both as if he were a human detective living in Baker Street and as if he were a fictional object created by Conan Doyle" (649). As Everett explains, readers and critics often speak about fictional characters as if they were real people:

> We enter inside the world of the text being discussed where fictional characters are flesh and blood people while simultaneously adopting a perspective from which we can recognize that the characters we are talking about are fictional objects and are modeled on, or used as the models for, other fictional objects in other texts. (Everett 640)

Similarly, in RPF, audiences talk about real people as if they were fictional characters. So, what is the difference between these two practices, and how do they impact our understanding of world building, canon, and (non)compliance?

Real and Fictional Bodies in RPF

Since *Method Act* begins with the body swap between Cumberbatch and Sherlock, it's not surprising that so much of the early fic focuses on the physical attributes of both characters.[6] After the first shock of discovering each other in the white box, Benedict notes how much Sherlock resembles him: "The man on the floor looked just like Benedict. *Exactly* like Benedict. And if he didn't have a concussion and his brain wasn't projecting hallucinations as he slowly bled, he *sounded* just like Benedict. It was the best goddamned body double he'd ever seen. Ever" (Splix71 chapter 1). Cumberbatch goes on to note how the double seems to be wearing his "costume" from "The Great Game" episode, "with the addition of a slick plastic apron" and "a pair of goggles" (Splix71 chapter 1). Benedict then immediately proceeds to catalog all of the seemingly distinct physical features that make him who he is: his unique eye color, his heterochromia, the facial scars he got from the National Theatre *Frankenstein* prosthetics, even his hands and feet were similar (Splix71 chapter 1, chapter 3).

As we've seen in other RPFs and fanfictions, Sherlock's hair receives extra attention in the story, especially the difference between dealing with the curls in the real world versus the fantasy of having perfect hair and skin all the time, as apparently is the case in *Sherlock*'s world. Benedict, comparing his *Sherlock*-world hair to his real-world hair, found that "his hair, usually wilting at the end of day's filming thanks to excessive product, was perfect" in *Sherlock*'s universe (Splix71 chapter 3). Benedict's *Sherlock* body in the fictional world seems to have all of his senses heightened, his physical appearance is flawless, and he has to make no effort to exercise or remain fit to retain his current figure, reflecting the idealized elements that fiction often brings to real-world objects. In contrast, poor Sherlock finds himself in the real world with hair that "had . . . ballooned. There was no other word for it. Half of it stuck out from his head in a sort of mad aureole, and the other half was plastered to his forehead. He stuck his fingers in it and gave it his usual quick tousle, but that did absolutely nothing" (Splix71 chapter 8). Sherlock struggles throughout the fic with adjusting to living in an imperfect world, with an imperfect, human body. The similarity between Benedict Cumberbatch's real body and the more idealized Sherlock version highlights both the ways in which all fiction is an idealization of the world as well as the close alliance between the real person and the fictional character Benedict is supposed to represent. For all intents and purposes, Benedict Cumberbatch *is* Sherlock Holmes. Or rather, Sherlock Holmes is Benedict Cumberbatch—just a hyperrealized 2.0 version.

Sherlock's fictionalized perfection gets further challenged later in the fic when he is confronted with Cumberbatch's real-life lisp. Midway through the story, Sherlock agrees to lunch with Tom Hiddleston and some of his friends. While they are out, one of Tom's friends asks Sherlock whether it's true that he (Cumberbatch) has a lisp. Sherlock, confident in his own physical perfection, absolutely denies it—and then is mortified when he discovers he can't deliver a perfect tongue-twister: "Nonchalantly waving Tom's protest away Sherlock gave Peter and Henry a smile that didn't come close to touching his eyes. 'Ready? Here goes: she thellth theesh—' Horrified, he stopped as Henry and Peter burst into laughter. . . . Heat flooded Sherlock's face. *Cumberbatch, you imbecile*" (Splix71 chapter 12). Even the fictional characters within the story expect Cumberbatch and Sherlock to be identical. Granted, Sherlock himself tells Benedict early in the story that while they may look and sound exactly alike—"you aren't me" (Splix71 chapter 1)—he believes that person and character are interchangeable.

Benedict and Sherlock both seem to have an easier job not confusing Martin Freeman and John Watson with their world counterparts. As is often the case in *Sherlock* fanfictions, *Method Act* has more description of and narration from Sherlock's character than from John's, as Benedict and Sherlock are the first-person narrators of their respective sections. Benedict seems to understand early in the swap that John Watson was not Martin Freeman: "Martin was a great actor," Benedict claims, "the best, but there was something different about [John's] eyes" (Splix71 chapter 5). When Sherlock first encounters Martin Freeman in the real world, he is immediately struck by Freeman's sense of style: "John!—in a pair of narrow cuffless trousers, a closely cut Blackwatch-tartan blazer, and—curiouser and curiouser—a silk foulard scarf wrapped around his throat. He looked absolutely ridiculous" (Splix71 chapter 4). As we saw with the RPFs from the *Martin Freeman Sexual Frustration* blog, the fic grounds Freeman's physical description in Freeman's real-world fashion sense and published pictures of similar outfits. But for Sherlock, seeing his John Watson in a silk foulard scarf is out of character:

> Because it *wasn't* John, was it? No, and not just because John Watson wouldn't have been caught dead in those clothes. It was another *actor*, an impostor, a John Watson look-alike who was now striding toward him, hitching one of those absurd carryalls, this one printed with the Union Jack, over his shoulder. (Splix71 chapter 4)

Being an actor makes Freeman, by default, an imposter in Sherlock's eyes. In no way could he ever live up to the real John Watson whom Sherlock knows and loves in his own world. The ability to act, however, is exactly what allows Splix71, other fan authors, and fanfic readers to engage in the fantasy world of fanfiction and of RPF in particular. It is a testament to Freeman and Cumberbatch's acting ability that their fans—and their own fictional counterparts—often cannot distinguish between the real and fictional worlds.

A Tale of Two Canons: Doyle and *Sherlock* World Building

The characters in *Method Act* (and *Sherlock* fans) are unable to differentiate between real and fictional personas, a situation complicated by the text's many layers of world building and metafiction. *Method Act* establishes early on that Sherlock has multiple world influences, including both the Doyle canon and the BBC television show. When Sherlock and Benedict initially meet in the metaphysical white box between worlds, Benedict has to tell Sherlock that he is, in fact, a fictional character, something Doyle, along with the *Sherlock* team, invented (Splix71 chapter 1). When he comes to in the real world, Sherlock begins researching Cumberbatch's claims on the internet and quickly Googles "Benedict Cumberbatch" and "Sherlock Holmes," "smugly" pleased to find his own name generates more search results: "80 million" (Splix71 chapter 4). Sherlock then remembers Cumberbatch's comment about Sherlock being a fictional character, and he decides to search "Arthur Conan Doyle" on Wikipedia: "'What had the actor said? Doyle canon?' Click. 'What the *hell*?' . . . 'Fictional?'" (Splix71 chapter 2). He quickly finds himself tumbling down the rabbit hole of Doylean canon: "An hour later, he was still reading, skimming through the fiction. Fiction, some of it oddly familiar. Just snatches here and there . . . so very odd. A Victorian predecessor in this universe, a work of fiction, layers and layers away" (Splix71 chapter 4). Even though Sherlock does not believe in alternate universes, he is still subconsciously drawn to the Doyle canon and recognizes the traces of that fictional world in his memories and lived experience. Rather than living a life of adventure and importance, as he'd thought, Sherlock is bitterly frustrated that he has become the butt of a cosmic joke and that "his work—*the* work, the *only* work, had been reduced to a television program. Entertainment" (Splix71 chapter 14).

After reading about himself and Doyle's fictional world online, Sherlock then proceeds to discover the video evidence of his own BBC *Sherlock* world. He stumbles upon the first *Sherlock* episode, "A Study in Pink," and is immediately struck by the fact that this is the same title as John's first blog post. He notes that the episode is told from John's point of view, but he's struck as well by how "oddly precise" the portrayal was. While he first tries to explain away the similarities by blaming them on the Doyle canon, Sherlock quickly recognizes that his world differs from the Doyle canon in substantial ways: "He'd scanned some of the stories on the train—Doyle's story had been called *A Study in Scarlet* and there were hardly any similarities at all to *what really had happened*, but this—" (Splix71 chapter 8; emphasis added). From Sherlock's point of view, his fictional world is real; he is a person, not a character, and his life history is "what really had happened," not these fictionalized accounts memorialized in Doyle's stories or the BBC television episodes.

Sherlock quickly finds himself addicted to watching his own story on the screen: "He couldn't stop watching. A strange, unfamiliar sensation slowly flooded him, a mangled hybrid of unease and incredulity" (Splix71 chapter 8). He's struck by how different Cumberbatch was in real life compared with his representation of Sherlock's character on-screen; he's similarly impressed with Martin Freeman's ability to perfect John Watson's character (Splix71 chapter 8). He quickly speeds through all of season one, noting the production additions of "superfluous" soundtracks and overblown titles (Sherlock questions whether "The Great Game" (S1E3) was really all that "great"). Watching the shows through the lens of the screen allows Sherlock a new point of view through which to reevaluate himself, John, and other persons in his life. When reencountering Sarah, John's boss and girlfriend from "The Blind Banker" (S1E2), Sherlock now has the perspective to realize that she "wasn't bad, as John's girlfriends went" (Splix71 chapter 8). Experiencing himself as a fictional character prompts Sherlock to think about the nature of reality, consciousness, and selfhood in ways that celebrities constantly experience in their personal and professional identities. He literally sees himself through the lens of his personal experiences at the same time that he's forced to see himself through the media's lens, and the result is that he has to come up with a combined, mediated version of his self that somehow works across worlds.

Although Sherlock's ego is initially infuriated to learn he is part of an historic fictional universe, John is actually proud of the legacy and the importance his character has played over the past century. In the alternate 221b *Sherlock* world, Benedict tells John late in the fic that while he is not actually Sherlock Holmes, the character of John Watson is famous:

> "Oh my God. I didn't – didn't I say? You're famous, you are, John Watson, and have been since the late eighteen hundreds. A man by the name of Sir Arthur Conan Doyle wrote dozens of stories about Holmes and Watson, and they've been best-sellers forever. There have been movies, earlier television series, animated versions, radio plays, et cetera, et cetera. Everyone loves you, and Sherlock too. The whole world knows the names of Sherlock Holmes and John Watson." (Splix71 chapter 20)

For John, learning that he's part of a long literary tradition gives his life more meaning than merely serving as Sherlock's sidekick in the contemporary 221b world. This literary history gets even more complicated when Cumberbatch tells Sherlock and John about the BBC's modern-day revision of Doyle's original canon, and much of the rest of *Method Act* is about exploring the complexities of fictionality, realism, and multilayered closed and open worlds.

Method Act spends more time discussing how Sherlock and John do or do not conform to the BBC *Sherlock* world than to how much they conform to Doyle's closed world (although one could argue that much of the BBC world originated in the nineteenth-century Doyle world). As Benedict explains to Mycroft after revealing his true identity, "It's not the Doyle canon as it was written, it's mostly a figment of Steven and Mark's imagination . . . the timeline's about the same" (Splix71 chapter 13). Steven and Mark's imagination, however, includes several tropes that clearly identify the BBC canon, as we've discussed throughout this book, including the show's modern London and 221b Baker Street set, identifiable speech patterns and syntax, and specific gestures or behaviors. Benedict notes immediately on entering the 221b world that the flat looks exactly like their theatrical set, although this version has actual ceilings (Splix71 chapter 1). The fic also reinforces several syntactic patterns fans see repeated in the show and throughout other *Sherlock* fanfic genres. For instance, even though Sherlock is in the real world, he still thinks in and uses recognizable syntactic patterns and catchphrases fans know from the show. While in an argument with Tom Hiddleston, for instance, Sherlock tries to check his impatient behavior by channeling one of John's chastisements from "The Reichenbach Fall" (S2E3): "*Timing, Sherlock*, John would have tutted" (Splix71 chapter 16). A few chapters later, he internalizes John again, telling himself "*Human lives, Sherlock. Do you care about that at all?*" (Splix71 chapter 18), a reference to the bomb plot in S1E3's "The Great Game" (S1E3). By repeating canonical/fanonical lines from the TV world, Splix71's Sherlock reinforces his ties to the fictional world, both for himself and for the reader.

In addition to syntax, *Method Act* also transports Sherlock's canonical behaviorisms and hobbies into the real world. Tom is surprised when he hears Sherlock tuning his violin in the real world, particularly because he admits that Benedict can't actually play in real life: "Tom groaned a little and stuck his head under the pillow. Benedict was a man of vast talents, but music wasn't among them" (Splix71 20). He's shocked, however, to hear Sherlock spontaneously begin to run through an arpeggio warm-up and then begin to play "sweet, upward-spiraling notes that wound into near silence, and then a tune that was familiar, something lovely and romantic, almost gentle. . . . It grew, quick-tempo, playful and a little whimsical, then returned to the familiar theme" (Splix71 chapter 20). Even though Tom knows, in real life, that Ben can't play the violin, he's struck by the actor's seeming ability to "be" the character he plays on TV. Tom frequently mentions in the fic that Ben seems to be channeling his role too often and bringing his work home with him; Tom can definitely see a difference between Benedict's loving, affectionate nature and Sherlock's cold rationality, but by bridging these characterizations through Benedict Cumberbatch's physical description, along with Sherlock's speech and characteristics, characters and readers easily become confused as to who is who and what is real and what is fictional.

Splix71 also cleverly uses world hopping to raise important questions about both the Doyle canon and the BBC *Sherlock* canon. Once Tom finally learns that Sherlock is not Benedict Cumberbatch, he's shocked to think about their sexual encounter earlier in the story. As Tom tells Sherlock "Jesus *Christ*. I thought you were meant to be asexual, anyhow," Sherlock demands, "Who said that?" When Tom replies, "It's canon . . . . Pretty explicitly, too. Sherlock Holmes is not interested in women." Sherlock "remains smugly silent" until Tom realizes his mistake—"Oh" (Splix71 chapter 20). Most fans assume Sherlock Holmes is asexual from the original Doyle stories, particularly from "A Scandal in Bohemia" when Watson writes: "All emotions, and that one [love] particularly, were abhorrent to his cold, precise but admirably balanced mind. He was, I take it, the most perfect reasoning and observing machine that the world has ever seen, but as a lover he would have placed himself in a false position. He never spoke of the softer passions, save with a gibe and a sneer" (Doyle, "Scandal"). BBC Sherlock has a companion scene in "A Study in Pink" (S1E1) in which John asks whether Sherlock has a girlfriend. Sherlock's response, "Girlfriend? Not really my area," prompts John to ask about a boyfriend, a question that Sherlock never actually answers ("A Study in Pink"). In having Tom confuse his BBC canonical reading of Sherlock with the Doyle canon, Splix71 highlights the ways in which the real and multifictional worlds collide, particularly in RPF.

Similar canon questions arise in the 221b fictional world, but this time they come from "Sherlock," that is, Benedict, himself. Cumberbatch asks John a popular question about the source of Sherlock's wealth, wondering if he made his fortune gambling. John clarifies: "He's got a little family money that's just about enough to live on," which confirms many Doyle scholars' ideas about Sherlock's wealth, thus eliding the two worlds and canons once again. John adds that the pair "do take payment for cases. He sort of charges by whim, though [which is also Doyle canon; see the ending of "A Scandal in Bohemia"], and only if the client's got money to burn. . . . Sometimes clients give him gifts, too, and most of the valuable ones get sold on eBay. He's got a really high seller rating" (Splix71 chapter 20). The verisimilitude of Sherlock having an eBay account and selling his case gifts on eBay further helps erase for the reader the distinction between Sherlock the fictional character and Benedict Cumberbatch as Sherlock in the real world. Since the reader sees Cumberbatch in her mind when imagining Sherlock, it becomes likewise simple to imagine the fictional character in real world scenarios, similar to how RPF operates with celebrity personas.

Not only does *Method Act* break down the real/fictional world boundaries of Cumberbatch and/as Sherlock, it also breaks down the world divisions in the text itself. For some inexplicable reason, both Sherlock and Cumberbatch are able to recall essential information they need to live as the other person in the alternate world. For instance, Benedict is able to use Sherlock's cell phone passcode without thinking, something that even the most knowledgeable codebreakers should be unable to do. To the contrary, Benedict "thumbed the code as if he'd always known it" (Splix71 chapter 7). Similarly, Sherlock is able to punch in Hiddleston's house alarm code without thinking. Dr. Paisley, the physicist Mycroft brings to the 221b world to help Sherlock and Benedict return to their primary worlds, hypothesizes that the two men are experiencing their double's "mental muscle memory"; they've "experienced a loss of density in what you might term the personal inflation field," which may "thin" the veil between worlds (Splix71 chapter 20). The "loss of density in the personal inflation field" implies, to a nonscientific reader, that the differences between Benedict Cumberbatch, celebrity, and Sherlock Holmes, fictional character, have *decreased* due to their cross-world experiences. That is, the more Cumberbatch *acts like* Sherlock Holmes, the more likely he is to *think like* and *be like* Sherlock Holmes. What's fascinating about RPF, and *Method Act* in particular, is the way in which this interchangeability is foregrounded, particularly in media and fandom.

Even though Benedict and Sherlock seem to retain some kind of "mental muscle memory" of the other's world and body, they both still express nostalgia for their own absent worlds. Sherlock, struck over and over again with the exhausting need to act like Benedict Cumberbatch, "missed the size and shape of his own world; he missed John. He was unmoored and isolated in a universe where he only existed on television, and on pages and pages of stories" (Splix71 chapter 14). Since he only exists on television and on the pages of stories in the real world, Sherlock's sense of self lacks the definition and permanence that real individuals experience. He is ephemeral, an idea. He also admits that his world, even though it is fictional, possesses a unique size and shape, which we've previously described through setting, description, and general world-building techniques. Even though the 221b world is fictional, it still retains elements of the world. In fact, Benedict deconstructs the idea that a difference exists between the real world and *Sherlock*'s fictional world. When thinking about Sherlock and John's relationship (or their potential for a romantic relationship) in the 221b world, he argues that "it didn't matter what happened in the real world—in *his* world, whether they played straight or gay or ambivalent or asexual—in this world, in this time and place, John Watson loved Sherlock Holmes and, God bless him, found the courage to tell him so in his own sort of roundabout way" (Splix71 chapter 17). While Cumberbatch initially makes a distinction between his real world and Sherlock's fictional one, he goes on to say that such distinctions don't matter: not *shouldn't* matter—*don't* matter. Because the man and the character are inextricably linked through their physicality, mannerisms, and behaviors, maintaining the generic distinctions between the persona and character seems both less viable and less necessary—particularly when it comes to fanfiction.

Fanfic and/as Fanfic: The Role of Fiction in RPF

In addition to using the multiverse metaphor to explore RPF's blurring between real actors' bodies and their fictional representation in fanfic, *Method Act* explicitly incorporates the concept and practice of fanfiction to introduce a metafictional and ontological exploration of identity, persona, and character. The story defines fanfic itself, explores the organizational principles of fic and fanfic archives—for example, the use of warnings, tags, and genres in structuring fanfic (Splix71 chapter 16)—and even includes excerpts from previously published and original *Sherlock* fanfic within the RPF itself (Splix71 chapter 14). Sherlock's first encounter with fanfic in the guise of a "Johnlock" fanvid he accidentally stumbles on during his search for Doyle canon references has him initially "snorting" with laughter (Splix71 chapter 8). The video prompts him into further research into fanfic, however, where he discovers various websites for posting and archiving fic like Fanfiction.net and the unnamed Archive of Our Own. Once again, he resorts to Wikipedia definitions of fanfiction as "a broadly defined fan labor term for stories about characters or settings written by fans of the original work, rather than by the original creator" (Splix71 chapter 14). Such entries help Sherlock further understand his own identity in relation to the real world and that of the source text. For him, the source text is his own world, which here is the television program: "*Sherlock* was the original work, those strange Victorian-era stories notwithstanding, and people wrote stories about him and John and their adventures" (Splix71 chapter 14). Sherlock makes an important distinction for his own sense of identity; he is not necessarily the Sherlock Holmes described in Doyle's original stories; rather, he is the creation and product of Steven Moffat and Mark Gatiss, a creation that is further normalized and concretized through Benedict Cumberbatch's distinctive performance.

Like his earlier internet searches about Benedict Cumberbatch, Sherlock Holmes, and Arthur Conan Doyle, Sherlock quickly learns that his BBC fandom is one of many different Sherlock Holmes fandoms on the internet.

> A bit of digging revealed that his iteration of Sherlock Holmes was the most popular one on the archive–and rightly so, obviously–but he spent a few minutes marveling over the differences of the different men who'd played Sherlock Holmes. The very lean and severe man from the black-and-white films with the ridiculous coat and hat–honestly, could one be more obvious and melodramatic? And that Watson was terribly bumbling and stupid; he wouldn't have lasted a day in the real world. Then there was the television version with the rather good-looking older fellow and a Watson who was marginally brighter. Then there was the scruffy Holmes with the large dark eyes and the handsome and sharp-tongued Watson—now there was a Watson to reckon with, though not a patch on *his* Watson. (Splix71 chapter 16)

Note how Sherlock avoids naming any of the other canonical actors who've played Sherlock Holmes but rather focuses on their physical appearance. Rather than discuss the different plot elements of the Basil Rathbone films as compared with Robert Downey Jr.'s more recent incarnations, the passage refers to them specifically by the actors' looks, costuming, and behaviors—the same methods we've been exploring within fictional world building and through the importance of characterization. For our Sherlock, his Sherlock Holmes is defined by his personal appearance, mannerisms, syntax, and the specific plot incidents in the various BBC episodes. He recognizes that he is not the same Sherlock Holmes as the ones he has found online. But when he studies Cumberbatch's portrayal of him, he has a much harder time distinguishing between himself and Cumberbatch-as-Sherlock-Holmes. As Cumberbatch ruminates in the middle of the story, "Maybe, in this universe, switching bodies and worlds with someone was no crazier than stealing corpses to simulate a terrorist attack" (Splix71 chapter 8)—a reference to Mycroft's "Coventry" plan in "A Scandal in Belgravia" (S2E1). RPF, then, and perhaps all fanfic, can be read as body switching and world swapping so that the two become intimately intertwined.

Ultimately, *Method Act* isn't so much about the various personas Cumberbatch portrays to the world but rather about what makes a specific character world compliant in a particular fandom. Cumberbatch recognizes that his acting and person directly contributed to the construction of the BBC *Sherlock* world. He notes to himself: "But it must mean something. This is your iteration of Holmes you've dropped into, not Jeremy Brett's or Basil Rathbone's or Robert Downey Junior's. In some small way, you've helped to create this universe—there must be a way for you to change places again" (Splix71 chapter 5). Once a particular actor is assigned to play a specific character in a fictional world, audiences are encouraged to associate that particular celebrity with the iconography of the character. As Sherlock himself notes in *Method Act*, "that was the problem with a work of fiction in the first place, wasn't it? Absolutely no control on the part of the creators once the thing had been released into the wild. People were free to make all sorts of stupid interpretations" (Splix71 chapter 14). In fact, multiverses and fanfics in general seem to be all about the infinite possibilities for storytelling, world building, and character exploration. Near the end of the story, when Sherlock and Benedict are about to return to their primary worlds, they find themselves no longer in the white box but in a black space "pierced with tiny pinpoints of stars." They are surrounded by "a massive web or net or hive of gossamer golden light . . . with other figures dimmed to near transparency. Were they people? Were they human?" (Splix71 chapter 20). Sherlock and Benedict's final encounter seems to place them in a literal spatial multiverse in which they are surrounded by other pairs. Some are in medieval cloaks, two women are seen in Renaissance dress, two are filaments of orange light. Is the reader supposed to take all of these pairings as alternate versions of Sherlock and John in multiple possible universes? Do they symbolize Sherlock and John throughout the literary and media history of Arthur Conan Doyle's world, or even within the various Sherlock Holmes fandoms on the internet? There is no clear way to tell. For Benedict, the possibility of "a thousand iterations of Holmes and Watson" gave him the space to imagine that perhaps in one of those nine hundred and ninety-nine they would be allowed to have a romantic relationship, even if so many other canonical versions seemed satisfied with simple friendship (Splix71 chapter 17). Once Sherlock returns to his 221b world, the very possibility of the multiple universes found in fanfiction allows him to act on his previously repressed romantic feelings for John. Facing John upon his return, Sherlock "thought of that other world. Millions of words about Sherlock and John" and proceeds to wrap John "in a tight embrace" (Splix71 chapter 20). The play on worlds and words in this final sentence seems more than coincidence; rather, it invites the reader to make explicit the connection between world building and fanfiction.

Method Act, particularly through its use of RPF, explicitly questions the relationship between realism and fiction. After Sherlock learns about the existence and proliferation of fanfic about him and John in their various worlds, he is plagued by questions of verisimilitude and realism: "Did they believe these stories, these fanfiction writers? He'd never been inclined much toward fiction himself; why lose yourself in the unreal when there was limitless potential in the reality of this world, its uproars and enigmas, its visceral tangabilities [*sic*] and idiosyncrasies?" (Splix71 chapter 14). Asking whether fans believe in the reality of fanfictions—and the worlds they represent—is perhaps less likely than readers believing the celebrity personas portrayed in the media and RPFs are real. Because Sherlock doesn't see himself as a fictional character, he doesn't understand the genre distinctions between fanfiction and RPF or even other canonical texts about his and John's adventures. Since he is real, all stories about Sherlock Holmes are potentially real. While contemporary readers know that Sherlock is a fictional character, they easily equate his character with the real-life physical elements of actor Benedict Cumberbatch's personal appearance, voice, and mannerisms.

Even when writing fictional stories about imagined encounters with *Sherlock*'s actors in the real world, fans reinforce the world primarily through Cumberbatch's and Freeman's consistent characterizations. Whether they are portrayed in a real-world scenario or in an alternate universe or as women, Sherlock's and John's characters remain engrained in Cumberbatch's and Freeman's bodies and unique portrayals of their characters. No matter how the trappings of the world change in various fanfic genres, the stories remain canon compliant as long as the characters remain consistent with Cumberbatch's and Freeman's bodies and portrayals.

SHERLOCK SEASON FOUR
The End of the World?

January 2017 saw the broadcast of the most recent *Sherlock* season. The much-anticipated season four attracted eleven million viewers, and after the BBC's alternate universe *Abominable Bride* Christmas special in December 2015 (and not counting the New Year's Eve fireworks broadcast), it was the most-watched program over the holidays. The fourth season followed the show's distinctive format of three ninety-minute episodes built loosely on canonical Arthur Conan Doyle stories: episode one, "The Six Thatchers," adapted the Doyle story "The Six Napoleons" into a story about Mary Morstan-Watson's spy/assassin background. Mary is hunted down by a captured teammate from A.G.R.A. (itself taken from the Doyle novella, *The Sign of the Four*, which first introduced Mary Morstan), who has hidden a top-secret thumb drive in one of six plaster busts of Margaret Thatcher. After unearthing the government mole who revealed A.G.R.A.'s location, Mary is shot to death trying to save Sherlock's life. John's anger over the loss of his wife carries over into episode two, "The Lying Detective," an adaptation of the Doyle story "The Dying Detective." In the original, Watson finds Holmes dying from a mysterious disease, only to learn the detective is using his illness to entrap Culverton Smith into admitting he poisoned his nephew. In the show, Sherlock becomes visibly strung out on drugs to lure John back into helping him catch media mogul Smith, now a serial killer with a guilty conscience. We later find that Sherlock's addiction is in response to a posthumous DVD Mary sent Sherlock instructing him to "Save John Watson" from his grief and isolation following her death. (Mary's plea to "save John" is one of many references to earlier *Sherlock* episodes, in this case "The Empty Hearse" (S3E1), in which Sherlock and Mary decipher a skip code telling them to "Save John Watson" from Charles Augustus Magnussen's Guy Fawkes Night bonfire.) The second episode comes to a close when John admits to Sherlock that he cheated on Mary by (inexplicably) sexting a red-haired stranger he met on the bus who, it turns out, is Sherlock's long-lost sister, Eurus, and also John's new therapist—who proceeds to shoot him in a classic *Sherlock* cliffhanger at the end of the second episode.

The final episode of season four, "The Final Problem," includes several nods to previous Arthur Conan Doyle stories and episodes in the *Sherlock* canon. On the surface, the episode title refers to Conan Doyle's infamous tale of the same name in which Holmes first meets and kills Moriarty while simultaneously faking his own death. Of course, *Sherlock* already adapted "The Final Problem" in "The Reichenbach Fall" (S2E3), in which Sherlock and Moriarty face off on the rooftop of St. Bart's Hospital, ending with Moriarty shooting himself in the head and Sherlock seeming to jump from the roof to his death. "The Final Problem" from season four, however, is a much more original, albeit far-fetched, episode that draws on several different Doyle stories to make up a larger bricolage.[1] The episode begins with a young girl waking up on a plane full of sleeping passengers and about to crash into London and continues with the revelation that Sherlock has blocked all memories of his younger sister, Eurus, after she murdered his childhood friend, Victor Trevor. (Holmes sublimated his memory of his friend and his fate into the now fanonical lost dog, Redbeard.) Sherlock confronts Mycroft with the knowledge that Eurus has escaped from her island prison, Sherringford, and is terrorizing Sherlock and John. The three men then break into Sherringford, where they are subsequently emotionally and psychologically tortured by Eurus before being mysteriously whisked away to the Holmes family manor, Musgrave House (an allusion to another Doyle story, "The Musgrave Ritual"), where Eurus leaves John to drown in a well (Victor's fate) until Sherlock reveals that she is actually the little girl on the plane and that she's been playing them all along. Eurus is miraculously "healed" by a hug from Sherlock, returned to her prison where she will no longer speak, and reunited with her parents (who had been told by Mycroft that she'd previously died in a fire). Through all of these dramatic leaps, incongruous storylines, and gaping narrative holes, Sherlock and John are returned to a (literally and metaphorically) damaged 221b Baker Street, where they put their lives back together and return to solving cases. The episode ends with a post-humous voice-over from Mary labeling John and Sherlock "the best and wisest men she has ever known. My Baker Street boys, Sherlock Holmes and John Watson" ("The Final Problem"). More on this ending a bit later.

While viewing numbers remained high, the season was criticized by critics and die-hard fans alike; even the most positive reviews found the final season an imperfect conclusion to a show that had met with a dazzling critical reception in its first season in 2010. Although one review claimed that the final episode "[blew] the doors off," others found the finale "mostly satisfying" or merely "imperfect" (Frost; Jeffrey, "*Sherlock* Series 4"). Most critics voice much stronger condemnations, however.[2] Declared a "mess" by *IndieWire* and *Vox*, the show was critiqued for its lack of logic, "frenzied plot twists," "implausible drama," "showiness," and "confusing" storylines (Romano). Others characterized the season as "anticlimactic," feeling it had "lost its way"; among the worst charges were that the showrunners were guilty of continued misogyny (Welsh) and of turning the show "into some kind of old-school teenage boy fantasy" (O'Connor). One of the most prevalent critiques of the show was disappointment that it had shifted away from the typical mystery/police procedural format that viewers had enjoyed in the first few seasons to a more James Bond superhero spy genre in which Sherlock and John dodge drone-carried patience grenades and have shoot-outs with master criminals. In season four, rather than watch Sherlock and John solve cases for clients, fans watched them deal with super villains and personal family drama, often outside the confines of 221b and their relationship with each other. The result of such departures from genre expectations was that many fans and critics felt the show had not only "lost its way," but that it had lost its *world*. *Sherlock* season four was characterized as "an all-out departure from the show's beginnings" (iTeam).

One major critique of season four was its lack of character development and its "out of character" behavior from the protagonists (Romano). In several scenes in "The Six Thatchers" (S4E1), for example, Sherlock is described as relying more on premonition, intuition, and sentiment than on intellect. When Sherlock and John first visit the home of the Conservative cabinet minister whose son has mysteriously disappeared, Sherlock notices the absence from a nearby table of a Margaret Thatcher plaster bust. At first, Sherlock can't explain what has brought him to the table, and when John questions him about it, he responds:

SHERLOCK: By the pricking of my thumbs.

JOHN: Seriously?

SHERLOCK: Intuition is not to be ignored, John. They represent data processes too fast for the conscious mind to comprehend. ("The Six Thatchers")

Sherlock's dependence on intuition in this scene, rather than on pattern recognition or other logical deductions, places him outside his typical characterization. In a later scene in the same episode, Sherlock and Mycroft discuss whether anything connected Moriarty and Thatcher, and Mycroft accuses Sherlock of depending on "premonition" rather than data to solve the mystery:

SHERLOCK: Something's coming.

MYCROFT: Are you having a premonition, brother mine?

SHERLOCK: The world is woven from billions of lives. Every strand crossing every other. What we call premonition is just movement of the web. If you could attenuate to every strand of quivering data, the future would be entirely calculable, as inevitable as mathematics.

MYCROFT: Appointment in Samarra?

SHERLOCK: Sorry?

MYCROFT: The merchant who couldn't outrun death. You always hated that story. Less keen on predestination then.

SHERLOCK: I'm not sure I like it now. ("The Six Thatchers")

Even though Sherlock claims that premonition is another form of deduction, Mycroft (and the audience) begin to fear that perhaps Sherlock is not acting like himself.

Not only is Sherlock behaving erratically, but John also acts out of character in several scenes in season four. Many critics noted the apparent incongruity between John Watson's foundational character trait of loyalty and his seemingly random decision to cheat on his wife in season four. Average John Watson's appeal to beautiful, younger, red-haired women in buses seems to imply more of a male fantasy than canonical characterization (even though Watson was known to be a "ladies' man" in the original tales). More troubling for some critics, however, was the hostility John showed to Sherlock and Mycroft throughout the season. In "The Six Thatchers," John no longer laughs at Sherlock's jokes or thinks his deductions amazing; at one point, he goads Sherlock for the solution to a young boy's death by preempting his deductions rather than enjoying Sherlock's mental leaps in solving the puzzle. Even more shockingly, John viciously takes out his anger at Mary's death on Sherlock by physically attacking him in "The Lying Detective" (S4E2). No humorous soundtrack à la "The Empty Hearse" dinner scene that opens season three lightens the mood; in "The Lying Detective" John brutally punches and then kicks Sherlock as he cowers, cornered, on the floor of the mortuary. Rather than getting the timeless Holmes-Watson friendship of old (despite some emotional conflicts), the characters in season four don't even seem to like each other anymore (Baker-Whitelaw).

Much of *Sherlock*'s world is based on characterization and setting. In the first three seasons, that world was grounded in "the real world of contemporary London," a setting many saw as "integral to [its] early success" (Burt, "Did *Sherlock* Lose Its Way"). In season four, most of the action happens *outside* of London and 221b Baker Street—in the London suburbs and English countryside; in hospitals, island prisons, and aquariums; on planes or in such exotic locations as Morocco. If audiences lose their sense of where the *Sherlock* world is located and of the diegetic objects and characters associated with that world, the entire construct risks falling apart. Rather than remaining in its world, the *Sherlock* of season four created its own alternate universe. Unlike *The Abominable Bride*'s (2015) explicit exploration of another time period and another London (later revealed as part of Sherlock's mind palace and thus actually part of the present), season four "went off the rails" (Burt, "Did *Sherlock* Lose Its Way") to such an extent that audiences were presented with something very different from the world they had come to love and expect.[3] Viewers missed the domestic setting of the 221b sitting room in which Sherlock and John met their clients and solved crimes over the breakfast table, and they missed the dark London streets down which the pair chased dangerous criminals. What they found instead was a series of improbable cases, with implausible motivations, in a variety of unsettled locations.

Showrunners Moffat and Gatiss seemed to sense that this version of *Sherlock* was not what viewers had come to expect from previous seasons.

In response to several critics' observations regarding the vast differences in characterization, setting, and story in the fourth season, Moffat and Gatiss proposed season four as a kind of "backstory" to the entire show (Jeffrey, "*Sherlock* Writers"). On the surface, the final season does serve as a backstory in that it provides an emotional context for Sherlock's character and the Holmeses' family dynamics; Mycroft tells Sherlock at one point in "The Final Problem," "Every choice you ever made, every path you've ever taken, the man you are today is your memory of Eurus" ("The Final Problem"). This backstory, however, comes completely out of the blue and undoes (in unconvincing ways) several threads and storylines from previous seasons. Gatiss's answer to that was to pose *Sherlock* season four as a kind of reboot of the entire show. By ending the season with a shot of Sherlock and John running out of Rathbone Place, Gatiss argued that the two men had somehow become the Rathbone and Bruce of the 1940s Sherlock Holmes films: "We never intended that to be, but the reason we leave it at Rathbone Place is that actually if we do come back, and we'd love to come back, we could very easily start with a knock on the door and Sherlock saying to John, 'Do you want to come out and play?'" (Jeffrey, "*Sherlock* Writers"). But shooting Cumberbatch and Freeman running out of Rathbone Place does not make them Rathbone and Bruce. Rather, Cumberbatch and Freeman's Sherlock and John are their own characters, with their own histories, characteristics, and storyworld, and to imply they have somehow "become" another franchise undermines the effort and creation Moffat and Gatiss have put into *Sherlock*'s world since its inception. Claiming they are only doing someone else's world relieves Moffat and Gatiss from any responsibility for where their world ended up.

Several critics saw season four as a reboot, noting "It was like our beloved characters had been restored to factory settings" (Hogan) and that the show was "back to square one" (Holub). These observations raised objections, however. For *Den of Geek*'s Kayti Burt, it seemed "amazing that Sherlock spent two seasons (and five years) doing narrative *dressage* only to end up back where it started"—literally (Burt, "Did *Sherlock* Lose Its Way"): one could read season four as a cap or bookend for many of the world elements initially introduced in *Sherlock*'s first season. As I noted earlier, "The Final Problem" (S4E3) concludes with Sherlock and John rebuilding 221b, taking cases together again, coparenting Rosie, and working with Lestrade and the Met to solve unsolvable crimes. The world is literally recreated right before the audience's eyes, and *Sherlock*'s world, albeit with the addition of Rosie, begins again at the opening episode, "A Study in Pink." *Den of Geek* effectively highlighted several ways *Sherlock*'s season four parallels season one in key elements: the focus on serial killers (Jeff Hope versus Culverton Smith); John Watson's nightmares and sleep issues; suicide themes (John in "A Study in Pink" and Faith in "The Lying Detective," as well as Eurus in "The Final Problem"); John (and now Sherlock) meeting with a therapist; Mycroft's surveillance (of John in "A Study in Pink" and of Sherlock in "The Lying Detective"); John's walking cane from season one and, in season four, Faith Smith's cane in "The Lying Detective"; and a group of detectives searching Sherlock's flat for drugs ("A Study in Pink," "The Lying Detective," and with Anderson and Sherlock's "fan club" in "The Empty Hearse").[4] One final notable parallel is Detective Inspector Lestrade's comment to John at the end of "A Study in Pink" that he hopes, one day, that Sherlock Holmes will be a good man as well as a great one. As Eurus is taken away at the end of season four's "The Final Problem," Lestrade is faced with another officer who is a "fan" of Sherlock Holmes:

> OFFICER: Is that him, then? Is that Sherlock Holmes?
> LESTRADE: Fan, are you?
> OFFICER: Well, he's a great man, sir.
> LESTRADE: No, he's better than that. He's a good one. ("The Final Problem")

Audiences are left uneasy at Lestrade's declaration, however. Is Sherlock Holmes a good man? What, in season four, has shown him to be "good"? What kind of moral compass does he possess now that he lacked in previous seasons? For most fans and critics, the answer is nothing. Sherlock has strayed so far from his original characterization and world that the only way to "reclaim" him is to start over from the beginning.

Many critics were struck by the inconsistency between season four and the previous seasons of *Sherlock*, particularly with the ways "The Final Problem" tried to reestablish the conclusion as a new beginning. For some, this return to "square one" perhaps signaled an even more important realization: the end of the show. Critics like Kaite Welsh for *IndieWire* noted the show "end[ed] on an oddly final note" with an almost "elegiac" tone. Similarly, Christian Holub for *Entertainment Weekly* read the fourth season's parallels to season one as indicating that "we've finally reached the end of the road. This episode clearly didn't know whether it was supposed to be a series finale or a temporary stopgap." Many of these rumors about season four being *Sherlock*'s final season actually came from the writers and actors themselves. As early as July 2016, writer and co-creator Steven Moffat told the *Telegraph* that he didn't know how long they would keep making the show (Foster). As he told the *Radio Times*, "Right at this moment, we really don't know about the future. . . . At the same time, because we love *Sherlock* the way we do, we don't want to keep it going past its natural term" (Dowell). In typical Moffat style, the writer both implied and denied that "The Final Problem" could, in fact, be the last *Sherlock* episode ever, reportedly stating at a London press screening for the episode, "If this is the last time—and I'm not planning on it to be, but it might be—it is possible that we could end it [with this episode]" (Tartaglione). Both writers were quite cagey about the show's future, with Gatiss reputedly claiming "It may be the final problem, you never know" (Tartaglione).

Both Benedict Cumberbatch and Martin Freeman have also helped spread rumors that *Sherlock* may, in fact, be over, or at least facing a much longer hiatus than the usual two-to-three-year break. Cumberbatch, when asked by *GQ* about "the last series of *Sherlock*," responded "It might be the end of an era. It feels like the end of an era, to be honest" ("Benedict Cumberbatch"). Similarly, Freeman, in a radio interview with Jim Norton and Sam Roberts, stated, "Life does sometimes have a way of telling you, 'This is probably it now.' This last [season] did have a feeling of . . . I don't know whether it has a finality to it, but certainly had a feeling of pause" (quoted in Sparks). Even the BBC's social media content creators implied *Sherlock*'s run was over, tweeting Mary's final lines of the show: "It's all about the legend. The stories. The adventures. Thank you for joining us for #Sherlock" (BBC One). And John's blog, an essential corporate transmedia storytelling extension developing the world outside the show, was terminated at the start of season four with this note: "John Watson is no longer updating this blog." The further comment, "For the latest *Sherlock* content on the BBC go to the *Sherlock* programme website" (Lidster), expressly highlights the world as a fictional construct and diminishes the illusion initially created by the show's content managers.

While the more cynical may suspect such speculations are merely meant to drum up audience anticipation again in the face of the degree of public criticism against the latest season, *Sherlock*'s creators and actors at the same time left open the possibility that the show would return for more episodes—but at a much later date. In Moffat's interview with the *Telegraph*, he claimed "it's unlikely that we've completely finished [*Sherlock*]. There would be nothing strange in stopping for a while. It could go on forever, coming back now and again" (Foster). These comments echo some Moffat and Gatiss remarks in previous years about returning to *Sherlock* over the next few decades as the actors naturally age and grow into their characters. Likewise, Cumberbatch's interview with *GQ* quotes him as saying "he'd love to revisit [*Sherlock*]," and "keep revisiting it"; "the idea of never playing him again is really galling" ("Benedict Cumberbatch"). Even though the BBC also seemed to hint that *Sherlock* was finished, headquarters has since commented that they are "reasonably hopeful" that *Sherlock* will return, possibly as early as two years after the fourth season ended (although the writers' and actors' comments seem to make that unlikely) (quoted in Burt, "*Sherlock* Season 5"). While the show's ratings may have dropped slightly during season four, the program remains one of the most-viewed television dramas in BBC history, and it continues to be a major revenue driver, so its discontinuance would not be dictated by low ratings or failure to generate revenue.

So what does all of this mean for *Sherlock* fanfiction? Fans' relationship to the show in a post-object world makes it difficult to predict the future of the fandom. Rebecca Williams defines post-object fandom as "fandom of any object which can no longer produce new texts" (Williams 269). Audiences remain unclear about *Sherlock*'s future: Has the last show taken place? Or is the series on hiatus? If so, will it come back and when? Will it have the same actors, writers, and canonical world? Given these open questions, perhaps a better way to consider the show's current state is as "zombie fandom." Whiteman and Metivier describe zombie fandoms as "online fan cultures that have entered into a state of atrophy, decline or impending demise" (270). While Sherlock fandom may not necessarily have entered a state of atrophy just yet, the show itself exists in a kind of "zombie time," "neither living nor dead, but somehow in between both orders. . . . The zombie narrative situates itself in that deferred space between catastrophe"—the final cancellation of the show—"and posthistory where the march of time begins to shamble and, as Harpold suggests, 'the end begins'" (Whiteman and Metivier 272). Because fans can't anticipate new episodes of *Sherlock*, however, does not necessarily mean they will abandon the fandom or stop creating fan works. They may continue to identify as *Sherlock* fans, purchase DVDs and merchandise, and talk about the show in online communities (Williams 269). But without a clear future or stable canonical world, *Sherlock* becomes a much less likely candidate for rich narrative world building; it becomes much harder for fans both to recreate the world and to recognize it in the work of others.

Many "big-name fans" have left *Sherlock* fandom, perhaps because of its unstable world or for political reasons, and many who've remained have chosen to explore alternate universes and storylines that better align with their desires for the show. Alternate universe and slash continue to be the most popular genres within the fandom, with most basing their versions on the world in its pre-season–three incarnation. More recently, a large group of fans have written "fix it fics" providing alternate endings to season four, including stories dealing with John and Sherlock's grief over Mary's death ("[Never] Turn Your Back to the Sea," "Where My Demons Hide"), confessing their love for one another ("The Pieces that Fall to Earth"), and parenting Rosie together ("Father"). Without new episodes on the horizon, and with such a drastically different canon/world for the final season, it would not be surprising if the *Sherlock* fanfiction phenomena lost momentum as fans turn to other fandoms and franchises that provide more open content and expanding worlds.

Perhaps *Sherlock*, like its nineteenth-century forerunner, has become a closed world, with the show's creators sealing off the possibilities for new innovative additions. Nonetheless, *Sherlock* fanfiction provides both a rich repository of creative work and a vast resource of cultural data on audience practices within contemporary popular culture. *Sherlock* fanfiction offers a fascinating and artful demonstration of audience engagement and participation in one of the most popular fictional worlds of the early twenty-first century. If the past 130 years have shown us anything, it is that Sherlock Holmes remains a perennial cultural favorite, and his world contains infinite resources for new imaginings. There is always room for a new Sherlockian world.

PERMISSIONS

Ann McClellan's work was originally published in the following publications:

A small portion of the Introduction was originally published as *"Tit-Bits*, New Journalism, and Early Sherlock Holmes Fandom," in *Transformative Works and Cultures* 23 (March 2017), http://dx.doi.org/10.3983/twc .2017.0816.

Portions of chapter 2 were previously published as "A Case of Identity: Role Playing, Social Media, and BBC *Sherlock*," in *The Journal of Fandom Studies* 1, no. 2 (2013): 139–57; in *The Baker Street Chronicle: "Sherlock" Special* S3 (2014); and as "'All that Matters Is the Work': Text and Adaptation in *Sherlock*," in *Sherlock Holmes in Context*, edited by Sam Naidu, 7–38 (New York: Palgrave MacMillan, 2017).

A previous version of chapter 4 was published as "Redefining 'Gender-swap' Fan Fiction: A *Sherlock* Case Study," in *Transformative Works and Cultures* 17 (September 2014), http://dx.doi.org/10.3983/twc.2014.0553.

NOTES

1. Consolidated viewing statistics for season three in 2014 estimated that more than twelve million viewers watched the show, making it the most watched BBC drama of the past decade, the show's highest ratings yet (P. Jones). *The Abominable Bride* Christmas special had more than 8.9 million UK viewers (Khonami).

2. Ironically, while London plays such an iconic role in *Sherlock*, from the distinctive opening credits to such key scenes as Moriarty robbing the Crown Jewels at the Tower of London in S2E3, most of the show was filmed in Cardiff, Wales, and on set. The production values of "importing" visual markers of these London landmarks, however, further establish the authenticity of *Sherlock*'s London world.

3. Abigail Derecho has challenged the use of "derivative" or "appropriative" when applied to fanfiction, arguing that the terms are both pejorative and imply too strong a relation to property, copyright, and ownership, which seems at odds with fanfiction practices. Instead, Derecho proposes authors and critics use the term *archontic*, from Jacques Derrida's theorization of the archive in his 1995 work *Archive Fever*. For Derecho, archontic literature is "composed of texts that are archival in nature and that are impelled by the same archontic principle: that tendency toward enlargement and accretion that all archives possess. . . . So all texts that build on a previously existing text are not lesser than the source text, and they do not violate the boundaries of the source text; rather, they only add to that text's archive, becoming a part of the archive and expanding it. An archontic text allows, or even invites, writers to enter it, select specific items they find useful, make new artifacts using those found objects, and deposit the newly made work back into the source text's archives" (Derecho 64–65).

4. Tolkien's legacy of "sub-creation" has haunted world building and fanfiction for decades. As William Proctor and Richard McCulloch articulate in their introduction to the May 2016 special issue of *Participations*, labeling the original source text (or even the real world) as the "primary" world and all other creations as "secondary" implies a hierarchy between realism and fiction and

between source text and transformative work. Such essentialist attitudes are easily deconstructed when we approach world building from the audience's experience. "If we each have different experiences" of the world and "see" different realities, Proctor and McCulloch conclude, there can be "no primary real world" (482).

5. Lisbeth Klastrup likewise distinguishes between "environments" and "worlds" when defining online worlds, specifically. For Klastrup, environments lack the requisite coherence, internal consistency (spatial or otherwise), and theme necessary for online worlds. Environments may be random in ways that worlds cannot be (*Towards a Poetics* 22).

6. Louisa Stein and Kristina Busse's early work "Limit Play: Fan Authorship between Source Intertext, and Context" provides an excellent framing of how authors of fanfiction work within, and challenge, existing canonical structures.

7. Paul Booth adds that even *Sherlock*'s storylines are "open": for instance, that Sherlock "both died (because in 1893 he had) and did not die (because Doyle resurrected him in the *Hound of the Baskervilles*) at the end of 'The Final Problem' means the narrative open-endedness of the character Sherlock is inscribed in canon for purist fans" (Booth, "*Sherlock* Fandom" 82).

8. Richard Gerrig argues that producers *intend* their audiences to be active participants within the world and in world building, and Umberto Eco notes that such worlds "incite audience participation in the form of speculation and fantasies" (Gerrig 122; Eco, quoted in Wolf 13).

9. Mark Wolf combines these two approaches in his definition of "world" and even adds characters' experiences as well, explaining: "To qualify as a fictional world, then, requires a fictional place . . . ; but a place is not always a world. The term 'world,' as it is being used here, is not simply geographical but 'experiential' that is, everything that is experienced by the characters involved, the elements enfolding someone's life (culture, nature, philosophical worldviews, places, customs, events, and so forth), just as world's etymological root word *weorld* from Old German refers to 'all that concerns humans,' as opposed to animals or gods" (Wolf 25).

10. Worlds are then defined by sets of extralinguistic objects (characters, settings, events) which the reader internalizes from the "window" of the text: "The idea of the textual world presupposes that the reader constructs in imagination a set of language-independent objects, using as a guide the textual declarations, but building this always incomplete image into a more vivid representation through the import of information provided by internalized cognitive models, inferential mechanisms, real-life experience, and cultural knowledge, including knowledge derived from other texts" (Ryan, *Narrative* 91).

11. In fact, an even earlier incarnation of Holmes's deerstalker can be seen in a few

unsigned illustrations for a reprint of Doyle's *Sign of the Four* in the June 14, 1890 *Bristol Observer*.

12. Deep media stories (like Jenkins's transmedia storytelling but without the emphasis on corporate sponsorship) are told across many media outlets and are nonlinear, participatory, gamelike, and immersive (Rose 3).

13. Originally, Doyle had difficulty publishing *A Study in Scarlet*, and spent nearly a year trying to do so before *Beeton's* finally agreed to publish it in 1886. He then had to wait another full year for it to come out in print. Doyle complained that he was paid a measly £25 for the publication and never earned another cent from it. *A Study in Scarlet* elicited little public response, and *The Sign of the Four*, published three years later in 1890, was similarly unsuccessful, at least in England (Payne 3; Carr 78).

14. For more information on the history of *The Strand Magazine*, its founders, and ultimate demise, see Reginald Pound's *Strand Magazine, 1891–1950* (London: Heinemann, 1966).

15. Doyle was quite vocal in his comments to friends and family about his hatred of Holmes. Likening his character to a "monstrous growth" and "an 'old man of the sea'" around his neck, he argued that killing Holmes was "justifiable homicide in self-defense, since, if I had not killed him, he would certainly have killed me" (Stashower 6, 147, 150). In his heart, Doyle felt that dedicating his life to Sherlock Holmes had robbed him of literary achievement. He frequently laments in his memoirs that he considered the stories "a lower stratum of literary achievement" and blamed Holmes from taking his mind "from better things," like the historical novels he loved (Doyle *Memories* 99, quoted in Stashower 126). His friend, Herbert Asquith, said Doyle once told him "he sometimes wished he had never written a word about Sherlock Holmes" (Pound 43).

16. Francesca Coppa, however, makes an important distinction between amateur fan practices, like writing fanfiction, and professionally penned pastiches: "If you only define fanfiction in terms of its engagement with other stories, copyrighted or not, there's no distinction between fanfiction and, say, Gregory Maguire's novel *Wicked* (which retells *The Wizard of Oz* from the Wicked Witch of the West's point of view), or Michael Chabon's *The Final Solution* (which features a beekeeping detective uncannily like Sherlock Holmes). But it seems there ought to be a distinction." Rather, "fanfiction isn't simply fiction created outside the market; it's fiction produced inside the community and within the culture of fandom" (Coppa, *Fanfiction* 7).

17. For more information on late nineteenth-century magazine promotions and fanfiction, see Ann McClellan's "*Tit-Bits*, New Journalism, and Early Sherlock Holmes Fandom."

18. Throughout the twentieth century, Sherlock Holmes references appeared in at least 50 films, 120 television shows, 55 stage plays (not including the three Doyle wrote himself), 162 radio plays, 37 records, two musicals, one ballet, more than 3,000 books and articles, and more than 700 published parodies and pastiches, more than 50 of which were published after 1970 (Herzinger 103). Herzinger's statistics extend up to 1992, when her essay was published; however, with the inclusion of contemporary fan creations in addition to the recent proliferation of pastiches, movies, and television shows, it has become virtually impossible to track the number of Holmes-inspired texts.

19. Holmesian pastiche and scholarship elicits many traditionalist views. Alistair Duncan maintains "the final requirement is that the stories must be filmed in the context of the time" (236). Similarly, David Stuart Davies, in his biography of Jeremy Brett, arguably the twentieth century's most famous Sherlock Holmes, claims that "fidelity was always at the forefront of Jeremy Brett's mind." Ironically, however, Davies continues to note that both Brett and producer Michael Cox used the Sidney Paget drawings as their reference point for Holmes's appearance and mannerisms, even though Doyle himself claimed Paget's illustrations did not match his conception of Holmes in the original stories (D. S. Davies 51). Thus, the Granada Holmes's "faithful" adaptation is itself based on another interpretation of the character rather than on the source texts themselves.

20. Trevor Hall disputes the commonly held assumption that Knox was the first scholar to hold Holmes up for serious literary study, arguing that Frank Sidgwick's "An Open Letter to Dr. Watson" in *The Cambridge Review* (January 23, 1902) was the first "higher criticism" analysis of Doyle's stories. Andrew Lang's "At the Sign of the Ship" (*Longman's Magazine*, July 1904) analyzing "The Three Students" was another such approach (Hall 4–5).

21. Vera Tobin similarly notes that while "the spectacle of supposedly rational adults engaging in such play was distasteful to many" in the early half of the twentieth century, contemporary audiences, surrounded as they are by fan communities, satire, comic books, and so on, view such activity as relatively normal (83).

22. Paul Booth has similarly observed that "if fandom was important to Conan Doyle's success, it is crucial for *Sherlock*'s. Of all the cult fan texts that thrive today, it is Sherlock Holmes that reveals the longevity and survival of fandom across decades, through multiple media representations, and with varied [and often surprising] results" (Booth, "*Sherlock* Fandom" 80).

23. Just recently, Sherlockian scholar and fan Mattias Boström has possibly traced the origin of Holmes's famous catchphrase, "Elementary, my dear Watson," to William Gillette's 1899 play, the script of which includes Holmes saying to

his partner, "Elementary, my dear fellow." Boström maintains that these specific lines along with the numerous iterations of "my dear Watson" in the play combined in the minds of audience members into a unique and memorable quotation. Boström cites seeing a parody from as early as 1901 of the famous phrase in a newspaper ad for Charles Forde's Bile Beans for Biliousness, as well as in several US and UK advertisements between 1901 and 1910. Boström concludes that the only thing linking the two international audiences that could possibly explain the parodization of Holmes's line on both continents was Gillette's play, which both played in London and toured in the United States during this period.

24. *Star Trek* fanfiction was the original source of many of the codes, genres, and distinctions later adopted by fan writers and online sites over the past forty-plus years (Busse, *Framing Fan Fiction* 202).

25. Henry Jenkins in *Textual Poachers* lays out ten different ways fans rewrite cult texts, ranging from "recontextualization," which fills in plot holes in the original storyline, to the ever popular "eroticization," which transforms characters' lives into erotic fantasies (165–80).

26. Mel Stanfill further explains that giving and returning gifts is required in such a highly structured environment: "This economy is not simply friendly and voluntary in the way that 'gifts' are colloquially understood as freely chosen expressions of affection. . . . Giving in a gift *economy* is, first, hierarchical . . . giving more produces status" (77). Profusive writing or commenting are additional ways fans show appreciation of other fans' labors.

27. Several excellent narratives about the history of fan studies have recently been published, including the *Routledge Companion to Media Studies* (2017), edited by Melissa A. Click and Suzanne Scott, and Kristina Busse's *Framing Fan Fiction: Literary and Social Practices in Fan Fiction Communities* (2017), the primary sources for much of the following history. Wiley-Blackwell Publishing is also preparing a new media fandom overview for publication in 2019.

28. Abigail Derecho defines fan fiction as "the literature of the subordinate," particularly because "most fanfic authors are women responding to media products that, for the most part, are characterized by an underrepresentation of women" (71).

29. Sheenagh Pugh argues that this desire for "more of, as well as more from" the source text prompted the creation of the first fanfiction (222).

30. Matt Hills provides an insightful reading of fan culture as a form of psychoanalytic "transitional space" wherein a specific text acts as a proper transitional object for a community (Hills, *Fan Culture* 108). I cautiously use "original" in this passage in the sense of new, noncopyrighted, world-based writing and not in the creative sense; fanfiction certainly provides original and creative inter-

pretations of canonical works. As for world "limits," I follow Louisa Stein and Kristina Busse's argument that "fannish creativity thrives not only because of the sense of pleasure of play within limits but also because of a sense of productive freedom borne of transformation. . . . Thus, fannish creative engagement spins on an axis of the embrace of limits and perceived rejection of limits" (Stein and Busse 195).

31. Interestingly, "canon" in the Great Game of mock Sherlockian scholarship refers to Sir Arthur Conan Doyle's original sixty Sherlock Holmes stories; these "sacred writings" are treated with the same reverence and respect as the Bible. So, the concept of canon has even more multilayered significance when analyzing Sherlockian stories, pastiches, and fanfiction.

32. Likewise, Rhiannon Bury claims, "the issue of canon is the one feature unique to fanfiction" (100). "Most important to treatments of fan texts are understandings of canon," concur Stein and Busse (9).

33. Martin Freeman in an interview reportedly called *Sherlock* "the gayest story in the history of television." "We all certainly saw it as a love story," Freeman told *The Telegraph* after picking up the Best Supporting Actor Award in 2011 (Walker).

34. As Kristina Busse articulates, "what is at stake" in fanfiction "is a power negotiation between fans and author over who has the authority to interpret a text, as well as the question over how a source text's canon ultimately is delineated, and by whom" (Busse, *Framing Fan Fiction* 99).

35. Recently, Santo has called for greater attention to "object-oriented" fans, that is, a focus on fans who purchase and collect merchandise related to fandom. Researching what merchandise fans buy and what they do with it helps increase understanding of what defines fandom, who has access, and how. Importantly, "merchandise constitutes one of the key components through which media industries have redefined their relationship with fan culture and have sought to define fandom not only in consumerist terms but also within existing frameworks for consumer product extension: namely, the reconstitution of fandom as a lifestyle category rather than a communal experience" (Santo 329).

36. Of course, exceptions can be made to this mimetic argument as well, including crack!fic and other genres in which characters are affected by their position within a different setting, genre, or alternate universe. While critics such as Sheenagh Pugh argue that acting "out-of-character" risks alienating the fan audience and "violating" the rules of the canon (70), Lisbeth Klastrup and others argue that knowing a character is acting out of character still reinforces the verisimilitude of the canon because recognizing the character is behaving

unusually indicates the readers' knowledge of canon compliance (Klastrup, *Towards a Poetics* 296).

37. Stein, Mittell, and Stam all argue that we must be careful of seeing genre as the end-all, be-all organizational principle for fan products. While fans frequently use genre distinctions to sort fan practices (publications, conferences, websites, and so on) and as methods to fulfill their personal reading preferences, genre distinctions are not inherent in the texts themselves (Mittell, "A Cultural Approach"); that is, categorization of slash fanfic, for example, is not ontological; it is a genre label that fan producers, audiences, and scholars assign a given work after the fact in recognition of its particular, previously determined characteristics, cultural values, and associations.

38. Derecho's specific argument was that early fans established and used headers primarily as a way to warn readers about (and attract them to) potentially triggering sexual content, such as rape stories, nonconsensual sex, and incest.

CHAPTER 1

1. I use *ur-text* here to avoid the implied hierarchies and pitfalls of "primary" and "secondary" texts or worlds.

2. Michael Saler has written extensively on nineteenth-century fans' investment in Sherlock Holmes's Victorian London, commenting on the role magazine letters, pages, and correspondence played in extending and adapting Holmes's world (95–97). Gatiss has also commented on the creators' desire to get out from under the dominant role the Victorian setting has played in previous adaptations (Digital Spy).

3. When Doyle created Sherlock Holmes, he was living in Portsmouth, England, and was relatively unfamiliar with London and its neighborhoods. He chose Holmes's address by looking at a street map and perhaps did not realize that, at the time, houses on Baker Street only numbered up to 100. It wasn't until 1930 that the Westminster City Council decided to extend Baker Street and 221 became a reality. The first tenants, the Abbey National Bank, immediately began receiving fan mail addressed to Sherlock Holmes, so much mail, in fact, that they hired a full-time secretary to reply to every piece of correspondence. For an entertaining selection of the most interesting letters sent to Baker Street over the years, see *The Sherlock Holmes Letters* (1987), by Richard Lancelyn Green. In 1990, when the Sherlock Holmes Museum opened at 239 Baker Street, the Westminster City Council realized the financial possibilities offered by the new tourist attraction and renumbered the street. Fans who now visit Holmes's home will note that the house numbering runs 235, 237, 221, 241, and up.

4. Polasek actually argues in her article that the BBC Sherlock adaptation "rewrites Conan Doyle's Victorian Sherlock Holmes out of existence, and in so doing purges from the real London landscape the simulacrum of 221b Baker Street with its Blue Plaque and its claim to authenticity" (195–96). I'm arguing here, however, that the real London landscape was already "purged" of "authenticity" by Doyle's fiction. It was Doyle's original stories that supplanted the reality of the London maps and replaced it with a fictional simulacrum powerful enough to draw fan letters and visitations, even when the real physical location did not (yet) exist.

5. Kellie Takenaka similarly recognizes the important role setting plays in *Sherlock*, noting that the show's "location is in fact hugely central to *Sherlock*" (20).

6. Air New Zealand has so completely embraced fans' interest in the filming locations used for *The Lord of the Rings* that the films now provide the theme of its in-flight safety video.

7. Avi Santo's recent research on "object-oriented fans" has raised important questions about the relationship between fandom and merchandise and the importance of studying the material realities of fandom (329). Santo argues that "Branded t-shirts, backpacks, and cell phone covers may transform fans into walking promotional platforms for particular franchises, but they also fulfill the entertainment industry's objective in creating veritable touch points for IP that integrate them into consumers' daily routines as branded lifestyle products" (331).

8. A diegetic extension is one "where an object from the storyworld gets released in the real world. Most diegetic extensions are objects featured in a series that do not bear much storytelling weight, such as Davy Crockett's coonskin cap" (Mittell, "Strategies" 259).

9. Paul Booth rightly warns, however, that such cross-promotion has significant impact on who gets to identify as a "fan." In "*Sherlock* Fandom: The Game is Afoot!" Booth observed fan practices at the 2010 first annual Sherlocked fan convention in London, noting how much of the fan experience was predicated on financial access: "Ticket prices ranged from a £29 single-day only ticket (for Saturday) to a £2995 VIP pass that included two autographs from each guest, two individual photos with each guest, and tickets to all the talks" (94). Individual talks cost money. Photo shots and autographs cost additional money. Fans were organized into different access lines based on how much money they'd been able to pay for tickets and access. What resulted, Booth concluded, was a clear fan class system that privileged those who had the time and money to buy more—and closer—access to the stars, and these discrepancies were clearly noticeable by the fans and quickly became a popular topic of discussion.

10. Janet Murray actually imagined a version of transmedia storytelling before Jenkins's *Convergence Culture* (2006) in *Hamlet on the Holodeck* (1997). There, Murray imagines a new kind of "integrated digital archive" that would showcase and share "virtual artefacts from the fictional world of the series." The archive could include various websites, diaries, photos, and other world-building artifacts, such as birth certificates, licenses, and other legal documents (255).

11. Freeman traces the rise of transmedia storytelling back to 1850s magazine culture and early twentieth-century newspapers, comic strips, and advertising. Early twentieth-century media outlets used strong visual content to steer audiences outside the magazines and newspapers to other related products. Having a comic character, for example, refer to a consumer product that audiences could purchase elsewhere helped establish the kinds of cross-promotional strategies that made modern advertising and storytelling so successful. These practices were then adopted by a few media-savvy writers like L. Frank Baum and Edgar Rice Burroughs, who used cross-promotional practices to create and promote tie-in products for their fictional stories (Freeman, "Advertising" 2365).

12. In *Convergence Culture*, Jenkins gives several examples of the multiple ways the transmedia franchise *The Matrix* creates radical intertextuality between the animated series and the main films, extending to "missing scenes" from the films that can only be experienced through the tie-in video games, and so on.

13. The BBC also experimented with the Twitter account @TheWhipHand for Irene Adler, a character in season two in 2012, but it was abandoned after just thirteen tweets.

14. Janet Murray predicted such a "hyperserial/integrated digital archive" in her foundational work, *Hamlet on the Holodeck* (1997): "Probably the first steps toward a new *hyperserial* format will be the close integration of a digital archive, such as a website, with a broadcast television program. . . . An integrated digital archive would present virtual artifacts from the fictional world of the series, including not only diaries, photo albums, and telephone messages but also documents like birth certificates, legal briefs, or divorce papers. . . . All of these artifacts would be available on demand, in between episodes, so that viewers could experience a continuous sense of ongoing lives" (254–55). Paul Booth similarly commented on realistic-looking TV character websites in *Digital Fandom* (2010).

15. In addition, Wolf also discusses the role of *transquels*—"an element, which would take place before, during, and after a previously-released sequence element (or elements)," usually used to provide broad historical context, and *paraquels*, where the same events from the show are shown from different

characters' points of view (209–10). The latter is usually created after the entire sequence or work is completed.

16. In addition to posting an interquel to inaugurate season three ("Many Happy Returns," October 5), the show's creators gifted fans with a seven-minute "webisode" posted on the BBC website on Christmas Eve 2013, showcasing Anderson's fall from the Yard, his wild theories about Sherlock's return, and John's continuing depression over Sherlock's alleged death. The webisode included a video that Sherlock apparently made for John's birthday before his "death."

17. Readers may already be familiar with such formats through the popular Bantam books 1980s and 1990s print series of "Choose Your Own Adventure" novels. Similar critiques of preprogrammed interactivity can be found in the history of hypertext design and other electronic literature.

18. Paul Booth argues that fictional character websites like John's blog and Sherlock's "Science of Deduction" give the appearance of greater interactivity with the character and fictional world (*Digital Fandom* 128).

19. As Mark Wolf explains, "Participatory worlds are a subset of interactive worlds, since while all participatory worlds are inherently open and interactive, not all interactive worlds allow the user to make permanent changes to the world, sharing in its authorship" (281).

20. A similar assumption was made in the early 1990s about the advent of hypertext. Building on the work of Roland Barthes and Jacques Derrida, George Landow's revolutionary *Hypertext: The Convergence of Contemporary Critical Theory and Technology* signaled a similar "paradigm shift." Landow argued that this new form of storytelling was the "ideal" text and had the power to revolutionize storytelling and reading by putting the power of the text in the reader's hands. Hypertext was participatory in the sense that it "blurred the boundaries between reader and writer" (755) until the reader, not the writer, actively "wrote" the text through her hypertextual choices. Even though Landow's book has gone through several editions and is still lauded as a foundational text in electronic literature studies, critics were not far behind in disputing his assumption that the death of the author necessarily meant the birth of the all-powerful reader or that the appearance of choice necessarily meant the reader had the ability to write a text that was not already there.

21. Mark Wolf argues that the presence of interactive media in traditionally non-interactive text/formats can actually make the user *more* aware of the limitations of the world rather than the limits of their participation within it (221).

22. Matthew Freeman defines commodity braiding as "the commercially designed interlocking of a range of commodities, be it media texts and/or consumer

products, through strategies of narrative or authorship as exemplified by the interlocking of pulp-based storyworlds" ("The Wonderful Game of Oz" 47).

23. All notifications use BBC press-release photos of the show's main characters/ actors, which also works to reinforce the verisimilitude and continuity of the world and app.

CHAPTER 2

1. See Albrecht-Crane and Cutchins 11–12, Dudley 31, Stam 57, and Cardwell for more on the history of fidelity and/in adaptation studies.

2. Fidelity has been a constant factor in previous Holmesian adaptations as well. Each new iteration "is scrutinised and analysed for its fidelity to, or commentary on, the Canonical stories" (Poore 168). Looking specifically at the 1980s Granada television series starring Jeremy Brett as Sherlock Holmes, Neil McCaw similarly commented on the importance of the Doyle source texts and on the show's commitment to the "authenticity" of Doyle's fictional world: "fidelity to this canon [was] seen as an indicator of cultural value and (seemingly) moral righteousness; there was a perceived *duty* to be loyal to the originating sources. This commitment to authenticity underpinned the development of the series and its diligent focus on the Doylean texts, a feature recognized by viewers and critics alike: 'the 32 Sherlock Holmes films which Michael Cox produced for Granada Television maintain the integrity of Doyle's texts in ways which other adaptations, including the famous series of films featuring Basil Rathbone and Nigel Bruce, do not'" (McCaw 38, quoting Trembly).

3. Critic Matt Hills labels this oscillation as a kind of "heretical fidelity," which lets Moffat and Gatiss reassure traditional Holmesian audiences that the "Canon remains as a sacred Ur-Text" (that is, as the primary "Work" underlying the show) at the same time that they clearly depart from it to create new, modernized stories of their own (Hills, *Fan Culture* 35).

4. Another possible explanation for the change from "based on Sir Arthur Conan Doyle's Sherlock Holmes" to "Based on the Works of Sir Arthur Conan Doyle" is that legal/copyright issues arose with the Doyle estate; however, this has not been confirmed by the showrunners or producers. I would argue, however, that the content of seasons two through four are much more adaptive than season one, as I go on to explain, which reflects the shift in language in the opening credits.

5. For example, "A Scandal in Belgravia" is a clear adaptation of Doyle's "A Scandal in Bohemia"; the BBC's "The Hounds of Baskerville" is an even closer adaptation of Doyle's *Hound of the Baskervilles*. Season two's "Reichenbach Fall" is

perhaps the most obscure; however, the script constantly invokes the original story title, "The Final Problem," through Moriarty's references to the conflict between him and Sherlock, which he refers to as "their problem. The final problem" (*Sherlock*, "The Reichenbach Fall").

6. In the BBC show, John and Mary Morstan do get married, but most of the embedded mysteries (other than Major Sholto's and Jonathan Small's names) come from other Holmes stories.

7. Several recent books have added important contributions to the history and development of Sherlock Holmes pastiches over the twentieth century—particularly, how *Sherlock*'s creators incorporate various versions in their own television appropriations (Stein and Busse, Porter, Ue and Cranfield, and Vanacker and Wynne).

8. Rather than feeling constrained, Louisa Stein and Kristina Busse argue that many fans "thrive" within these structures because of the "pleasure of play within limits" (195).

9. In fact, while Tumblr maintains old posts in user archives, Twitter, due to the amount of traffic, does not allow users to search back more than three thousand or so tweets, so it becomes difficult for users and researchers to use the archives. Tumblr lacks date stamps as well, so it is impossible to tell when a post originated other than by looking through the user's monthly archives. The lack of easily searchable archives poses a significant problem for current and future social media research.

10. Louise Rosenblatt's "transactional theory" of reading and writing is fundamental here. Rosenblatt claims: "Every reading act is an event, a transaction involving a particular reader and a particular configuration of marks on a page, and occurring at a particular time in a particular context. . . . The 'meaning' does not reside ready-made in the text or in the reader, but happens during the transaction between reader and text" (4).

11. Ika Willis, in her discussion of "Mary Sue" narratives and queer identity in fanfiction, argues that textual gaps are a definitive feature of all fanfiction. Willis writes: "It is only through the idea of supplementation, I would argue, that fanfiction can be understood (as it often is, both by academics and by fans) as 'filling in the gaps' in canon. For these gaps may only become visible—may only, indeed, be gaps—when the text is read from a position that refuses the illusion of continuity; and textual gaps are filled in according to an associative, not deductive, logic. Writing fanfiction is not simply adding the final piece of a jigsaw—completing a text with a known unknown, whose correct shape and dimensions can be deduced: rather, writing fanfiction first of all makes gaps in a text that the cultural code attempts to render continuous, and then, rather than filling them in, supplements these gaps with intertexts which are

not docile but which—like both Sedgwick's promise to her younger self . . . and Barthes's Brecht intercalation—make the tacit things explicit" (158).

12. A subgenre within fanfiction, *crack!fic* is defined by its tenuous connections to canon, with particular emphases on bizarre plotlines, out-of-character behavior, and humor. While each Sherlock in the aforementioned scene is "consistent" with the show's characterization (demanding, selfish), the idea of John being bombarded with a slew of such characters, all demanding tea at the same time, is both humorous and, of course, impossible. As crack!fic, the scene violates virtually all of the "rules" established for world building in RPNs. By simultaneously reinforcing and challenging the world of the show, crack!fic demonstrates that not all readers desire fidelity all the time.

13. Lisbeth Klastrup identifies similar connections between immersion and realism in role playing. For Klastrup, immersion is "the initial creation of and then continuous on-off belief in the world, the pretend-moments when the player consciously pretends that all that happens in the online world is 'real,' and accordingly interprets events in conjunction with their in-game or in-world meaning" (Klastrup "Worldness").

14. Unlike fan productions, which treat seriously and fulfill fans' desire for a homoerotic relationship between Sherlock and John, *Sherlock*'s creators repeatedly turn this possibility into a joke rather than a viable representation of the kinds of love individuals may share and experience in real life. John's constant denial of any sexual attraction to Sherlock and his "confirmed bachelor" nickname from "The Reichenbach Fall," for instance, reinforce the message that a romantic relationship between the two men is, literally, a joke.

15. Several fans have shared theories that Moffat and Gatiss have been laying the groundwork to reveal a romantic relationship between Holmes and Watson at a later date. Known as the "Johnlock Conspiracy," or TJLC, these fans argue that the writers are simultaneously conspiring to both fuel and thwart audience's desires for a romantic culmination to the characters' on-screen relationship.

16. Similar forays are being made in fanfiction as well. "The Sensation of Falling as You Just Hit Sleep" by Greywash, for example, deftly interweaves traditional narrative fanfiction with a variety of digital images and screencaps (Greywash).

17. While such designations seemingly increased the authenticity of the account, Facebook does not actually "verify," designate, or even acknowledge specific accounts as role-play accounts, nor do they have criteria by which they evaluate them. Any person could add or customize the viral tag as they saw fit, perhaps as a way to legitimize one role-playing character over others with the same persona.

18. The sherlock holmes-bbc profile disappeared during this time but was soon replaced by that of Shock Holmes, perhaps indicative of a deleted account.

CHAPTER 3

1. The term *slash* comes from the virgule ("/"), a punctuation mark used between two same-sex characters' names to delineate a homoerotic pairing (for example, Kirk/Spock or Holmes/Watson).

2. Most scholars posit slash's origin in the *Star Trek* fandom in the early- to mid-seventies, when several fans, primarily women, began to write and share stories imagining Captain Kirk and Spock in various romantic and erotic scenarios. Scholar Raven Davies, however, has argued that slash fiction actually started much earlier, in 1920s cinema culture. "In the 1920s, an underground group of gay fans of the new technical sensation, cinema, created a new way of seeing the unfolding story," Davies wrote. "Changing the starring characters to their own sexual orientation they began writing stories to illustrate their own life experiences and fantasies, while maintaining a close similarity to the personae originated by the characters" (R. Davies 197).

3. Francesca Coppa recently wrote about the impact of genderswapping James Bond's iconic "M" character as a woman. With Judi Dench's casting in 1995's *Goldeneye*, the film franchise "took a page from fanfiction by changing the gender of a primary character, and, as fans have long known, to change a character's gender is to change the parameters of the universe" (*Fanfiction Reader* 121–22).

4. Critics like Elizabeth Woledge and Catherine Driscoll, for example, see less of a distinction between pornography and romantic fiction within slash. For Driscoll, "the dominant mode of the use of sex in fanfiction" is sexual intercourse that "closes the narrative to resolve plot and character, even if some other kind of sex had preceded it" (86).

5. Mulvey, Penley, and others have more recently been criticized for their essentialism (much like the similar argument among evolutionary biologists): Mulvey for assuming a white, heterosexual, male audience and Penley for assuming that only white, middle-class, heterosexual women write and read slash. Critics Eden Lackner, Barbara Lynn Lucas, and Robin Anne Reid warn against assuming all slash writers and readers are heterosexual women or that slash is written by straight women for other straight women and is always about gay male sex (194). For instance, many readers were surprised when popular fan author bendingsignpost revealed himself to be a man. Many commenters on his popular fics like "34 Minutes," "Stranger at the Gate," and the "Watches 'Verse'" assumed he was a woman writing gay male slash *Sherlock* fic.

6. Catherine Tosenberger warns against situating slash and other queer readings of the canon in opposition to the source texts, claiming "the insistence that slash must transgress the existing canon rather troublingly assigns to the canon a heteronormativity it may not necessarily possess. Moreover, it reinforces the assumption that queer readings are always readings 'imposed' from the outside" (187).

7. Slash readings aren't new to the Holmesian universe, however. Some scholars cite Rex Stout's 1941 essay, "Watson Was a Woman," from Baker Street Irregular founder Christopher Morley's *Saturday Review of Literature,* as one of the first intimations that Holmes and Watson were in a more domesticated relationship than most Victorian fans imagined.

8. Controversially, Moffat and Gatiss recently gave an interview at the 2016 San Diego Comic-Con about Moffat's participation on a panel discussing representation of minority characters on screen. In the interview, Moffat accused fans of "trivializing" a "serious subject" matter by turning it into confirmation that the Johnlock Conspiracy was real and that John and Sherlock would end up in a romantic relationship. Gatiss went on to claim that all of the Johnlock queer references in the show were a reference to the "joke" in Billy Wilder's film *The Private Life of Sherlock Holmes,* thus implying that their inclusion was similarly a joke. Even though *Sherlock*'s creators stated that fans could "write whatever they like and have a great time extrapolating"—"once we hand the show to them"—they've "explicitly said this was not going to happen." The reality was that the show and its characters were "theirs" (Parker). While Gatiss maintained that the show shouldn't have to—and could not—be responsible for addressing social issues like queer representation, both writers maintained that fans could do what they chose with the show at the same time that they denied their interpretation of the context and their desires for its resolution (Parker).

9. As Catherine Tosenberger explains, many slash fics are based on television shows and movies that follow the "buddy" movie format, with a pair of male protagonists who complement one another physically, psychologically, and emotionally. (John and Sherlock's physical and behavioral compatibility—Sherlock's tall figure to John's shorter one, Sherlock's dark curls to John's ash-blond hair, and so on—were mentioned briefly in the introduction to this book.) In "buddyslash" fics, two male characters, already strongly emotionally connected through the sacred bonds of friendship, transform that friendship into a romantic and sexual relationship of equals. The men are represented as "soul mates" who know each other like no others in their lives possibly can (Tosenberger 192).

10. Actor Benedict Cumberbatch's hands are frequently an object of fan study and

adoration, and several Tumblr blogs and hashtags (#handporn) feature photos, screenshots, and gifs of Cumberbatch's hands both in real life and in his
acting.

11. Fetishization of the actors' bodies becomes a particular focal point for critics
of real person slash or real person fic. Many fans view such appropriations of
the actors' real bodies as a violation of their privacy; however, most fanfiction
writers don't seem to experience the same conflict when appropriating actors'
bodies for other genres.

12. Catherine Driscoll notes that developing romances within slash fictions are
often "substituted or supplemented with sexualized encounters of building
intimacy and explicitness" (86).

13. Author emmagranto1 herself seemed to recognize the separation between
John's image of Sherlock and Sherlock's own experiences in these scenes, and
as a result she began rewriting the entire fic from Sherlock's point of view so
audiences could get a better sense of his emotional and sexual well-being. Unfortunately, the fic at this time remains unfinished.

14. "First time" fics are popular within fandoms as they signify a masculine vul-
nerability and emotional trust and intimacy between the partners. Anal sex, in
particular, is often seen as the ultimate physical and emotional connection in
slash fic. Many male protagonists are subsequently portrayed as "anal virgins"
and "the loss of their anal virginity affirms a bond they share with no one else,
and 'first time' slash stories are extremely popular" (Salmon and Symons 98).

CHAPTER 4

1. The essential source on genderswap fanfiction to date is by Kristina Busse
and Alexia Lothian ("Bending Gender"). Both Busse and Lothian have also
blogged independently on the issue (Busse, "Is Fandom"; Lothian, "Doing
Boys"), and Hannah Ellison dedicated a small section of her recent *Glee*
(2009–) kink meme article to "girl!peen" fiction (stories about women with
male genitalia; 2013). Freund and Fielding ("Research Ethics") also touch on
the subject. Additionally, a few other recent articles—on cosplay, in particular—have included discussions of gender bending (Gilligan "Having Cleavages"; Leng "Gender"), and Jordan Youngblood recently published an article
on gender embodiment in video games (2013).

2. Jeremy Brett's Sherlock Holmes from the much-lauded Granada TV series in the
1980s was a similar mix of arrogant masculine intellect and effete, prissy self-
centeredness. Thus, Cumberbatch's fluidly gendered Sherlock is not the first
complexly gendered Holmes in media history.

3. On the website Archive of Our Own, one of the only truly searchable fan sites,
fans use several different terms to describe the genre, including "genderswap,"

"gender!swap," "sexswap," "genderswitch," "gender-switch," "genderflip," or adding "girl!" or "fem!" before a character's name. This variety illustrates the multiple ways in which fans envision gender identity, thus complicating researchers' ability to gather definitive data on the subject. Other labels in research on genderswap fanfiction use "genderfuck" and "gender bending" interchangeably (Busse and Lothian 105).

4. The genderswap entry in the Fanlore wiki is one of the few places where this discrepancy is noted. "While it should correctly be called *sexswap*, since the biological sex is being swapped (and the social gender only as a consequence of the biological change)," the site explains, "the term is established for a number of likely reasons, e.g., the conflation of sex and gender in discourse or the better flow of words" (http://fanlore.org/wiki/Genderswap). This definition assumes, however, that social gender is only a consequence of biological sex rather than an integral part of an individual's holistic gender identity. "Sex," as Susan Stryker notes, "is not the foundation of gender in the same way that an apple is not the foundation of a reflection of red fruit in the mirror; 'sex' is a mash-up, a story we mix about how the body means, which parts matter most, and how they register in our consciousness or field of vision" ("(De)Subjugated Knowledges" 9).

5. Some readers may fairly question whether one can claim that genderswap fails to attend to the body when so many of these stories are sexually explicit. While this is certainly true, here we explore what those bodies mean and how they affect characters' sense of identity rather than merely what bodies do in sexual situations.

6. Some scholars, for example, Monique Wittig and Judith Butler, argue that our understanding of nature and the natural at the root of the biological argument underpinning our concept of sex are as culturally constructed as our understanding of gender. As Wittig explains, we often take sex "as an 'immediate given,' 'a sensible given,' 'physical features,' belonging to a natural order. But what we believe to be a physical and direct perception is only a sophisticated and mythic construction, an 'imaginary formation,' which reinterprets physical features (in themselves as neutral as others but marked by a social system), through the network of relationships in which they are perceived" (Wittig, quoted in Butler, *Bodies That Matter* 155).

7. Of course, all of these parameters can be problematized in specific circumstances: infertility, castration, vasectomy, hysterectomy, mastectomy, and so on. Even the most obvious cultural and biological determinants of sex identity can be altered. In addition to basic reproductive genitalia, some people also include secondary sex characteristics, such as mammary glands and facial hair, as bodily signs of biological sex. Intersexed individuals—people who ex-

hibit biological characteristics of more than one sex—clearly challenge the underlying concepts defining Western society's male/female sex/gender classification; however, most of Western culture remains structured by this simplified binary system.

8. For Butler, gender is performative in the sense that "as in other ritual social dramas, the action of gender requires a performance that is repeated. This repetition is at once a reenactment and re-experiencing of a set of meanings already socially established; and it is the mundane and ritualized form of their legitimation" (Butler, *Bodies That Matter* 191). Therefore, gender has "no ontological status apart from the various acts which constitute its reality" (185). In more recent transgender research, such arguments have come under fire for ignoring the material reality of the body in a post-9/11 surveillance state that is much more invested in defining, maintaining, and policing boundaries between sex and gender, the self and the state, nation and nation.

9. The term *cisgender* attempts to highlight the typically unnamed assumption of nontransgender status in the terms *man* and *woman*. Some transgender theorists dislike the term, however, arguing that it still situates nontransgender, or cisgender, as the norm. Nontransgender, they argue, positions transgender identities as central, which, for some, is a more political act.

10. Many scholars and individuals reject the transsexual label, claiming it is too old-fashioned and narrow to encompass all transgender people and experiences; many others refuse it due to its unfortunate pathological associations with the *Diagnostic and Statistical Manual of Mental Disorders*, connecting it to gender identity disorder and gender dysphoria. While transsexuals and transgender people both experience similar dissociation between their gender identities and/or gender expression and their biological sex, transsexuals are often described as individuals who seek to alter their bodies, either through hormone treatment or sex assignment surgery, while transgender people "may have little or no intention of having sex-reassignment surgeries or hormone treatments" (Nagoshi and Brzuzy 432). Transgender, rather than transsexual, has become the accepted term within North American trans* activism—most likely since it is considered more inclusive and addresses a wider range of gender and sex identities.

11. Transgender theorists Nagoshi and Brzuzy argue that previous poststructural theories about the social construction of gender that do not take embodiment and biology into account are now inadequate: "Bodies are involved more actively, more intimately, and more intricately in social processes than theory has usually allowed," they elaborate. "Bodies participate in social action by delineating courses of social conduct—the body is a participant in gender so-

cial practice" (Nagoshi and Brzuzy 435). As a result, Susan Stryker and Aren Z. Aizura note in their introduction to the recently published *Transgender Studies Reader 2* (2013) previous transgender scholarship's "explicit whiteness, U.S.-centric, and Anglophone bias" (4) and the ways in which transgender bodies are increasing becoming a Foucauldian field of knowledge through post-9/11 surveillance strategies. They add, "'Gender' is not merely the representation in language and culture of a biological sex; it is also an administrative or bureaucratic structure for the maintenance of sexual difference and reproductive capacity (the ticking off of M's and F's on state-issued or state-sanctioned forms). In this sense, and to the extent that gender identity is understood as the psychical internalization and somaticization of historically contingent modes of embodied personhood, transgender is intimately bound up with questions of nation, territory, and citizenship, with categories of belonging and exclusion, of excess and incorporation, and with all the processes through which individual corporealities become aggregated as bodies politic" (8).

12. Notably, transgender research has shifted in the last decade away from the pathological, linguistic, and performative histories of gendered bodies to focus on the various ways in which bodies are politicized through gender, sexuality, race, class, nation, able-bodiedness, etc. Current trans* theory is particularly interested in the ways in which bodies act, are acted upon, and are materially defined in/by systems of power.

13. Jane Clare Jones's "Is Sherlock Sexist? Steven Moffat's Wanton Women" from *The Guardian* and Helen Lewis's rebuttal in the *New Statesman* prompted a small but passionate media and internet firestorm around the show's female characters—or lack thereof. Bloggers such as Foz Meadows, Wellingtongoose, Rileyo, and Addyke all wrote insightful meta commentary on the show's women characters, their portrayals, and audience responses.

14. Since *Sherlock*'s first broadcast in 2010, CBS launched its own genderswapped version of John Watson in Lucy Liu's Joan Watson on *Elementary. Elementary*'s creators removed many of the canonical elements that defined John Watson's character, however: his military background, his experience with fire arms, and so on, so Liu's Joan Watson was left with little character motivation and little purpose other than to serve as Sherlock's babysitter. In subsequent seasons, the showrunners had Joan get self-defense training, and she ultimately started her own detective service to rival Sherlock's, thus putting her on a more equal footing with Johnny Lee Miller's Holmes. Fans have shown little interest in Liu's genderswapped character, however, perhaps because she doesn't retain the canonical elements defining Watson's character in the original Arthur Conan Doyle world.

15. To help situate the popularity of genderswap stories in Sherlock fandom, consider that Archive of Our Own (AO3) lists 35,669 BBC *Sherlock* fanfiction entries, 260 of which are specifically tagged "genderswap"; AO3 reports 3,353 "genderswap" narratives across all fandoms. Keeping in mind the variants within statistical reporting, when searching BBC *Sherlock* and the following tags, AO3 revealed: Femlock, 147; Gender Changes, 210; Female John, 1,019; Fem!John, 31; Girl!John, 122; Female Sherlock, 1,440; Fem!Sherlock, 0; Girl!Sherlock, 0; Transgender, 34.

16. While such masculine and feminine labels are limiting and, to some extent, the entire point of this critique, they remain a useful shorthand for how most of North American society categorizes such behaviors.

17. In other genderswap stories, guy!John is not as comfortable with his feminine behaviors as Martin Freeman appears to be on BBC *Sherlock*. In one story, guy!John has a minor gender-identity crisis when he realizes he's the one who's insisting on having a romantic relationship with Sherlock instead of casual sex, exclaiming, "Oh God, I'm the woman in this relationship" (Violet_ Pencil). In another, fem!Sherlock and John have a disagreement about Sherlock's ex-boyfriend, Sebastian, who claimed one of them wasn't "suited" to being a wife. Fem!Sherlock assumes he is speaking about her, but guy!John thinks it's really a comment about his role in their relationship. He explains: "Sherlock, I'm the one who does the washing up, and I practically have to bully you into doing the drying. I do the cooking, and if anything gets tidied around here it's because I do it. And he was looking at you as he said it, and I figured he knew that if anyone's the stereotypical 'wife' here, it's me" (Blind Author). Clearly, not all genderswap stories are as political about dissociating sex and gender, and some may, in fact, reinforce such notions, all of which serves as a strong reminder not to generalize that all genderswap fanfiction stories are feminist or counter hegemonic.

18. Kristina Busse points out the ways in which cultural expectations for women's gendered behavior are often contradictory: "When women act according to stereotype, their behaviors get dismissed as feminine; when they act against stereotype, their behaviors get dismissed as aberrant or get reinscribed negatively as feminine nevertheless" ("Geek Hierarchies" 74).

19. This may be because John's femininity is largely canonical. Even though he is the primary narrator for virtually all of the Arthur Conan Doyle Holmes/Watson stories, he is subordinate to Holmes in ability, always a step behind, concerned over Holmes's health and drug habits, and so on. This feminized subordination becomes reified in the various film and television portrayals of the characters, particularly Nigel Bruce's Watson in relation to Basil Rathbone's Holmes. The BBC *Sherlock*'s Martin Freeman keeps Watson's military acumen

at the forefront of his characterization, which perhaps mitigates the possible threat of his femininity for traditional audiences.

20. Such criticisms of allegedly feminized behavior are striking when taken in the context of fan studies as a discipline, since the historical etymology of *fan, fanatic*, is rooted in the highly gendered and criticized practice of women audiences' pursuit of male matinee idols in the early twentieth century, as discussed by Henry Jenkins, among others (Jenkins, *Textual Poachers* 17).

21. Of the 35,669 BBC *Sherlock* fanfiction stories currently listed on Archive of Our Own, only 34 are tagged transgender. Of the 891,202 works listed on AO3 to date, only 645 are tagged transgender.

22. Male-to-female Sherlock transgender fanfiction stories are quite rare; in my research, I only uncovered one: Red's "Like Normal People." John stumbles upon Sherlock in the bathroom injecting himself with an unknown substance. Based on Sherlock's history with drug addiction, John immediately assumes it is a narcotic, and when he learns Sherlock is injecting estrogen instead, it completely changes their relationship. John continues to treat Sherlock the same way he had before—only now he is the one providing the legally obtained, regulated hormones and managing Sherlock's transition—but it allows John to acknowledge his latent sexual feelings for his flatmate.

23. Contemporary theorists like Susan Stryker and Judith Butler deny that the existence of biological sex always already determines an individual's gender identity. For Stryker, "the sex of the body does not bear any necessary or deterministic relationship to the social category in which that body lives" ("(De)Subjugated Knowledges" 11). Butler's poststructuralist argument is a bit more nuanced, claiming that sex cannot be viewed as the prediscursive forbear of gender—that is, sex does not somehow come before gender, nor is gender based on sex (*Gender Trouble* 152). Instead, sex itself is culturally constructed and a gendered category, one that politically situates nature and the natural to serve to the economic benefit of heterosexuality and reproduction. In contrast, gender for Butler is "a kind of becoming or an activity" (152).

24. Even though gender may be "artificial," as Nagoshi and Brzuzy argue, this does not mean it is easy to change.

25. Transgender theorist Cressida Heyes explained her own physical/psychic dissociation as follows: "In some ways, I feel as though the body I have is the *wrong* body: too large, too female in some respects, too clumsy. Surely an incisive intellectual mind requires an equally lean and skillful body?" (1097–98).

26. Richard Ekins and Dave King describe four subprocesses by which transgender individuals transition from one gender to another: substituting, concealing, implying, and redefining. *Substituting* involves replacing one sex's genitalia with the other's. *Concealing* involves hiding or masking specific sex character-

istics: binding breasts, tucking the penis, etc. *Implying* involves suggesting the presence of certain sexed body parts, most often through the use of clothing. *Redefining* is the most complex and subtle of the processes; individuals re-name and reclassify traditionally sexed characteristics (a beard becomes facial hair or a penis becomes a "growth" between the legs) (583–85). Fanfiction writer Ishmael uses several of these processes in her series "Bodies" to illustrate the ways in which FTM!Sherlock expresses his gender and sex identities.

27. Interestingly, Red's "Like Normal People," the sole MTF!Sherlock story I found, uses the same pronoun shift midway through the story. In the first half, John refers to Sherlock as "he" until he discovers Sherlock in their bathroom injecting estrogen; then the pronoun shifts to "she" in the second half, where John and MTF!Sherlock become romantically involved. As an aside, one problematic element of this story is John's speculation that perhaps Sherlock transitioned to female "for his benefit," so that John would consider her as a sexual partner, which negates the very significant personal reasons why an individual might feel the need to transition to another sex/gender.

28. One important sociopolitical movement we don't see much of in *Sherlock* fanfic is racebending—where fan writers change the racial identity of canonical figures from the show's world. Anne Kustritz and Melanie E. S. Kohnen co-authored a wonderful chapter in *Sherlock and Transmedia Fandom* on the TV show's problematic attitudes toward race and orientalism, in particular, "The Blind Banker" (S1E12). I have not, however, encountered any explicitly raced *Sherlock* fanfics in my research thus far. As many current fan studies critics have noted, expanding the field to cover race, ethnicity, and representations of both are essential pursuits as it moves forward.

CHAPTER 5

1. Linda Hutcheon makes similar arguments about adaptations in general. Hutcheon first paraphrases Jonathan Culler that "known adaptations obviously function similarly to genres: they set up audience expectations" before characterizing the interaction as working "through a set of norms that guide our encounter with the adapting work we are experiencing" (Hutcheon 121). Fanfics, I argue, are forms of adaptations that work to similar ends. These "audience expectations" are foundational as readers approach various fan works, particularly with AUs, since so much of the traditional canonical world has been stripped away, leaving the fic at risk of being seen as out of character or inconsistent with the overall elements of the world.

2. One obvious exception to all canonical rules is crack! fanfiction, which completely violates all canonical tenets in the name of humor. In contrast to AU fanfic, crack is not intended to be taken as a serious extension of or commen-

tary on the fictional world but rather as a playful, ironic, even ridiculous departure from it.

3. Crossover fanfic is often derided in the media, in particular, as the most uncreative fanfic genre. Ewan Morrison, for example, recently published a scathing review of fanfic in *The Guardian* in which he called crossover fanfic "the most postmodern and aesthetically bankrupt of all fanfic." In Morrison's diatribe, crossovers "warp" character motivations and narratives to conform to the writer's own personal agenda.

4. Sherlock's canonical hair ruffle is repeated in several AU fanfics as a foundational element establishing his character. For example, in earlgreytea68's *The Bang and the Clatter,* John watches in fascination as "Sherlock ruffled his hands through his hair, not that it made it any more unruly than it already was. It was clearly an absent-minded gesture, not calculated for seduction. Nevertheless, John's mouth watered just a bit, a situation not helped by Sherlock abruptly fixing him with that pale, sparking gaze" (chapter 4).

5. Watson first describes Holmes sitting in his armchair and "putting his fingertips together, as was his custom when in judicial moods" in "The Red-Headed League," one of the original stories published in *The Adventures of Sherlock Holmes* (263). The mannerism is afterward repeated frequently; it becomes an identifiable character element in the canon and is often seen in film and television adaptations.

6. Sherlock having Asperger syndrome is even jokingly referenced in a scene between John and Lestrade in "The Hounds of Baskerville" (S2E2), when John tells Lestrade that Sherlock is actually happy to see him in the countryside.

7. Fanfic author bendingsignpost has an even more extreme AU/AU in "No Fixed Point," which combines three different alternate universes from the Watches series, *Stranger at the Gate*, and another fic, "Behavioural Modification," which is more of a slash fic than an AU. The summary explains: "The summary for 'No Fixed Point' states: '(Original prompt: "ECM!John gets hurt again, and ends up with a few more lives. By overwriting Stranger at the Gate!John and Behavioural Modification!John." Thus, Watches "Verse" with Behavioural Modification and Stranger at the Gate, spoilers for everything. Prompted and filled on LiveJournal. NOT an official continuation of any of these "verses.")'" (bendingsignpost, "No Fixed Point" Summary). While the fic is too complicated to go into here, especially because it depends on prior knowledge of three other alternate universes, it merits more in-depth analysis at a later date.

CHAPTER 6

1. V. Arrow argues that RPF's close affiliation with the "lesser forms" of bandoms such as NSYNC and, more recently, One Direction, has particularly contrib-

uted to RPF's negative image, in that young female fans allegedly use such fictions to validate their fan knowledge and devotion or to "legitimize" their Beloved Slash Objects (BSO) (325–26).

2. Hagen conversely argues that this very invention of an imaginary inner life "indirectly reinforces their fakeness through the assumption that their media presentation is purely performed and does not reflect their true personalities" (49).

3. More recently, sociologists like David C. Giles (2002) and fan studies scholar Matt Hills ("From Para-Social") have begun to challenge these negative perceptions and offer new ways to apply, expand upon, and reconceptualize parasocial relationships in a digital and participatory environment. For Hills, parasocial models seem too limiting and pejorative to describe fan practices. Rather than being a one-sided, nondialectical, delusional experience, as Horton and Wohl depicted traditional parasocial relationships in the 1950s, Hills notes how fans participate in broader communal networks through which they share information, create materials for others, and perform fan service in support of the larger community. Thus, rather than labeling such activities *parasocial*, as in *alongside* real social relationships, Hills posits the term "multisocial interaction" as a more appropriate description of the ways fans "draw on celebrities as a resource within their self-narratives and share and perform these narratives with multiple fan others" (Hills, "From Para-Social" 471).

4. According to Mercer, fans and media have an "obsessive" interest in male celebrity bodies, in particular, seeing "the male body as index of masculinity, as marker of virility and, more problematically, increasingly as site of desire" (88).

5. Fan scholar Anne Jamison reported on the incident on her blog, noting that once performers enter the public arena and make money off their bodies through paparazzi photographs, clothing, and general promotion, then "You're part of that material now." Jamison continued: "You don't have to watch or look at fan culture created about these virtual versions of you or your loved ones who work in the industry. You don't have to comment on it. But if you're going to comment, it's probably wise to learn a little about what you're commenting on. And, people in powerful positions shouldn't contribute to mocking people in less-powerful positions. But it's hard to remember when you yourself feel attacked by some of those less-powerful people! And the internet makes it all feel up-close and personal even when it isn't" (Jamison, "It's Not Jane Austen").

6. For the sake analysis here, I am referring to Splix71's portrayal of Benedict Cumberbatch as a fictional character in the same way that I refer to the BBC's Sherlock and John characters.

1. For example, references to "The Three Garridebs" and "The Dancing Men" appear in the episode, as well as oblique references to the character Victor Trevor from "The Gloria Scott" and the name "Norbury" from "The Adventure of the Yellow Face." Moffat and Gatiss also include lines from "The Final Problem." For instance, the episode ends with a posthumous voice-over from Mary parroting Watson's famous lines from "The Final Problem": "The best and wisest [men] I know."

2. The iNews website collated a helpful list of the most vitriolic critical reactions to *Sherlock* season four.

3. *Den of Geek*'s Kayti Burt wasn't the only critic to label *Sherlock* season four an "alternate universe." Gavia Baker-Whitelaw in *The Daily Dot* similarly critiqued season four for veering far from the show's original world. For Baker-Whitelaw, however, all of *Sherlock*'s world is, in a sense, an "alternate universe" where "almost everyone in London is white" and Sherlock can break the law without consequence.

4. For more details on the parallels between *Sherlock* season four and season one, see *Den of Geek*'s "34 Things You Might Have Missed in 'The Lying Detective.'"

BIBLIOGRAPHY

1001 Fangirls. "Sleeping Whispers (Sherlock X Reader)." *Tumblr.com*. November 25, 2016. http://1001fangirls.tumblr.com/post/153654160933/sleeping-whispers -sherlock-x-reader.

Abercrombie, Nicholas, and Brian Longhurst. *Audiences: A Sociological Theory of Performance and Imagination*. London: Sage, 1998.

Abundantlyqueer. *Two Two One Bravo Baker*. Archiveofourown.org. April 8, 2011. https://archiveofourown.org/works/180121/chapters/264839.

Addyke. "*Sherlock* Meta: This Woman's Work: In Defense and Affection of BBC *Sherlock's* Depiction of Irene Adler." LiveJournal.com. February 7, 2012. https://addyke.livejournal.com/2359.html.

Albrecht-Crane, Christa, and Dennis Cutchins. "Introduction." *Adaptation Studies: New Approaches*, 11–14. Madison: Farleigh Dickinson Univ. Press, 2010.

Andrew, Dudley. "Adaptation." In *Film Adaptation*, edited by James Naremore, 28–37. London: Athlone Press, 2000.

Anonymous. "A Comic Con Fantasy." *Martin Freeman Sexual Frustration*. July 26, 2012. http://mfsexualfrustration.tumblr.com/post/28070336293/a-comic-con -fantasy.

———. "A Day at the Beach." *Benedict Cumberbatch Sexual Frustration*. April 15, 2014. http://bcsexualfrustrationblog.tumblr.com/.

———. "Drive." *Martin Freeman Sexual Frustration*. January 17, 2014. http:// mfsexualfrustration.tumblr.com/post/73626692771/freesmut-drive.

———. "The One Where Martin Role-Plays as Dr. Watson," Part 2, Part 3, Part 4. *Martin Freeman Sexual Frustration*. July 12, 2011. http://mfsexualfrustration .tumblr.com/post/7546499027/my-tmi-tuesday-would-be-martin-dressed-up -as-a.

———. "Over Pancakes and Django." *Martin Freeman Sexual Frustration*. October 21, 2012. http://mfsexualfrustration.tumblr.com/post/34212852718 /over-pancakes-and-django.

———. "A Quick Hob-Nob." *Benedict Cumberbatch Sexual Frustration*. April 15, 2014. http://bcsexualfrustrationblog.tumblr.com/.

———. "A Study in an Education." *Benedict Cumberbatch Sexual Frustration*. April 15, 2014. http://bcsexualfrustrationblog.tumblr.com/.

———. "A Summer's Day." *Benedict Cumberbatch Sexual Frustration.* April 15, 2014. http://bcsexualfrustrationblog.tumblr.com/.

Applegate, K. A. "Facebook Bans RP Characters." *The Preternatural Post.* February 1, 2011. http://www.preternaturalpost.com/2011/facebook-bans-rp -characters/.

———. "Roleplayer vs. Average Facebook User." *The Preternatural Post.* February 2, 2011. http://www.preternaturalpost.com/2011/role-player-v -average-facebook-user/.

Arrow, V. "Real Person(a) Fiction." In *Fic: Why Fanfiction Is Taking Over the World*, edited by Anne Jamison, 323–32. Dallas, TX: Smart Pop, 2013.

Bacon-Smith, Camille. *Enterprising Women: Television Fandom and the Creation of Popular Myth.* Philadelphia: Univ. of Pennsylvania Press, 1992.

Baker-Whitelaw, Gavia. "*Sherlock* Season 4 Premiere Disappoints Despite Huge Plot Twist." *The Daily Dot.* January 2, 2017. https://www.dailydot.com/parsec /sherlock-season-4-six-thatchers-review/.

Bakhtin, Mikhail M. "Forms of Time and of the Chronotope in the Novel." In *The Dialogic Imagination: Four Essays*, edited by Michael Holquist, 84–258. Austin, TX: Univ. of Texas Press, 1981.

Barthes, R. *S/Z.* Translated by Richard Miller. London: Jonathan Cape, 1975.

BBC. *Sherlock* (web page). http://www.bbc.co.uk/drama/sherlock/disclaimer .shtml.http://www.bbc.

BBC One. "Steven Moffat and Mark Gatiss—Coming Up?—*Sherlock*—BBC One." YouTube. August 9, 2010. https://youtu.be/kcv__1Fzoos.

———. Twitter Post. January 15, 2017, 6:28pm. https://twitter.com/hashtag/bbc1 ?lang=en.

bendingsignpost. "Behavioural Modification." Archiveofourown.org. February 7, 2012. https://archiveofourown.org/works/334595/chapters/540799.

———. "Elsewhere Come Morning." Archiveofourown.org. February 7, 2012. https://archiveofourown.org/works/334822/chapters/541207.

———. "No Fixed Point." Archiveofourown.org. July 12, 2013. https://archiveof ourown.org/works/881081/chapters/1695898.

———. *The World on His Wrist.* Archiveofourown.org. February 7, 2012. https:// archiveofourown.org/works/334557/chapters/540728.

"Benedict Cumberbatch Covers *GQ's* November Issue." *GQ.* September 30, 2017. http://www.gq-magazine.co.uk/article/benedict-cumberbatch.

Bennett, James. *Television Personalities: Stardom and the Small Screen.* London: Routledge, 2011.

Black, David A. "Character, or, The Strange Case of Uma Peel." *Cult Television*, edited by Sarah Gwenllian-Jones and Roberta Pearson, 99–114. Minneapolis: Univ. of Minnesota Press, 2004.

Blind Author. "Five Times Sherlock's Gender Didn't Matter (And One Time It Did)." *Fanfiction.net*. March 4, 2011. https://www.fanfiction.net/s/6796277/1/.

Bonnstetter, Beth E., and Brian L. Ott. "(Re)Writing Mary Sue: Écriture Feminine and the Performance of Subjectivity." *Text and Performance Quarterly* 31, no. 4 (2011): 342–67.

Booth, Paul. *Digital Fandom: New Media Studies*. New York: Peter Lang, 2010.

———. "Rereading Fandom: MySpace Character Personas and Narrative Identification." *Critical Studies in Media Communication* 25, no. 5 (2008): 514–36.

———. "*Sherlock* Fandom: The Fandom is Afoot!" In *Crossing Fandoms: SuperWhoLock and the Contemporary Fan Audience*, edited by Paul Booth, 79–103. London: Palgrave, 2016.

Bordwell, David. *Narration in the Fiction Film*. London: Methuen, 1985.

Boström, Mattias. "'Elementary, My Dear Watson': The Birth of a Quotation." *I Hear of Sherlock Everywhere* (blog). August 17, 2016. http://www.ihearof sherlock.com/2016/08/elementary-my-dear-watson-birth-of.html#.Wdkn cltSzX4.

Bowman, S. L. *The Functions of Role-Playing Games: How Participants Create Community, Solve Problems and Explore Identity*. Jefferson, NC: McFarland, 2010.

Burt, Kayti. "Did *Sherlock* Lose Its Way when It Abandoned Realism?" *Den of Geek* (blog). January 17, 2017. http://www.denofgeek.com/us/tv/sherlock /261502/did-sherlock-lose-its-way-when-it-abandoned-realism.

———. "*Sherlock* Season 5: Is *Sherlock* Over?" *Den of Geek* (blog). January 18, 2017. http://www.denofgeek.com/us/tv/sherlock/257303/sherlock-season-5 -is-sherlock-over.

Bury, Rhiannon. *Cyberspaces of Their Own: Female Fandoms Online*. New York: Peter Lang, 2005.

Busse, Kristina. *Framing Fan Fiction: Literary Practices in Fan Fiction Communities*. Iowa City: Univ. of Iowa Press, 2017.

———. "Geek Hierarchies, Boundary Policing, and the Gendering of the Good Fan." *Participations* 10, no. 1 (2013): 73–91.

———. "'I'm Jealous of the Fake Me': Postmodern Subjectivity and Identity Construction in Boy Band Fan Fiction." In *Framing Celebrity: New Directions in Celebrity Culture*, edited by Su Holmes and Sean Redmond, 253–67. London: Routledge, 2006.

———. "Is Fandom Gonna Have to Choke a Bitch? Language and Gender in Fanfiction." Presentation at Writercon 2009, Minneapolis, MN, July 31. http:// www.kristinabusse.com/cv/research/writercon09gender.html.

Busse, Kristina, and Alexis Lothian. "Bending Gender: Feminist and

(Trans)Gender Discourses in the Changing Bodies of Slash Fanfiction." In *Internet Fiction(s)*, edited by Ingrid Hotz-Davies, Anton Kirchhofer, and Sirpa Leppänen, 105–25. Cambridge: Cambridge Scholars, 2009.

Butler, Judith. *Bodies That Matter: On the Discursive Limits of "Sex."* New York: Routledge, 1993.

———. *Gender Trouble.* New York: Routledge, 2006.

Campbell, Mark. *Sherlock Holmes.* Harpenden, UK: Pocket Essentials, 2007.

Cardwell, Sarah. *Adaptation Revisited: Television and the Classic Novel.* Manchester: Manchester UP, 2002.

Carlson, N. "Are a Third of Facebook Users Fake?" *Business Insider.* April 3, 2010. http://articles.businessinsider.com/2010-07-02/tech/29993371_1_friend -requests-report-links-facebook-ceo-mark-zuckerberg.

Carr, John Dickson. *The Life of Sir Arthur Conan Doyle.* London: John Murray, 1949.

Carter, Lin. *Imaginary Worlds: The Art of Fantasy.* New York: Ballantine, 1973.

The Civic Imagination Project (website). Part of the MacArthur Foundation Research Network on Youth and Participatory Politics. https://www.civic imaginationproject.org/about.

Click, Melissa A., and Suzanne Scott, eds. *The Routledge Companion to Media Fandom.* New York: Routledge, 2017.

Coker, Catherine. "Earth 616. Earth 1610, Earth 3490—Wait, What Universe Is This Again? The Creation and Evolution of the Avengers and Captain America/ Iron Man Fandom." *Journal of TWC* 13 (2013). http://dx.doi.org/10.3983/twc .2013.0439.

Coppa, Francesca. *The Fanfiction Reader: Folk Tales from the Digital Age.* Ann Arbor: Univ. of Michigan Press, 2017.

———. "Writing Bodies in Space: Media Fan Fiction as Theatrical Performance." In *Fan Fiction and Fan Communities in the Age of the Internet,* edited by Karen Hellekson and Kristina Busse, 225–44. Jefferson, NC: McFarland, 2006.

Cumbertrekky. "Benedict Cumberbatch—Oz Comic Con (via cumberbitchen)." *Tumblr.com.* April 15, 2014. http://muchadoaboutbenedict.tumblr.com/search /oz+comic+con.

Davies, David Stuart. *Bending the Willow: Jeremy Brett as Sherlock Holmes.* Ashcroft, BC: Calabash Press, 2002.

Davies, Raven. "The Slash Fanfiction Connection to Bi Men." *Journal of Bisexuality* 5, no. 2–3 (June 2005): 195–201.

De Certeau, Michel. *The Practice of Everyday Life.* Translated by Steven F. Rendall. Berkeley, CA: Univ. of California Press, 2011.

Derecho, Abigail. "Archontic Literature: A Definition, a History, and Several

Theories of Fanfiction." In *Fan Fiction and Fan Communities in the Age of the Internet*, edited by Karen Hellekson and Kristina Busse, 61–78. Jefferson, NC: McFarland, 2006.

Dhaenens, Frederik, Sofie Van Bauwel, and Daniel Biltereyst. "Slashing the Fiction of Queer Theory: Slash Fiction, Queer Reading, and Transgressing the Boundaries of Screen Studies, Representations, and Audiences." *Journal of Communication Inquiry* 32, no. 4 (October 2008): 335–47.

Digital Spy. "Mark Gatiss on *Sherlock*." YouTube.com (online video clip). July 22, 2010.

DiscordantWords. "(Never) Turn Your Back to the Sea." Archiveofourown.org. April 15, 2017. https://archiveofourown.org/works/9848774/chapters/22100969.

Dowell, Ben. "*Sherlock* Fans Could Have a Long Wait for Series 5." *Radio Times*. January 20, 2017. http://www.radiotimes.com/news/2017-01-15/sherlock-fans-could-have-a-long-wait-for-series-5/.

Doyle, Sir Arthur Conan. *The Adventures of Sherlock Holmes*. Project Gutenberg. https://www.gutenberg.org/files/1661/1661-h/1661-h.htm. Accessed April 18, 2011.

———. *Memories and Adventures*. London: Greenhill, 1988.

———. *A Study in Scarlet*. Project Gutenberg. http://www.gutenberg.org/files/244/244.txt. Accessed July 12, 2011.

Driscoll, Catherine. "One True Pairing: The Romance of Pornography and the Pornography of Romance." In *Fan Fiction and Fan Communities in the Age of the Internet*, edited by Karen Hellekson and Kristina Busse, 79–96. Jefferson, NC: McFarland, 2006.

Duncan, Alistair. *Eliminate the Impossible: An Examination of the World of Sherlock Holmes on Page and Screen*. Hertfordshire: MX, 2008.

Dyer, Richard. *Stars*. London: BFI, 2004.

earlgreytea68. *The Bang and the Clatter [B&C]*. Archiveofourown.org. April 1, 2014. https://archiveofourown.org/works/744242/chapters/1386629.

———. *Nature and Nurture*. Archiveofourown.org. March 21, 2013. https://archiveofourown.org/works/729134/chapters/1354275.

Eco, Umberto. "*Casablanca*: Cult Movies and Intertextual Collage." In *Travels in Hyper Reality*, 197–212. Translated by William Weaver. New York: Harcourt, Brace Jovanovich, 1986.

Edwards, Tim. "Medusa's Stare: Celebrity, Subjectivity and Gender." *Celebrity Studies* 4, no. 2 (2013): 155–68.

Ekins, Richard, and Dave King. "Towards a Sociology of Transgendered Bodies." *Sociological Review* 47, no. 3 (1999): 580–602.

Elliot, Patricia, and Katrina Roen. 1998. "Transgenderism and the Question of Embodiment: Promising Queer Politics?" *GLQ: A Journal of Lesbian and Gay Studies* 4, no. 2 (1998): 231–61.

Ellis, John. "Star/Industry/Image." In *Star Signs: Papers from a Weekend Workshop*, edited by Jeremy G. Butler. London: BFI, 1982.

Ellison, Hannah. "Submissives, Nekos, and Futanaris: A Quantitative and Qualitative Analysis of the Glee Kink Meme." *Participations* 10, no. 1 (2013): 109–28.

emmagrant01. "Alternate and Missing Scenes from 'A Cure for Boredom.'" Archiveofourown.org. April 4, 2012.

———. "A Cure for Boredom." Archiveofourown.org. March 28, 2012.

———. "eep." *Tumblr.com*. February 17, 2014.

Ericsson, Martin. "Interaction vs. Participation." Vimeo.com (online video clip). March 22, 2012.

Etothepii. "Seems So Easy for Everybody Else." Archiveofourown.org. May 12, 2011. http://archiveofourown.org/works/198418.

Evans, Elizabeth. *Transmedia Television: Audiences, New Media and Daily Life*. New York: Routledge, 2011.

Everett, Anthony. "Against Fictional Realism." *The Journal of Philosophy* 102, no. 12 (December 2005): 624–49.

Fanlore "RPF." http://fanlore.org/wiki/RPF#Fiction_About_Famous_People. Accessed September 1, 2012.

Fiske, John. *Television Culture*. London: Methuen, 1987.

Foster, Patrick. "Next Series of *Sherlock* Could Be Last, BBC Show's Creator Warns." *The Telegraph*, July 15, 2016. http://www.telegraph.co.uk/news/2016/07/15/next-series-of-sherlock-could-be-last-bbc-shows-creator-warns/.

Foxycop678. "I'm Not Your Sniffer Dog." Livejournal.com. August 17, 2010. http://astudyinpink.livejournal.com/1403.html.

Freeman, Matthew. "Advertising the Yellow Brick Road: Historicizing the Industrial Emergence of Transmedia Storytelling." *International Journal of Communications* 8 (2014): 2362–81.

———. "Branding Consumerism: Cross-Media Characters and Story-Worlds at the Turn of the Twentieth Century." *International Journal of Cultural Studies* 18, no. 6 (2015): 629–44.

———. "The Wonderful Game of Oz and Tarzan Jigsaws: Commodifying Transmedia in Early Twentieth-Century Consumer Culture." *Intensities: The Journal of Cult Media* 7 (August 2014): 44–54.

Freund, Katharina, and Dianna Fielding. "Research Ethics in Fan Studies." *Participations* 10, no. 1 (2013): 329–34.

Frost, Caroline. "*Sherlock* Review: 13 Times Season 4 Finale 'The Final Problem'

Shocked, Surprised and Felt Unmistakably Final." *Huffington Post*. January 16, 2017. http://www.huffingtonpost.co.uk/entry/sherlock-the-final-problem -review_uk_587bfe24e4b0f3b82a37ca4d.

Genette, Gerard. *The Architext: An Introduction*. Translated by Jane E. Lewin. Berkley: Univ. of California Press, 1979.

Gerrig, Richard J. *Experiencing Narrative Worlds: On the Psychologic Activities of Reading*. New Haven, CT: Yale Univ. Press, 1993.

Giles, David C. "Parasocial Interaction: A Review of the Literature and a Model for Future Research." *MediaPsychology* 4 (2002): 286–305.

Gilligan, Sarah. "Heaving Cleavages and Fantastic Frock Coats: Gender Fluidity, Celebrity and Tactile Transmediality in Contemporary Costume Cinema." *Film, Fashion and Consumption* 1, no. 1 (2012): 7–38.

Gledhill, Christine. "Signs of Melodrama." In *Stardom: Industry of Desire*, edited by C. Gledhill, 207–29. Routledge, 1991.

Goffman, Erving. *The Presentation of Self in Everyday Life*. Woodstock, NY: Overlook, 1973.

Goodman, Nelson. *Ways of Worldmaking*. Indianapolis: Hackett, 1978.

Gray, Jonathan. *Show Sold Separately: Promos, Spoilers, and Other Media Paratexts*. New York: New York Univ. Press, 2010.

Gray, Jonathan, Cornel Sandvoss, and C. Lee Harrington, eds. *Fandom: Identities and Communities in a Mediated World*. New York: New York Univ. Press, 2007.

Green, Richard Lancelyn. *The Sherlock Holmes Letters*. Iowa City: Univ. of Iowa Press, 1987.

Gregoriou, Christiana. "The Televisual Game Is On: The Stylistics of the BBC's Modern-Day *Sherlock*." *Crime Across Cultures: Moving Worlds* 13, no. 1 (2013): 49–61.

Greywash. "The Sensation of Falling as You Just Hit Sleep." Archiveofourown.org. July 31, 2012. http://archiveofourown.org/works/324584/chapters/522817.

Grossman, Lev. "The Boy Who Lived Forever." *Time* (web). July 7, 2011. http:// content.time.com/time/arts/article/0,8599,2081784,00.html.

Guignon, Charles. *On Being Authentic*. London: Routledge, 2004.

Hagen, Ross. "'Bandom Ate My Face': The Collapse of the Fourth Wall in Online Fan Fiction." *Popular Music and Society* 38, no. 1 (2015): 44–58.

Hall, Trevor H. *Sherlock Holmes: The Higher Criticism: A Lecture Delivered to The School of English, The University of Leeds*. Leeds: W. S. Maney and Sons, 1971.

Hassapopoulou, Marina. "Spoiling Heroes, Enhancing Our Viewing Pleasure: NBC's *Heroes* and the Re-Shaping of the Televisual Landscape." In *Writing and the Digital Generation: Essays on New Media Rhetoric*, edited by Heather Urbanski. Jefferson, NC: McFarland, 2010.

Hayot, Eric. *On Literary Worlds*. Oxford: Oxford Univ. Press, 2012.

Hellekson, Karen, and Kristina Busse, eds. *Fan Fiction and Fan Communities in the Age of the Internet: New Essays*. Jefferson, NC: McFarland, 2006.

Herman, David. "Storyworlds." In *Routledge Encyclopedia of Narrative*, edited by David Herman, Manfred Jahn, and Marie-Laure Ryan, 569–70. London: Routledge, 2005.

Herzinger, Kim. "Inside and Outside Sherlock Holmes: A Rhapsody." In *Critical Essays on Sir Arthur Conan Doyle*, edited by Harold Orel. New York: G. K. Hall, 1992.

Heyes, Cressida. "Feminist Solidarity after Queer Theory: The Case of Transgender." *Signs* 28, no. 4 (2003): 1093–120.

Hills, Matt. *Fan Culture*. London: Routledge, 2002.

———. "From Para-Social to Multisocial Interaction: Theorizing Material Digital Fandom and Celebrity." In *A Companion to Celebrity*, edited by P. David Marshall and Sean Redmond. West Sussex, UK: Wiley Blackwell, 2016.

———. "*Sherlock's* Epistemological Economy and the Value of 'Fan' Knowledge: How Producer-Fans Play the (Great) Game of Fandom." In *Sherlock and Transmedia Fandom: Essays on the BBC Series*, edited by Louisa Ellen Stein and Kristina Busse. Jefferson, NC: McFarland, 2012.

Hogan, Michael. "*Sherlock* Episode 3: The Final Problem Review: 'An Exhilarating Thrill Ride.'" *Telegraph*. January 17, 2017. http://www.telegraph.co.uk/tv/0 /sherlock-episode-3-final-problem-review-exhilarating-thrill/.

Hollmes, Sherlock. ". . . No. It Really Wouldn't." Facebook.com. Accessed February 4, 2012. http://www.facebook.com/SherlockHolmesbbc.

Holmes, Shock. "We Post What WE Like . . ." Facebook.com. April 29, 2013. http:// www.facebook.com/shockholmesbbc?ref=ts&fref=ts.

Holub, Cristian. "*Sherlock* Recap: 'The Final Problem.'" *Entertainment Weekly*. January 16, 2017. http://ew.com/recap/sherlock-season-4-finale/.

Horton, Donald, and R. Richard Wohl. "Mass Communication and Para-Social Interaction: Observations on Intimacy at a Distance." *Participations* 3, no. 1 (May 2006). Web. http://www.participations.org/volume%203/issue%201/3 _01_hortonwohl.htm. First published in *Psychiatry* 19 (1956): 215–29.

Hutcheon, Linda. *A Theory of Adaptation*. New York: Routledge, 2006.

"Imagines." Angelfire.com. http://www.angelfire.com/falcon/moonbeam/terms .html#I. Accessed November 3, 2016.

Iser, Wolfgang. *The Act of Reading: A Theory of Aesthetic Response*. London: Routledge, 1976.

———. *The Implied Reader: Patterns of Communication in Prose Fiction from Bunyan to Beckett*. Baltimore: Johns Hopkins Univ. Press, 1974.

Ishmael. "Body of Evidence." Archiveofourown.org. June 2, 2011. http://archiveof ourown.org/works/207027.

iTeam. "*Sherlock* Series 4: The Most Furiously Outraged Critics." *iNews.co.uk*. January 16, 2017. https://inews.co.uk/essentials/culture/television/sherlock -outraged-critical-reviews/.

Itsallfine. "The Pieces that Fall to Earth." Archiveofourown.org. March 17, 2017. https://archiveofourown.org/works/9566708/chapter Accessed 2 October 2017.

Jamison, Anne. *Fic: Why Fanfiction Is Taking Over the World*. Dallas, TX: Smart Pop, 2013.

———. "It's Not Jane Austen." *Tumblr.com*. January 30, 2014. http://annejamison .tumblr.com/post/75080601852/my-conversation-with-the-millions-elizabeth -minkel.

Jann, Rosemary. *The Adventures of Sherlock Holmes: Detecting Social Order*. New York: Twayne, 1995.

Jeffrey, Morgan. "*Sherlock* Series 4, Episode 3 Review: 'The Final Problem' Puts Heart Above Brains . . . and It Mostly Works." *Digital Spy*. January 15, 2017. http://www.digitalspy.com/tv/sherlock/review/a818925/sherlock-season-4 -episode-3-finale-review-spoilers-bbc-moriarty/.

———. "*Sherlock* Writers Open Up about Show's Future after Series 4 Finale: 'We Could End It There.'" *Digital Spy*. January 15, 2017. http://www.digitalspy.com /tv/sherlock/news/a818954/sherlock-writers-open-up-about-shows-future -after-series-4/.

Jenkins, Henry. "Afterword." In *Fandom: Identities and Communities in a Mediated World*, edited by Jonathan Gray, Cornel Sandvoss, and C. Lee Harrington, 357–64. New York: New York Univ. Press, 2007.

———. *Convergence Culture: Where Old and New Media Collide*. New York: New York Univ. Press, 2006.

———. "Excerpts from 'Matt Hills Interviews Henry Jenkins.'" In *Fans, Bloggers, and Gamers: Exploring Participatory Culture*. New York: New York Univ. Press, 2006.

———. *Reading in a Participatory Culture: Re-Mixing* Moby Dick *in the English Classroom*. New York: Teachers College Press, 2013.

———. *Textual Poachers: Television Fans and Participatory Culture*. New York: Routledge, 1992.

———. "Transmedia 202." *Confessions of an Aca-Fan*. Blog. August 1, 2011. http:// henryjenkins.org/2011/08/defining_transmedia_further_re.html.

Jenkins, Henry, Sam Ford, and Josh Green. *Spreadable Media: Creating Value and Meaning in a Networked Culture*. New York: New York Univ. Press, 2013.

Jenkins, Henry, Sangita Shresthova, Liana Gamber-Thompson, Neta Kligler-Vilenchik, and Arley Zimmerman. *By Any Media Necessary: The New Youth Activisim*. New York: New York Univ. Press, 2016.

Jones, Jane Clare. "Is Sherlock Sexist? Steven Moffat's Wanton Women." *Guardian*, January 3, 2012. http://www.theguardian.com/commentisfree /2012/jan/03/sherlock-sexist-steven-moffat.

Jones, Paul. "*Sherlock* Is Most Watched TV Drama for Over a Decade." *RadioTimes*, January 22, 2014. http://www.radiotimes.com/news/2014-01 -22/sherlock-is-most-watched-bbc-drama-series-for-over-a-decade/.

Jones, Sara Gwenllian. "The Sex Lives of Cult Television Characters." *Screen* 43, no. 1 (Spring 2002): 79–90.

Jung, Susanne. "Queering Popular Culture: Female Spectators and the Appeal of Writing Slash Fan Fiction." *Gender Forum* 8 (2004). http://www.genderforum .org/issues/gender-queeries/queering-popular-culture-female-spectators -and-the-appeal-of-writing-slash-fan-fiction/.

Jupiter_Ash. "A Study in Winning." Archiveofourown.org. March 21, 2012. https:// archiveofourown.org/works/366788/chapters/596177.

Kaplan, Deborah. "Construction of Fanfiction Character through Narrative." In *Fan Fiction and Fan Communities in the Age of the Internet*, edited by Karen Hellekson and Kristina Busse. Jefferson, NC: McFarland, 2006.

Kate_Lear. "The Love Song of John H. Watson." Archiveofourown.org. February 14, 2011. https://archiveofourown.org/works/183801?view_adult=true.

Kestner, Joseph A. *Sherlock's Men: Masculinity, Conan Doyle, and Cultural History*. Aldershot: Ashgate, 1997.

Khonami, Nadia. "*Sherlock* Draws Largest Festive Audience." *The Guardian*, January 2, 2016. Web. https://www.theguardian.com/tv-and-radio/2016/jan /02/sherlock-draws-largest-festive-tv-audience.

Klastrup, Lisbeth. "Online Worlds." In *The Johns Hopkins Guide to Digital Media*, edited by Benjamin J. Robertson, Lori Emerson, and Marie-Laure-Ryan. Baltimore, MD: Johns Hopkins Univ. Press, 2013.

———. "Towards a Poetics of Virtual Worlds: Multi-User Textuality and the Emergence of Story." PhD diss., IT University of Copenhagen, 2004.

———. "The Worldness of EverQuest: Exploring a 21st Century Fiction." *Game Studies* 9, no. 1 (2009). http://gamestudies.org/0901/articles/klastrup.

Klastrup, Lisbeth, and Susana Tosca. "*Game of Thrones*: Transmedial Worlds, Fandom, and Social Gaming." In *Storyworlds across Media: Toward a Media-Conscious Narratology*, edited by Marie-Laure Ryan and Jan-Noel Thon. Lincoln: Univ. of Nebraska Press, 2014.

Koten, Jiří. "Fictional Worlds and Storyworlds: Forms and Means of . Classification." In *Four Studies of Narrative*, edited by Bohumil Fort, Alice Jedlickova, Jiří Koten, and Ondrej Sladek. Prague: Institution of Czech Literature, 2010.

Kranz, David L. "Trying Harder: Probability, Objectivity, and Rationality in

Adaptation Studies." In *The Literature/Film Reader: Issues of Adaptation*, edited by James M. Welsh and Peter Lev, 77–104. Lanham, MD: Scarecrow, 2007.

Kustritz, Anne. "Slashing the Romance Narrative." *The Journal of American Culture* 26, no. 3 (September 2003): 371–84.

———. "'They All Lived Happily Ever After. Obviously': Realism and Utopia in *Game of Thrones*–Based Alternate Universe Fairy Tale Fan Fiction." *Humanities* 5, no. 43 (2016): 1–16.

Kustritz, Anne, and Melanie E. S. Kohnen. "Decoding the Industrial City: Visions of Security in Holmes's and *Sherlock*'s London." In *Sherlock and Transmedia Fandom: Essays on the BBC Series*, edited by Louisa Ellen Stein and Kristina Busse. Jefferson, NC: McFarland, 2012.

Lackner, Eden, Barbara Lynn Lucas, and Robin Anne Reid. "Cunning Linguists: The Bisexual Erotics of *Words/Silence/Flesh*." In *Fan Fiction and Fan Communities in the Age of the Internet*, edited by Karen Hellekson and Kristina Busse. Jefferson, NC: McFarland, 2006.

Lamb, Jonathan. "'Lay Aside My Character': The Personate Novel and Beyond." *The Eighteenth Century* 52, no. 3–4 (2011): 271–87.

Lamb, Patricia Frazer, and Diana L. Veith. "Romantic Myth, Transcendence, and *Star Trek* Zines." In *Erotic Universe: Sexuality and Fantastic Literature*, edited by Donald Palumbo. New York: Greenwood, 1986.

Landow, George. "Excerpt from *Hypertext 2.0*." In *Criticism: Major Statements*, edited by Charles Kaplan and William Anderson. New York: Bedford St. Martin's, 1999.

Lane, Riki. "Trans as Bodily Becoming: Rethinking the Biological as Diversity, Not Dichotomy." *Hypatia* 24, no. 3 (2009): 136–57.

Leng, Rachel. "Gender, Sexuality, and Cosplay: A Case Study of Male-to-Female Crossplay." *Phoenix Papers* 1, no. 1 (2014): 89–110.

Levenworth, Maria Lindgren. "Transmedial Narration and Fanfiction." In *Storyworlds across Media: Toward a Media-Conscious Narratology*, edited by Marie-Laure Ryan and Jan-Noel Thon. Lincoln: Univ. of Nebraska Press, 2014.

Levenworth, Van. "The Developing Storyworld of H.P. Lovecraft." In *Storyworlds across Media: Toward a Media-Conscious Narratology*, edited by Marie-Laure Ryan and Jan-Noel Thon. Lincoln: Univ. of Nebraska Press, 2014.

Lewis, C. S. *An Experiment in Criticism*. Cambridge, UK: Cambridge Univ. Press, 1961.

Lewis, Helen. "*Sherlock*'s Sexy, but Not Sexist." *New Statesman*, January 16, 2012. http://www.newstatesman.com/television/2012/01/sherlock-moffat-doctor.

Lidster, Joe. "The Personal Blog of John H. Watson Blog." http://www.john watsonblog.co.uk/. Accessed October 2, 2017.

Lothian, Alexis. "Doing Boys Like They're Girls, and Other (Trans)Gendered Subjects: The Queer Subcultural Politics of 'Genderfuck' Fanfiction." Paper presented at the Los Angeles Queer Studies Conference, October 11, 2008.

Lury, Karen. "Television Performance: Being Acting and 'Corpsing.'" *New Formations* 27 (1995): 114–31.

Mad_Lori. *Performance in a Leading Role*. Archiveofourown.org. July 19, 2011. https://archiveofourown.org/works/225563/chapters/341590.

Mad_Maudlin. "In Arduis Fidelis." Archiveofourown.org. September 18, 2010. http://archiveofourown.org/works/118501.

Marshall, P. David. "The Promotion and Presentation of the Self: Celebrity as Marker of Presentational Media." *Celebrity Studies* 1, no. 1 (2010): 35–48.

Marszal, Andrew. "*Sherlock* Finale Another Ratings Triumph." *The Telegraph*, January 16, 2012. http://www.telegraph.co.uk/culture/tvandradio/9017545/Sherlock-finale-another-ratings-triumph.html.

McCaw, Neil. "Sherlock Holmes and a Politics of Adaptation." In *Sherlock Holmes and Conan Doyle: Multi-Media Afterlives*, edited by Sabine Vanacker and Catherine Wynne, 36–48. New York: Palgrave MacMillan, 2014.

McClellan, Ann. "*Tit-Bits*, New Journalism, and Early Sherlock Holmes Fandom." *Transformative Works and Cultures* 23 (2017). http://dx.doi.org/10.3983/twc.2017.0816.

McGee, Jennifer. "'In the End, It's All Made Up': The Ethics of Fanfiction and Real Person Fiction." In *Communication Ethics, Media, & Popular Culture*, edited by Phyllis M. Japp, Mark Meister, and Debra K. Japp. New York: Peter Lang, 2005.

Meadows, Foz. "Sexism in *Sherlock*." *Shattersnipe: Malcontent and Rainbows* (blog). December 12, 2011. http://fozmeadows.wordpress.com/2011/12/12/sexism-in-sherlock/.

Mellor, Louisa. "*Sherlock*: 34 Things You Might Have Missed in 'The Lying Detective.'" *Den of Geek* (blog). January 10, 2017. http://www.denofgeek.com/us/tv/sherlock/261361/sherlock-34-things-you-might-have-missed-in-the-lying-detective.

Mercer, John. "The Enigma of the Male Sex Symbol." *Celebrity Studies* 4, no. 1 (2013): 81–91.

Merriman, Rebecca. "Sherlock Holmes Isn't Straight or Gay—He's Not Interested in Sex at All." EntertainmentWise.com. March 31, 2015.

m-holmes (Lestrade-Holmes, Mycroft). "You're Old News, Holmes . . . ." Tumblr.com. Accessed April 3, 2012. http://m-holmes.tumblr.com/post/20436260484/richardbrookonline-replied-to-your-post.

Mittell, Jason. "A Cultural Approach to Television Genre Theory." *Cinema Journal* 40, no. 3 (2001): 3–24. http://dx.doi.org/10.1353/cj.2001.0009.

———. "Strategies of Storytelling on Transmedia Television." In *Storyworlds across Media: Toward a Media-Conscious Narratology,* edited by Marie-Laure Ryan and Jan-Noel Thon. Lincoln: Univ. of Nebraska Press, 2014.

Moffat, Steven, and Mark Gatiss, creators. *Sherlock.* Hartswood Films, 2010–2017.

Montgomery, John Warwick. *The Transcendent Holmes.* Ashcroft, BC: Calabash, 2000.

Moran, Caitlin. "The Seven Wonders of *Sherlock.*" *The Times,* August 5, 2010. http://www.thetimes.co.uk/tto/arts/tv-radio/article2673621.ece.

Morgan, Jeffrey. "*Sherlock*: Edinburgh Festival Masterclass—Live Blog." *Digital Spy,* August 24, 2012.

Morrison, Ewan. "In the Beginning, There Was Fan Fiction: From the Four Gospels to Fifty Shades." *The Guardian,* August 13, 2012. https://www .theguardian.com/books/2012/aug/13/fan-fiction-fifty-shades-grey.

Mulvey, Laura. "Visual Pleasure and Narrative Cinema." *Screen* 16, no. 3 (October 1975): 6–18.

Murray, Janet H. *Hamlet on the Holodeck: The Future of Narrative in Cyberspace.* Cambridge, MA: MIT Press, 1997.

———. *Inventing the Medium: Principles of Interaction Design as a Cultural Practice.* Cambridge, MA: MIT Press, 2011.

Nagoshi, Julie L., and Stephanie Brzuzy. "Transgender Theory: Embodying Research and Practice." *Affilia* 25, no. 4 (2010): 431–43.

Nomdeplume. "Father." Archiveofourown.org. January 15, 2017. https://archiveof ourown.org/works/9327989.

O'Connor, Rosie. "*Sherlock* Season 4 Has Morphed into a Grotesque Parody of the Witty, Faithful TV Adaptation It Once Was." *The Independent,* January 4, 2017. http://www.independent.co.uk/arts-entertainment/tv/features/sherlock -season-4-episode-one-benedict-cumberbatch-martin-freeman-tv-series -mary-watson-amanda-a7509261.html.

O'Hare, Kate. "*Sherlock* Season 3: Amanda Abbington and Martin Freeman's Not-Wedding." *Zap 2 It* (blog). January 26, 2014. http://blog.zap2it.com /frominsidethebox/2014/01/sherlock-season-3-amanda-abbington-and -martin-freemans-not-wedding.html.

Osborne, H. "Performing Self, Performing Character: Exploring Gender Performativity in Online Role-Playing Games." *Transformative Works and Cultures* 11 (2012). http://journal.transformativeworks.org/index.php/twc /article/view/411/343.

Parachute_Silks. "Astronomy." LiveJournal.com. November 1, 2010.

———. "Categories." LiveJournal.com. November 22, 2010. https://parachute -silks.livejournal.com/2348.html.

Parker, Valerie. "SDCC 2016: Sherlock & A Case of Sexual Identity" (blog). Withanaccent.com. July 27, 2016.

Parrish, Juli J. "Metaphors We Read By: People, Process, and Fanfiction." *Journal of Transformative Works and Cultures* 14 (2013). http://dx.doi.org/10.3983/twc .2013.0486.

Pavel, Thomas G. *Fictional Worlds*. Cambridge, MA: Harvard Univ. Press, 1986.

Payne, David S. *Myth and Modern Man in Sherlock Holmes: Sir Arthur Conan Doyle and the Uses of Nostalgia*. Bloomington: Indiana Univ. Press, 1992.

Pearce, Celia. *Communities of Play: Emergent Cultures in Multiplayer Games and Virtual Worlds*. Cambridge: MIT Press, 2009.

Pearson, Roberta E. "Anatomising Gilbert Grissom: The Structure and Function of the Televisual Character." In *Reading CSI: Crime TV Under the Microscope*, edited by Michael Allen. London: I. B. Tauris. 2007.

———. "Barbies, Bardies, Trekkies, and Sherlockians." In *Sherlock and Transmedia Fandom: Essays on the BBC Series*, edited by Louisa E. Stein and Kristina Busse. Jefferson, NC: McFarland, 2012.

———. "Kings of Infinite Space: Cult Television Characters and Narrative Possibilities." *Scope: An Online Journal of Film Studies* (2003): 1–14. https://www .nottingham.ac.uk/scope/documents/2003/november-2003/pearson.pdf.

Penley, Constance. "Brownian Motion: Women, Tactics, and Technology." *Technoculture* (1991): 135–62.

———. "Feminism, Psychoanalysis, and the Study of Popular Culture." In *Visual Culture: Images and Interpretations*, edited by N. Bryson, M. Holly, and K. Moxey. Hanover, NH: Wesleyan Univ. Press, 1994.

Phillips, Tom, and Matthew Tucker. "38 Pictures of Benedict Cumberbatch Photobombing Things." Buzzfeed.com. March 3, 2014. https://www.buzzfeed .com/tomphillips/pictures-of-benedict-cumberbatch-photobombing -things?utm_term=.ieXR6Ldpj#.oaMDmnqYJ.

Piper, Melanie. "Real Body, Fake Person: Recontextualizing Celebrity Bodies in Fandom and Film." *Journal of Transformative Works and Cultures* 20 (2015). http://journal.transformativeworks.org/index.php/twc/article/view/664/542.

Plakotaris, Michael. *Murder in His Eyes: Sherlock Holmes and Panoptic Power*. Leicestershire, U.K.: Upfront, 2003.

Polasek, Ashley. "Sherlockian Simulacra: Adaptation and the Postmodern Construction of Reality." *Literature/Film Quarterly* 40, no. 3 (2012): 191–96.

Poore, Benjamin. "Sherlock Holmes and the Leap of Faith: The Forces of Fandom and Convergence in Adaptations of the Holmes and Watson Stories." *Adaptation* 6.2 (2013): 158–71.

porcupinegirl. "My Fandoms, Let Me Show You Them: Is *Sherlock* Sexist?"

Tumblr.com. August 24, 2012. http://bbc-sherlock-afghanistan.tumblr.com
/post/30104689429/my-fandoms-let-me-show-you-them-is-sherlock-sexist.

Pound, Reginald. *The Strand Magazine, 1891–1950*. London: Heinemann, 1966.

Proctor, William, and Richard McCulloch. "Exploring Imaginary Worlds:
Audiences, Fan Cultures and Geographies of the Imagination." *Participations*
13, no. 1 (May 2016): 479–87.

Pugh, Sheenagh. *The Democratic Genre: Fanfiction in a Literary Context*. Glasgow:
Bell and Bain, 2005.

Ramachandran, V. S. "Phantom Penises in Transsexuals." *Journal of
Consciousness Studies* 15, no. 1 (2008): 5–16.

reckonedrightly. *No Bangs Without Foreign Office Approval*. Archiveofourown
.org. July 1, 2013. https://archiveofourown.org/works/864779/chapters/1658749.

Red. "Like Normal People." Archiveofourown.org. August 1, 2011. http://archiveof
ourown.org/works/232508.

———. "A Room Untended." Archiveofourown.org. March 28, 2012. http://
archiveofourown.org/works/370720.

Rennison, Nick. *Sherlock Holmes: The Unauthorized Biography*. London: Atlantic
Books, 2005.

Rileyo. "A Response to 'Is *Sherlock* Sexist? Steven Moffat's Wanton Women.'"
Rileyo: Just Another Blog. January 7, 2012. http://rileyo.wordpress.com/2012
/01/07/a-response-to-is-sherlock-sexist-steven-moffats-wanton-women/.

Rixon, Paul. "*Sherlock*: Critical Reception by the Media." In *Sherlock and
Transmedia Fandom: Essays on the BBC Series*, edited by Louisa Stein and
Kristina Busse, 165–78. Jefferson, NC: McFarland, 2012.

Romano, Aja. "*Sherlock* Season 4, Episode 3: 'The Final Problem' Might Be the
Series Finale. If It Is, It's a Huge Disappointment." *Vox* (website). January 16,
2017. https://www.vox.com/2017/1/16/14279588/sherlock-finale-final-problem
-review.

Rosalia. "Sunscreen." June 4, 2012. http://mfsexualfrustration.tumblr.com/post
/24437128604/sunscreen.

Rose, Frank. *The Art of Immersion: How the Digital Generation Is Remaking
Hollywood, Madison Avenue, and the Way We Tell Stories*. New York: W. W.
Norton, 2011.

Rosenblatt, Louise. "Technical Paper No. 416: Writing and Reading: The
Transactional Theory." Champaign: Univ. of Illinois, 1988. https://www.ideals
.illinois.edu/bitstream/handle/2142/18044/ctrstreadtechrepv01988i00416_opt
.pdf.

Rubin, Henry S. "Phenomenology as Method in Trans Studies." *GLQ: A Journal of
Lesbian and Gay Studies* 4, no. 2 (1998): 263–81.

"Rule 63." TVtropes.com. March 19, 2013. http://tvtropes.org/pmwiki/pmwiki
.php/Main/RuleSixtyThree.

Russ, Joanna. "Pornography by Women, for Women, with Love." In *Magic
Mommas, Trembling Sisters, Puritans and Perverts: Feminist Essays*, edited by
Joanna Russ. Trumansburg, NY: Crossing Press, 1985.

Ryan, Marie-Laure. "Story/Worlds/Media: Tuning the Instruments of a Media-
Conscious Narratology." In *Storyworlds across Media: Toward a Media-
Conscious Narratology*, edited by Marie-Laure Ryan and Jan-Noel Thon.
Lincoln: Univ. of Nebraska Press, 2014.

———. *Narrative as Virtual Reality: Immersion and Interactivity in Literature and
Electronic Media*. Baltimore, MD: Johns Hopkins Univ. Press, 2001.

Ryan, Marie-Laure, and Jan-Noel Thon. "Introduction." In *Storyworlds across
Media: Toward a Media-Conscious Narratology*, edited by Marie-Laure Ryan
and Jan-Noel Thon. Lincoln: Univ. of Nebraska Press, 2014.

———, eds. *Storyworlds across Media: Toward a Media-Conscious Narratology*.
Lincoln: Univ. of Nebraska Press, 2014.

Saler, Michael. *As If: Modern Enchantment and the Literary Prehistory of Virtual
Reality*. Oxford: Oxford Univ. Press, 2012.

Salmon, Catherine, and Don Symons. "Slash Fiction and Human Mating
Psychology." *The Journal of Sex Research* 41, no. 1 (February 2004): 94–100.

Sanders, Julie. *Adaptation and Appropriation*. London: Routledge, 2006.

Sandvoss, Cornel. "The Death of the Reader? Literary Theory and the Study
of Texts in Popular Culture." In *Fandom: Identities and Communities in a
Mediated World*, edited by Jonathan Gray, Cornel Sandvoss, and C. Lee
Harrington. New York: New York Univ. Press, 2007.

Santo, Avi. "Fans and Merchandise." In *The Routledge Companion to Media
Fandom*, edited by Melissa A. Click and Suzanne Scott. New York: Routledge,
2017.

Sawyer, Andy. "Fables of Irish Fandom: Fan Fiction in the 1950s and '60s." In *Fic:
Why Fanfiction Is Taking Over the World*. Dallas, TX: Smart Pop, 2013.

Shadowfireflame. "Sherlock Holmes Genderswap Recs (fem!Sherlock)."
LiveJournal.com. February 23, 2011. https://shadowfireflame.livejournal.com
/32941.html.

Sherlock: The Network (mobile application). Apple iOS and Android. The Project
Factory & Hartswood Films. 2014.

Sherlock: Season One. 2010; London: BBC Home Entertainment, 2010. DVD.

Sherlock Holmes Society of London. "About the Society." 2016. http://www
.sherlock-holmes.org.uk/about-the-society/.

Sherlockology. "Benedict Cumberbatch Narrates Jaguar XKR-S Commercial."
YouTube.com (online video clip). September 3, 2011.

Shreffler, Philip A. Introduction to *Sherlock Holmes by Gas-Lamp: Highlights from the Four Decades of the Baker Street Journal*, edited by Philip A. Shreffler, 1–7. New York: Fordham Univ. Press, 1989.

SilentAuror. "Where My Demons Hide." Archiveofourown.org. January 11, 2017. https://archiveofourown.org/works/9286244.

SomeoneElsesDream. "And Then You Wake." Archiveofourown.org. September 7, 2011. http://archiveofourown.org/works/250385/chapters/387257.

Sparks, Lily. "*Sherlock*: Is Season 4 the Final Chapter?" TV Guide.com. December 18, 2016. http://www.tvguide.com/news/sherlock-season-4-final-chapter/.

Splix71. *Method Act*. Archiveofourown.org. September 14, 2014. http://archiveof ourown.org/works/1139576/chapters/2304953.

———. "Real Person Slash Post." Tumblr.com. February 17, 2014.

Stam, Robert. "Fidelity: The Dialogics of Adaptation." In *Film Adaptation*, edited by James Naremore, 54–78. London: The Athlone Press, 2000.

Stanfill, Mel. "The Fan Fiction Gold Rush, Generational Turnover, and the Battle for Fandom's Soul." In *The Routledge Companion to Media Fandom*, edited by Melissa A. Click and Suzanne Scott. New York: Routledge, 2017.

Stashower, Daniel. *Teller of Tales: The Life of Arthur Conan Doyle*. London: Penguin, 1999.

Stasi, Mafalda. "The Toy Soldiers from Leeds: The Slash Palimpsest." In *Fan Fiction and Fan Communities in the Age of the Internet*, edited by Karen Hellekson and Kristina Busse. Jefferson, NC: McFarland, 2006.

Stein, Louisa E. "'Emotions-Only' versus 'Special People' and Genre in Fan Discourse." *Transformative Works and Cultures*, no. 1 (2008). https://doi.org /https://doi.org/10.3983/twc.2008.043.

———. "'This Dratted Thing': Fannish Storytelling through New Media." In *Fan Fiction and Fan Communities in the Age of the Internet*, edited by Karen Hellekson and Kristina Busse. Jefferson, NC: McFarland, 2006.

———. "Tumblr Fan Aesthetics." In *The Routledge Companion to Media Fandom*, edited by Melissa A. Click and Suzanne Scott. New York: Routledge, 2017.

Stein, Louisa E., and Kristina Busse. "Limit Play: Fan Authorship between Source Text, Intertext, and Context." *Popular Communication* 7 (2009): 192–207.

———, eds. *Sherlock and Transmedia Fandom: Essays on the BBC Series*. Jefferson, NC: McFarland, 2012.

Stryker, Susan. "(De)Subjugated Knowledges: An Introduction to Transgender Studies." In *The Transgender Studies Reader*, edited by Susan Stryker and Stephen Whittle. New York: Routledge, 2006.

———. *Transgender History*. Berkeley, CA: Seal Press, 2008.

Stryker, Susan, and Aren Z. Aizura. "Introduction: Transgender Studies 2.0." In

The Transgender Studies Reader 2, edited by Susan Stryker and Aren Z. Aizura. New York: Routledge, 2013.

Takenaka, Kellie. "21st Century Digital Boy." *The Sherlock Holmes Journal* 30, no. 1 (2010): 20–21.

Tartaglione, Nancy. "*Sherlock* Creators and Cast on Season 4 Finale's Thrills and Heart; Is This Really the 'Final Problem' for the Baker Street Boys?" *Deadline.* January 15, 2017. http://deadline.com/2017/01/sherlock-season-4-finale -spoilers-cast-creators-reactions-1201887426/.

Textsfromjohnandsherlock. "6:17pm." Tumblr.com. June 3, 2013. http://textsfrom johnandsherlock.tumblr.com/page/2.

Thomas, A. "Fanfiction Online: Engagement, Critical Response and Affective Play through Writing." *Australian Journal of Language and Literacy* 29, no. 3 (2006): 226–39.

Thomas, Bronwen. "Fans Behaving Badly? Real Person Fic and the Blurring of the Boundaries between the Public and the Private." In *Real Lives, Celebrity Stories: Narratives of Ordinary and Extraordinary People Across Media.* London: Bloomsbury, 2014.

Thomas, L., and N. Enoch. "Most Popular Show on BBC's iPlayer this Year? Elementary . . . the *Sherlock* Episode with the Nude Scenes Watched by 2.5m." *The Daily Mail*, May 29, 2012. http://www.dailymail.co.uk/sciencetech/article -2151933/Sherlock-popular-BBC-iPlayer-2011-Lara-Pulver-nude-scene-watched -2-5m.html.

Tobin, Vera. "Ways of Reading Sherlock Holmes: The Entrenchment of Discourse Blends." *Language and Literature* 15, no. 1 (2006): 73–90.

Tolkien, J. R. R. "On Fairy Stories." In *The Monsters and the Critics and Other Essays*, edited by Christopher Tolkien. London: George Allen and Unwin, 1983.

Tolson, Andrew. "'Being Yourself': The Pursuit of Authentic Celebrity." *Discourse Studies* 3 (2001): 443–57.

Tosenberger, Catherine. "Homosexuality at the Online Hogwarts: Harry Potter Slash Fanfiction." *Children's Literature* 36 (2008): 185–207.

Ue, Tom, and Jonathan Cranfield. *Fan Phenonena: Sherlock Holmes.* Exeter, UK: Intellect, 2014.

Vanacker, Sabine, and Catherine Wynne, eds. *Sherlock Holmes and Conan Doyle: Multi-Media Afterlives.* New York: Palgrave MacMillan, 2014.

Violet_Pencil. "Take Me to Bed (Or Lose Me Forever)." Archiveofourown.org. March 10, 2011. http://archiveofourown.org/works/169066.

Walker, Tim. "Sherlock is the 'Gayest Story in the History of Television,' says Martin Freeman." *The Telegraph*, May 24, 2011. http://www.telegraph.co.uk /culture/tvandradio/8531671/Sherlock-is-the-gayest-story-in-the-history-of -television-says-Martin-Freeman.html.

Ward, Susannah, dir. *Unlocking Sherlock*. 2014; London: Midnight Oil Pictures, 2015. DVD.

Wellingtongoose. "The Hidden Heroines of Sherlock." LiveJournal.com. October 7, 2012. https://wellingtongoose.livejournal.com/11505.html.

Welsh, Kaite. "*Sherlock* Review: 'The Final Problem' Proves to Be a Problematic Season Finale." IndieWire.com. January 15, 2017. http://www.indiewire.com/2017/01/sherlock-review-the-final-problem-season-4-episode-4-spoilers-finale-1201769310/.

Whiteman, Natasha, and Joanne Metivier. "From Post-Object to 'Zombie' Fandoms: The 'Deaths' of Online Fan Communities and What They Say About Us." *Participations* 10, no. 1 (May 2013): 270–98.

Wikipedia. "Lupercalia." Wikipedia.org. Accessed September 25, 2017. https://en.wikipedia.org/wiki/Lupercalia.

Williams, Rebecca. "'This Is the Night TV Died': Television Post-Object Fandom and the Demise of *The West Wing*." *Popular Communication* 9 (2011): 266–79.

Willis, Ika. "Keeping Promises to Queer Children: Making Space (for Mary Sue) at Hogwarts." In *Fan Fiction and Fan Communities in the Age of the Internet*, edited by Karen Hellekson and Kristina Busse. Jefferson, NC: McFarland, 2006.

Wiltse, Ed. "'So Constant an Expectation': Sherlock Holmes and Seriality." *Narrative* 6, no. 2 (May 1998): 105–22.

Woledge, Elizabeth. "Intimatopia: Genre Intersections Between Slash and the Mainstream." In *Fan Fiction and Fan Communities in the Age of the Internet*, edited by Karen Hellekson and Kristina Busse, 97–114. Jefferson, NC: McFarland, 2006.

Wolf, Mark J. P. *Building Imaginary Worlds: The Theory and History of Subcreation*. New York: Routledge, 2012.

Youngblood, Jordan. "'C'mon! Make Me a Man!': Persona 4, Digital Bodies, and Queer Potentiality." *Ada: Journal of Gender, New Media, and Technology* 2. http://adanewmedia.org/2013/06/issue2-youngblood/.

Youngs, Ian. "The *Doctor Who* Fan Who Created the Show's New Titles." BBC.com. August 23, 2014. http://www.bbc.com/news/entertainment-arts-28871058.

Zipfel, Frank. "Fiction Across Media: Toward a Transmedial Concept of Fictionality." In *Storyworlds across Media: Toward a Media-Conscious Narratology*, edited by Marie-Laure Ryan and Jan-Noel Thon. Lincoln: Univ. of Nebraska Press, 2014.

INDEX

Fandom & Culture